A WOMAN'S PLACE IS IN THE BOARDROOM

PENINAH THOMSON
AND **JACEY GRAHAM**
WITH **TOM LLOYD**

palgrave

First published 2005 by
PALGRAVE MACMILLAN
Houndmills, Basingstoke, Hampshire RG21 6XS and
175 Fifth Avenue, New York, N.Y. 10010
Companies and representatives throughout the world

PALGRAVE MACMILLAN is the global academic imprint of the Palgrave Macmillan division of St. Martin's Press, LLC and of Palgrave Macmillan Ltd. Macmillan® is a registered trademark in the United States, United Kingdom and other countries. Palgrave is a registered trademark in the European Union and other countries.

ISBN-13: 978–1–4039–9683–1
ISBN-10: 1–4039–9683–0

This book is printed on paper suitable for recycling and made from fully managed and sustained forest sources.

A catalogue record for this book is available from the British Library.

Library of Congress Catalog Card Number: 2005044659.

10 9 8 7 6 5 4 3 2
14 13 12 11 10 09 08 07 06

Printed and bound in Great Britain by
Creative Print & Design (Wales), Ebbw Vale

To our families, friends and colleagues who have
inspired and sustained us in our careers and to the
children in our lives: may you reach your potential and
play your own part in shaping the future

Also by Peninah Thomson:

"Public Sector Human Resource Management: An Agenda for Change" in *Strategies for Human Resource Management* (ed.) Michael Armstrong, Kogan Page, 1992.

"Public Sector Management in a Period of Radical Change 1979–1992": pp. 33–40 in *Change in the Civil Service: A Public Finance Foundation Reader* (ed.) Norman Flynn, CIPFA, the Chartered Institute of Public Finance and Accountancy, 1994.

"Aftermath: Making Public Sector Change Work: Part 1", *Public Policy Review*, **3**(1): 54–6, 1995.

"A Paradigm Shift: Making Public Sector Change Work: Part II", *Public Policy Review,* **3**(2): 60–4, 1995.

The Changing Culture of Leadership: Women Leaders' Voices, Elizabeth Coffey, Clare Huffington, Peninah Thomson, The Change Partnership, 1999.

"Making the Case for Business: the Change Agenda" in *Work–Life Strategies for the 21st Century*, pp. 40–3. Report by The National Work–Life Forum, 2000.

"Introduction" in *10 Things That Keep CEO's Awake and How to Put Them to Bed* in Coffey, E. et al., McGraw-Hill Business Books, The Change Partnership Whitehead Mann, 2002.

"Corporate Governance, Leadership and Culture Change in Business", Royal Society of Arts, Manufactures and Commerce, 2003.

Also by Jacey Graham:

"Shell Oil Company US: the 2004 Catalyst award winner for diversity initiatives". With Leslie Mays and Susan Vinnicombe, in *Supporting Women's Career Advancement: Challenges and Opportunities* (ed.) Cary Cooper. Edward Elgar, 2005.

Also by Tom Lloyd:

Dinosaur & Co. Studies in corporate evolution, RKP, 1984; Penguin, 1985.
The "Nice" Company, Bloomsbury, 1990; Calmann-Levy, France, 1992; FrancoAngeli, Italy, 1993.
Entrepreneur!, Bloomsbury, 1992.
The Charity Business, John Murray, 1993.

Contents

LIST OF ILLUSTRATIONS, FIGURES AND TABLES

Illustrations

Figures

Tables

PREFACE

Halfway through this book we describe the circumstances that brought us together, how we began to work as partners in the field of women's career advancement and how, in particular, the FTSE 100 Cross-Company Mentoring Programme came into being. What prompted us to write a book about the scarcity of women in the boardrooms of our large companies? Given the progress women have made in the corporate world in recent years, why did we feel another book on the subject was needed? There has been some progress over the past decade, but not enough had changed or seemed likely to change in the near future for what we both see as a serious inefficiency in the market for executive talent to be left to work itself out.

This book emerged not from a dispassionate, academic interest in the numbers or from a passionate, political interest in equality and women's rights, but from our experience over many years in executive coaching and diversity and talent management. We know about the inefficiency called the "glass ceiling" at first hand, because as professionals we talk every day to senior men and women who know it intimately, either as an obstacle in their efforts to find the talent their companies need to win a competitive advantage or as an obstacle to personal advancement. We have heard stories from both the "demand" side of the ceiling (from chairmen and CEOs who want to appoint more women to their boards) and from the "supply" side (from the women who want to be appointed to these positions, but who find the cultures of their organizations increasingly abrasive, the closer they get to the top echelons of management).

"You can't drill a hole through the floor", said one British comedian to another. "Why not? It's my floor", the other replied. "No, halfway down it's their ceiling." The glass ceiling looks different depending on the side from which it's viewed. In this book we have explored and compared these two points of view and revealed, we believe, something of the nature of this strange, poorly understood barrier that prevents women from making what research suggests is or could be a distinctive and immensely valuable contribution to the guidance and governance of the large companies that shape our world.

Our work with people on both sides of the glass ceiling has also taught us how to break or dissolve a barrier that consists of assumptions and habits embedded so deeply in cultures and business processes that they're below the threshold of conscious awareness. We know what works for organizations and for women; what strategies make the most difference; what tactics cause the least disruption and male resentment; and what kind of processes, practices and institutions are most effective in dismantling a barrier that impoverishes us all.

This book will be of interest to people who aspire to or already have the power to change the gender balance in the higher echelons of their organizations. Chairmen and chief executives, who are concerned about but have not yet begun to address the problem, should find the views of their peers illuminating and informative, and human resource (HR) directors and other senior executives, to whom the responsibility for bringing more women up through the pipeline will fall, should find some useful ideas, prescriptions and approaches.

Headhunters will be interested in what the various stakeholders think about their complicity, or otherwise, in this market inefficiency, and female candidates for board positions will be interested in the views of headhunters, chairmen and CEOs.

There's much here too for non-executive directors who take their duty seriously; for those who suspect that the presence of women on boards will improve standards of corporate governance; for those who believe that women have valuable (but different) contributions to make to the problems of strategic change and understanding the customer; and for ambitious businesswomen who want to equip themselves with arguments and evidence that will help them to secure the support they need to move up corporate hierarchies.

Students of and practitioners in organizational development and human capital management should also find some useful insights here, and we very much hope this book will help talented and ambitious young women contemplating business careers to confront issues and barriers of which they have as yet no inkling.

The problems that face our world are so complex and difficult that we will need all the talent available to solve them. Our deepest wish is to contribute to solving these problems by helping those with power and authority to recognize and try to staunch the enormous waste of resources represented by the scarcity of women at the top of our large companies.

PENINAH THOMSON AND JACEY GRAHAM

The authors can be contacted at:

peninah.thomson@praesta.com   jacey.graham@brookgraham.com
www.praesta.com   www.brookgraham.com

Acknowledgements

This book was made possible by the contribution of many people in many ways. We would like to thank the chairmen and CEOs who gave freely of their time, experience and insights: Roger Carr – chairman of Centrica and Mitchells & Butlers, Dick Cavanagh – president and CEO of The Conference Board, Greg Dyke – former director-general of the BBC, Peter Erskine – CEO of O_2, Joe Forehand – chairman of Accenture, Russ Fradin – CEO of Bisys Group, Howard Frank – vice-chairman and chief operating officer of Carnival Corporation, Harvey Golub – retired chairman and CEO of American Express, Rob Margetts CBE – chairman of Legal & General plc and BOC Group, Charles Miller Smith – chairman of ScottishPower, Sir Mark Moody-Stuart KCMG – chairman of Anglo American, Sir John Parker FREng – chairman of National Grid, Jim Preston – retired chairman and CEO of Avon, Sir Gerry Robinson – chairman of Allied Domecq, Bryan Sanderson CBE – chairman of Standard Chartered plc, Paul Skinner – chairman of Rio Tinto, Maarten van den Bergh – chairman of Lloyds TSB.

We are grateful for the views expressed by women directors and aspiring women directors who shared their personal experiences and insights with us: Ruth Anderson, Darlene Ayers-Johnson, Patricia Barron, Heather Bell, Ruth Cairnie, Carolyn Cattermole, Anita Chandraker, Isabel Doverty, Sheila Forbes, Pamela Gillies, Claire Hamon, Ali Harrison, Lois Hedg-Peth, Lorraine Heggessey, Nina Henderson, Sally-Ann Hibberd, Karen Hoggard, Vivienne Hole, Bella Hopewell, Mary-Jo Jacobi, Gwen Jones, Nancy Karch, Alison Levett, Ruth Markland, Anna Mazzone, Debbie McGowan, Chris Meda, Sonia Mills, Kate Nealon, Laurel Powers-Freeling, Susan Reilly, Michèle Romaine, Helen Stevenson, Jacqui Sutton, Moira Wallace OBE, Helen Weir and Alison Wheaton.

The picture we paint would not have been complete without the insights of executive search consultants. Our thanks go to them for the information they shared with us: Julie Daum, head of the Spencer Stuart Board Practice in the US; Carol Leonard, chairman of the Whitehead Mann Board Services Practice; Samantha Allen, Gill Carrick, Katushka Giltsoff, Chris Leslie, Gerard Clery-Milan and Karin Barnick also of Whitehead Mann; Kenneth MacLennan, former UK managing director of Korn/Ferry International; and Ruth Tait, partner in the UK board practice of Heidrick and Struggles.

We are grateful to the people who provided us with case studies and information about initiatives worldwide: Gunilla Ahrén, Anne Griswold, Marit Hoel, Stephanie MacKendrick, Rhodora Palomar-Fresnedi, Susan Schiffer Stautberg, Debbie Soon, Adam Travis and Mirella Visser. Thanks too to Jude Rich for his personal input and for introducing us to many American interviewees.

Our thanks and appreciation also go to our fellow members of Women Directors on Boards: Sarah Churchman of PricewaterhouseCoopers, Hilary Samson-Barry of the Department of Health, Leslie Mays of Shell and Professor Susan Vinnicombe OBE of the Cranfield School of Management. We would also like to thank our advisers: Baroness Pauline Perry; Anne Watts OBE; Natalie Miller; Dr Val Singh of Cranfield School of Management; Stephen Lawrence, former chief executive of Whitehead Mann; Clare Huffington, director of the Tavistock Consultancy Service; Richard Keys, partner at PricewaterhouseCoopers; Nigel Nicholson, professor of Organisational Behaviour at London Business School; Dame Stephanie Shirley, founder and life president of Xansa; Dr Sue Henley, director of Saville Consulting; Professor Dame Sandra Dawson, director, Judge Business School and Richard Stone.

Jacey would like to thank Lesley Brook, her business partner and co-founder of Brook Graham LLP, for her contribution, insights and support in the writing of this book; Jane Harris for her encouragement and pragmatism in their shared experiences of women's advancement and her close colleagues in Lloyds TSB and Shell who, over the years, helped to pioneer some of the ideas in this book.

The Change Partnership has sponsored the FTSE 100 Cross-Company Mentoring Programme since its inception in 2004, and the Partnership has, in addition, been a committed sponsor of this book. Sponsorship of the Programme has since July 2005, been provided by Praesta Partners LLP. Peninah would like to thank Peter Hogarth and all her other colleagues past and present for the work they do to help women executives fulfil their potential. Particular thanks to Chris Cooper and John Coleman for advice on aspects of the text, and to Mairi Eastwood for her sustained belief in, and commitment to, this book. We also want to thank our researcher, Lynda Knill, and our graphic designer Barbara Shore for her wonderful cartoons. Jo Gavin and Nanette Webb have worked on more drafts of the text than they probably ever dreamed possible – our warm thanks to them.

Our co-author, Tom Lloyd, helped to review the findings from our research, clarify our thinking, synthesize our ideas and get them down on paper. The way the three of us have worked together – apart from the occasional impassioned debate about commas – has been a model of cheerful and effective teamwork, and we can't promise not to do it again!

We would like to take this opportunity of thanking all the chairmen and mentors who have signed up to the FTSE 100 Cross-Company Mentoring Programme. In addition to those already acknowledged on page xvii, we would like to thank the following for their enlightened approach and commitment to improving the gender balance of the board pipeline: John Allan CBE – CEO of Exel; Donald Brydon – chairman of Smiths Group; Patrick Cescau – chief executive of Unilever; Sir Richard Evans CBE – chairman of United Utilities; Iain Ferguson CBE – CEO of Tate & Lyle; Niall Fitzgerald – chairman of Reuters Group; Sir Roy Gardner – CEO of Centrica; Tom Glocer – CEO of Reuters; Stephen Green – group chief executive of HSBC Holdings; Anthony Habgood – chairman of Whitbread & Bunzl; Baroness Sarah Hogg – chairman of 3i Group; Sir Tom McKillop – CEO of AstraZeneca; Dick Olver – chairman of BAE Systems; David Reid – chairman of Tesco; Matt Ridley – chairman of Northern Rock; James Smith – chairman of Shell UK; Lord Dennis Stevenson – chairman of HBOS; and to all the mentees, some of whom would prefer not to be identified. Our thanks also go to the following people for their encouragement of the Programme at the early stages of its development: Dr Dina Consolini, Clara Freeman OBE, Rt Hon Patricia Hewitt MP, Norma Jarboe, Angela Mason OBE, Diane Morris, Helene Reardon-Bond, Stephen Spivey, Dr Laura Tyson, and Tracy Vegro. We would also like to thank our publisher, Stephen Rutt and his team, for their support, guidance and enthusiasm.

We thank those in our "personal support systems" who have encouraged us and provided much needed distraction at times. Jacey would like to thank Jimmy and Jacque Graham, James and Paula Graham, Constance Skeels, Clare, Laura, Evelyn and Malcolm Dias. Peninah would like to thank Alastair and Diana Thomson, Lorraine and Ron de Jong, Christine and Geoff Dean, John Scott, Jane Spencer, Jacquie Rawes and Richard Simmons.

There's a saying that runs: "Behind every successful senior woman in business there is a man without a chip on his shoulder." Many women, as well as men, have over the years provided each of us with support, encouragement and fellowship: but we would like to single out two men without chips on their shoulders, Ed Smith and Peter Dias, with love and thanks.

Finally, we would like to acknowledge the part played by the children and young people with whom we share our lives in influencing our thoughts and hopes about the future: James, Tristan, Ben, Eleanor, Kate, Tom, Tamsin, Rory and Stephanie.

B2B	business-to-business
B2C	business-to-consumer
BBC	British Broadcasting Corporation
CBI	Confederation of British Industry
CEO	chief executive officer
CFO	chief financial officer
CSR	corporate social responsibility
DTI	Department of Trade and Industry
ED	executive director
FD	finance director
FTSE 100	Financial Times/Stock Exchange 100
GDP	gross domestic product
GMAT	Graduate Management Admission Test
HR	human resources
IOD	Institute of Directors
IT	information technology
MBA	Masters Degree in Business Administration
MLQ	Multifactor Leadership Questionnaire
MPs	Members of Parliament
NASDAQ	National Association of Securities Dealers Automated Quotations
NEDs	non-executive directors
NYSE	New York Stock Exchange
OD	organization development
ROE	return on equity
S&P500	Standard & Poors 500
SSBI	Spencer Stuart Board Index
TSRs	total shareholder returns
VP	vice president
WDoB	Women Directors on Boards

The way we live, our material well-being and the extent to which we realize our dreams for ourselves and our families are all deeply influenced by the large capitalist corporations that create most of the world's wealth and to the service of which most of us devote our skill, talent and working lives. We will argue that these large, increasingly global institutions that shape our world and our lives are themselves misshapen, because they are led and governed almost entirely by men.

But you will find no accusations of sex discrimination here, no revelations of male chauvinist conspiracy, no catalogue of man's inhumanity to working woman. It is not that kind of book. Nor will we suggest that these male-led organizations are irredeemably predatory, irresponsible or corrupt. On the contrary – it seems to us that they have been, and remain, a powerful force for good in a troubled world. They would be a more potent force for good, however, a more powerful engine of economic growth and a more prolific creator of value for shareholders if more women were more directly involved in their guidance and governance. There are four main reasons for this.

The first is that the success of groups of individuals who work together to create value for their shareholders by meeting the needs of customers will depend partly on how well their leaders understand and empathize with their customers. Other things being equal, such as their leaders' innate and learned abilities, companies will create more value for their shareholders if the minds of their leaders resemble more closely the "mind" of their market. To argue otherwise would be to assert that understanding and empathy have no value in business.

On the face of it, therefore, the ideal leadership team would have slightly more women than men, because women currently account for a little over half the population of the developed world. One could argue that the balance of power in leadership teams should actually favor women even more than this, because women shop more than men, and probably have more influence on men's buying decisions than men have on theirs.

It does not follow from this, and we will not argue, that women should hold some 60 percent of large company directorships. But population numbers and studies of purchasing behavior do suggest that if companies want to be better adapted to their customers, women should hold more than the 16 percent of S&P 500 and 10 percent of FTSE 100 directorships they currently hold.

The second reason why shareholders and stakeholders of large corporations would benefit if women were more intimately involved in their guidance and governance is that such organizations are hard to manage, and by failing to appoint women to senior positions, companies are denying themselves access to half the talent pool. This self-denial seems particularly unwise now, at a time when corporate governance reforms are effectively creating a serious shortage of directors by reducing the number of directorships an individual can hold.

The third reason why we believe large companies would benefit if women were more involved in their leadership is that women bring distinctive qualities and sensibilities to the tasks of management, and companies have more need now for the feminine qualities most evident in women than the masculine qualities most evident in men.

The final reason why we believe large companies would benefit if women were more involved in their leadership follows from the first three and the logic of competition. If companies with more women in senior positions are more attuned to their customers and better managed, those that appoint more women to senior positions than their competitors will, other things being equal, gain a competitive advantage. By the same token, companies that make no attempt to do so will put themselves at a disadvantage, and be in breach of their duty to shareholders to maximize shareholder value.

Some argue that demographic and educational trends and the inexorable logic of the "war for talent" will in due course correct the gender imbalance on boards. According to this view, the imbalance is a market inefficiency, and markets correct their inefficiencies eventually. Our view is that although there is some merit in this – companies will come under growing pressure to correct the gender imbalance on their boards – it would be unwise to assume that the correction will happen automatically, or any time soon. Markets do tend to correct their inefficiencies, but only when they are closed systems, and in the age of globalization, markets for directors are far from being closed systems. While demographic trends are reducing the national pools of potential male directors in some countries, such the US and the UK, they are increasing them in other countries such as India and China.

But it is one thing to acknowledge all this, and quite another to achieve a better balance between the sexes on the bridge of the ship of business. Our research has convinced us that there is no conspiracy and that if there is a glass ceiling, it is not of man's deliberate making.

There are many reasons for the scarcity of women in leadership positions at large companies, and they interact in subtle and complex ways. Some of them are historical, some stem from the nature of organizations themselves, some are to do with deep-rooted differences in the male and female mind (and the differences in outlooks, attitudes and appetites these generate), and there is no denying that the childbearing and child-rearing roles assigned to women by nature contribute to their rarity at the top of large companies, although not as much, we believe, as is usually supposed.

Moreover, focusing on the numbers themselves will change nothing except the numbers. Women-only short lists for board seats would arouse understandable howls of protest from men. And, although they would help to redress the sex imbalance, the additional women would add no more than a cosmetic value (no pun intended) if their arrival left the organization unchanged. The reason large companies should appoint more women to senior management positions is that it will improve their performance, not that it will earn them "brownie points" and higher rankings in diversity league tables.

There are no quick or easy solutions to the problem. It will take time and a lot of innovative thinking to adapt businesses to a marketplace in which the customer is queen, and reap the rewards of women's management touch. We hope this book will help company leaders in the US and the UK, where our attention is mostly focused, to understand why appointing more women to their boards will create more value for their shareholders, and identify and find ways around the obstacles on the path to achieving better balanced boards.

We begin, in Chapter 1, by summarizing recent research on the rise of women as the dominant purchasing sex and exploring its implications for so-called "customer-focused" organizations. We summarize the results of research on women executives at large US and UK companies, identify the main trends and suggest that the manifest fact that today's customer is not "king", as the traditional wisdom has it, but "queen" helps to explain the evidence, such as it is, that companies with more women directors than average create more shareholder value than average.

We demonstrate the extent of the female talent pool, which is largely untapped by businesses, by summarizing evidence that shows girls do better than boys at school and in higher education, and thus represent the higher quality as well as the larger proportion of available talent at graduate level.

In Chapter 2 we provide some tools and concepts for thinking about why the market has so far failed to acknowledge the opportunity cost created by the imbalance and made so little progress toward correcting it. Our purpose in suggesting companies are kingdoms is not to contribute to the psycho-logical debate, but to provide a framework for thinking about the kinds of problems companies wishing to achieve better balanced boards must solve.

Chapter 3 summarizes conversations we have had with the chairmen and chief executives (CEOs) of several large US and UK companies and reveals, amongst other things, that these corporate kings are not averse to appointing more women to their boards. On the contrary, although some believe that the "male" nature of their industries (engineering, mining, and so on) makes women board members less necessary or appropriate, most seem keen to appoint more women to their boards. We end the chapter by identifying the main themes that emerged from these conversations.

Following on from this, Chapter 4 summarizes the views of several female executives in the "marzipan layer" (as Laura Tyson, dean of London Business School and author of the 2003 Tyson Report, calls the manage-ment layer just below the board) at US and UK companies. Company lead-ers need to understand the views and concerns of such women, because they are the vanguard of a large and growing contingent of business talent that companies cannot afford to ignore.

In Chapter 5 we describe the origins and report on the progress so far of the FTSE 100 Cross-Company Mentoring Programme, a new mentoring scheme we developed and launched in 2004, which brings together the protagonists of Chapter 3 (male chairmen and CEOs) with the protagonists of Chapter 4 (senior female executives at other companies who aspire to board roles). The Programme has received a substantial amount of press coverage in the UK and has attracted interest from other countries. We believe it has the makings of a powerful new alliance between male leaders, who recognize the need for more women on their boards, and ambitious women eager to meet that need.

In Chapter 6 we discuss some of the differences between the manage-ment and leadership styles of men and women and argue that companies are in need of female styles of management now, as they try to reconcile the apparently conflicting needs of shareholders and stakeholders; respond to demands for higher standards of corporate governance; and search for ways to attract and keep good people in the war for talent. We do not suggest that the female style of leadership is better than the male style. Our argument is that the styles are complementary and since the female style is underrepre-sented in the boardroom at present, companies that appoint more women to their boards or executive committees will gain a competitive advantage.

In Chapter 7 we present the views of women who have made it to the board. In Chapter 8 we present the views of executive search professionals (head-hunters) who seek candidates for board appointments at large companies.

Chapters 9 and 10 comprise the main prescriptive section of the book. Chapter 9 describes a "gender pipeline strategy" for bringing women up the management hierarchy to the boardroom, and discusses what women can do to further their own careers while their companies remain male. The absence of women from their boardrooms is a long-term problem for companies, but there are steps they can take in the short term to improve the gender balance on their boards while long-term cultural change takes effect.

Chapter 10 explains how to promote the long-term cultural changes needed to make companies androgynous, so that ultimately women do not have to play the game by "male" rules, but can pursue their careers in a gender-balanced environment. We conclude that change is required on the personal, interpersonal and system levels. We suggest that, although this book is about how to get more women onto boards, many of our prescriptions should also be of benefit to other minority groups.

We begin Chapter 11 by confronting the difficult question of what "good" would look like on a board in the future, in terms of its gender balance. Having suggested some figures, we look at trends in this direction outside the US and the UK, and speculate how business will change if and when those figures are reached. We end the book by arguing that society at large, as well as companies, needs to get many more women into leadership positions if we are to solve the pressing economic and social problems of our time.

CHAPTER 1

The customer is queen

The directors of Cisco Systems were assembled in the boardroom waiting for their new CEO, John Chambers. They knew the boss was in the building, because he had been spotted. Had he forgotten? Didn't he realize the importance of his inaugural board meeting? Chambers turned up half an hour late. He said he was sorry, but he'd been busy sorting out a customer's problem.

Was it bad manners or, as the Wharton Business School Professor George Day interpreted it, a "clear sign that customers were a top priority"? Day argues that "pervasive market orientation" should be "woven into the fabric of the organization" and says that "markets eventually punish firms with arrogant and unresponsive cultures".[1]

History does not record the gender of the customer who delayed the arrival of Cisco's CEO that day. Chances are it was a man, because Cisco makes the routers, hubs and switches that link the internet together and most of its customers are companies managed by males. Moreover, the year was 1995 when there were fewer women than there are now in middle and senior management positions. At the time of writing in April 2005 three of Cisco's 32-strong executive team were women.[2]

Had Cisco been a B2C (business-to-consumer) rather than a B2B (business-to-business) company, the chances are that the customer who delayed Chambers would have been a woman. The conventional wisdom that George Day and other management writers often urge companies to believe passionately in, rather than glibly espouse, is "the customer is king". The conventional wisdom is wrong. The customer isn't king, she's queen.

According to management guru Tom Peters, a self-confessed UTTER LUNATIC (his capitals) about the importance of women as customers, women in the US "are instigators-in-chief of most consumer purchases". To wit:

All consumer purchases	83 percent
Home furnishings	94 percent
Vacations	92 percent
New homes	91 percent
DIY ("home projects")	80 percent
Consumer electronics	51 percent

Cars	61 percent (+ influence another 30 percent)
New bank accounts	89 percent
Healthcare	80 percent decisions, 66 percent spending

He says two-thirds of working women in the US and more than 50 percent of working wives earn over half their family's income, and women write 80 percent of checks (cheques), pay 61 percent of all bills and own 53 percent of stocks (equities).

According to Peters' research, the power of women as company purchasers is also grossly underestimated. They account for over half of US purchasing managers and agents, their dominance of corporate HR functions gives them control of huge budgets for health plans, pensions, and so on, and they make up more than 50 percent of corporate admin officers "with awesome power when it comes to opening (or not) the commercial purse".[3] Moreover they own 38 percent of US businesses, which together employ over 27 million people and generate over $3.5 trillion in annual revenues.

Other research estimates that women purchase, or influence the purchase of, 80–95 percent of consumer goods, including 50 percent or more of the traditionally "male" categories, such as cars, consumer electronics and PCs, 80 percent of healthcare products and 92 percent of holidays.[4]

Comparable figures for the UK are hard to come by, but according to Henley Centre, the UK futures consultancy, 71 percent of "main shoppers" (people who make over 60 percent of their family's purchases) are women. It seems a fair bet that a substantial proportion of the 29 percent of the men who are main shoppers take lists written by women to the shops with them.

According to Peter Frost of Rethink Pink, an annual UK conference focusing on female consumers, women influence over 85 percent of global consumer decision making, buy over 50 percent of new cars, comprise 40 percent of business travelers and start 35 percent of new businesses.[5]

Research carried out by the Centre for Economics and Business Research for the Liverpool Victoria financial services group found that women currently own 48 percent of Britain's personal wealth, and the study predicted this will to rise to 60 percent by 2025, because women perform better than men in secondary, further and higher education and live longer.[6]

There is nothing "niche" about women. They're the primary consumers in all modern, industrialized economies. They are the market.

Companies that wish to be market-driven, therefore, effectively wish to be women-driven. Which is not to say that men are incapable of understanding women (many of the leading women's fashion designers are men, after all) or that male-driven businesses have no access to information about women's tastes, preferences and needs. They can – and most B2C compa-

© Barbara Shore

THE CUSTOMER IS QUEEN!

nies do – get women in for consultation and go to considerable lengths to adapt their products or services to the women-dominated marketplace.

The point is that although it is very useful to get women "in", it is more competitively advantageous in the long term to get women "on" boards, because that will lead to a deeper cultural adaptation to the marketplace. Getting women in for consultation outsources female input. Getting women on the board embeds the feminine in the company's culture by feminizing the corporate persona. To put the same point another way, it's hard to weave, as Day advocated, "pervasive market orientation into the fabric of the organization" when the dominant gender of the market is unrepresented in its leadership.

As Tom Peters put it, "if a board does not at all resemble the market being served then something big is badly wrong".[3]

It's one thing to make an assertion, however, and quite another to provide corroboration. What evidence is there that having more women on the board will lead to a "deeper cultural adaptation to the marketplace"? And, given

WHAT'S THE FEMALE PERSPECTIVE?
— WE NEED A FOCUS GROUP

© Barbara Shore

that the ultimate objective of all companies is to make their shareholders as well off as possible, what purpose would such an adaptation serve?

Shareholders of publicly listed companies perceive value in monetary terms and the money value of their investments is ultimately driven by financial performance. So, our question boils down to: "What evidence is there that companies with women on their boards perform better financially than those with all-male boards?" The short answer is "some".

Women directors and corporate performance

The Female FTSE Report, published annually by Cranfield University's School of Management, tracks the number of women on the boards of the constituents of the UK's main equities index, the Financial Times/Stock Exchange (FTSE) 100.[7]

In her foreword to the 2004 report, Patricia Hewitt, the then UK secretary of state for trade and industry and cabinet minister for women, welcomed the 9 percent rise in the number of women directors of FTSE 100 constituents from 101 in 2003, to 110 (less than 10 percent of all directors on FTSE 100 boards and the vast majority of these female directors are non-executive), and said that a growing number of executives realized that "equality for women isn't just a moral issue – it's something which has a positive impact on their businesses too."

Ms Hewitt was referring to a finding in the 2004 report that, over the previous three years, the 69 companies with women directors had recorded an average return on equity (ROE) of 13.8 percent, compared to an average ROE of only 9.9 percent for the 31 companies which had all-male boards.

The Cranfield team also found that market capitalization was highly correlated with the presence of women directors – the bigger the company, the more likely it was to have women directors. That this was consistent with a 2003 US study,[8] but inconsistent with a 1997 US study,[9] suggests this relationship between market capitalization and women directors has emerged quite recently. They found no correlation between financial performance and the proportion of women on boards.

The number of companies with female executive directors had only increased from 10 to 13 since 2000 and there was still only one female CEO, Marjorie Scardino, of Pearson, the publishing group that owns the *Financial Times* (or one-and-a-half if you include Marie Melnyk, joint managing director of the Morrisons supermarket chain). This compares with seven female CEOs (down from nine the previous year) of constituents of the Standard & Poors 500 (S&P 500) US index, as at July 15, 2004, according to the 2004 Spencer Stuart Board Index (SSBI).[10]

CEO	Company
Carol A. Bartz	Autodesk
Andrea Jung	Avon Products
Margaret C. Whitman	eBay
Marion O. Sandler	Golden West Financial (co-CEO)
Carleton S. Fiorina	Hewlett-Packard
Patricia F. Russo	Lucent Technologies
Anne M. Mulcahy	Xerox

Carly Fiorina has since left Hewlett-Packard and been replaced by a man.

Of the 13 female executive directors of FTSE 100 companies, six were chief financial officers (CFOs) and two were HR directors. Professor Susan Vinnicombe and Dr Val Singh, the authors of the Cranfield report, said executive directors were especially important, because they are "everyday role models" for other women, "indicating that executive career tracks do go right to the boardroom … for women as well as men." They expect the 13 companies with female executive directors to prove "better able to recruit and … retain talented and ambitious women in the future, with the symbolic value of their female executive directors."

A study by Catalyst, America's leading not-for-profit organization focusing on female advancement in the workplace, reached broadly similar performance conclusions. Published in 2004 under the title *The bottom line: connecting corporate performance and gender diversity*, the study measured ROE and total shareholder returns (TSRs; capital gains plus reinvested dividends) during the second half of the 1990s at the 353 Fortune 500 constituent companies for which diversity data were available.[11]

The study ranked the companies by the representation of women on their top teams and found that the top quartile (top 25 percent) significantly outperformed the bottom quartile on both measures – by 35 percent on ROE and 34 percent on TSRs.

Catalyst talks of top teams rather than boards, because the composition of boards is different in the two countries. UK boards include executive and non-executive directors (NEDs), in more or less equal numbers. US boards normally include only one or two insiders – the chairman/CEO and the CFO. The roles of chairman and CEO are normally separate in UK companies, but have historically been combined in US companies. That's changing. According to the 2004 SSBI, 74 percent of S&P 500 companies combined the roles of CEO and chairman in 2004, compared to 77 percent in 2003 and 80 percent in 1999.

Despite these important differences in board composition, however, the big numbers are comparable at a deeper level, because the executive committees that run US companies supply many of the outside or independent directors. In other words, if you are on your company's executive committee, there is a fair chance of you being, or becoming an independent director at another S&P 500/Fortune 500 company. You're less likely than you were, however, to be an independent director of more than one company. According to the 2004 SSBI, the average number of outside directorships of S&P 500 CEOs fell below one for the first time in 2004 to 0.9, from 1.0 in 2003 and 1.6 in 1999.

To take account of differences in sector performances – the pharmaceutical sector, for example, dramatically outperformed the utilities sector during the period – the Catalyst study analyzed performance within sectors. It found that in each of the five industries analyzed, the companies in the top 25 percent of the gender diversity rankings achieved a higher average ROE than did those in the bottom 25 percent, and in four of the industries analyzed, the top 25 percent recorded higher average TSRs than the bottom 25 percent.

Statistically, the results of both the studies are highly significant. They show a strong positive relationship between the representation of women on boards and financial performance. They tell us nothing, however, about the nature of this relationship. As the authors of the Catalyst report pointed out, the relationship could be "causative", in the sense that more women on the board causes the better performance, or it could be "spurious", in the sense that more women on the board is related to another variable, such as size (as suggested by the Cranfield study), which is the real cause of the better performance. So the issue remains open. The studies corroborate the hypothesis that firms with women directors perform better financially than those with all-male boards, but they do not prove it. Corroboration is all that can be expected at this stage, however.

The drivers of financial performance are many and varied and although some companies are making good progress (see box) the number of female

---

Companies with relatively high numbers of women directors

According to the 2004 SSBI, the boards of four S&P 500 constituents had 40 percent or more female members:

Golden West Financial	56 percent	financial services
Avon	55 percent	cosmetics
Albertsons	50 percent	grocery retailing
Pepsi Bottling	40 percent	soft drinks

According to Cranfield's *Female FTSE Report 2004* the boards of 12 FTSE 100 constituents had 20 percent or more female members:

John Lewis Partnership	35 percent	retailing*
Marks & Spencer	31 percent	retailing
AstraZeneca	31 percent	pharmaceuticals
J. Sainsbury	27 percent	grocery retailing
Shell	27 percent	oil
BAA	25 percent	airports
Prudential	23 percent	financial services
Reckitt Benckiser	22 percent	household products
Aviva	21 percent	financial services
Legal & General	21 percent	financial services
3i Group	20 percent	venture capital
Centrica	20 percent	utility
Kingfisher	20 percent	retailing

* Not a FTSE 100 constituent, because unlisted, but see Chapter 6.

executive directors remains far too low to expect a clear causative link between gender diversity on boards and performance to emerge. But companies that wait until such a clear causative link emerges may find they've waited too long. As in other areas of business, companies that wish to lead change in a changing environment, rather than follow it, must act before all the evidence is in. For reasons we will be discussing later, it will take time to achieve a more appropriate gender balance on a board – a long time, a lot of effort, and top-level commitment. If competitive advantage is to be gained by such a rebalancing, it will also require the courage to act before the competitive need to act is obvious.

That the US figures for female directors are higher than the UK's, but not much higher, gives the lie to those who claim the imbalance of the genders on UK boards requires no corrective action, because it is just a matter of time before trends already in train bring the number of women on UK boards up to the US level. The gender imbalance would hardly be "corrected" by an increase in the proportion of female FTSE 100 directors from 9.7 percent, in the *Female FTSE Report 2004* to 16 percent in the SSBI 2004, or 16.9 percent of Fortune 100 boards in a May 2005 report by The Alliance for Board Diversity.[12] Moreover, the increase in the US percentage from 12 percent in 1999 has been partly (perhaps mostly) due to deliberate corrective action by US companies.

Inaction is clearly not an option and the time to act is now. The evidence summarized above, that more women on the board leads to improved financial performance, is not conclusive, but neither is it negligible and there are good commonsense reasons to give it more credence than the numbers deserve on their own.

Reasonable conjectures

It seems reasonable to assume that companies in which leadership positions are "open", in the sense that they are as accessible to women as they are to men, will acquire (not initially perhaps, but eventually) more able and talented leaders than companies in which leadership positions are "closed" to women. This follows from the demonstrable, generally accepted fact that ability and talent are distributed evenly between the sexes.

We do not think that the *same* abilities and talents are distributed evenly between the sexes. As a very general rule, men have more of some abilities and talents than women, and women have more of other abilities and talents than men. We will explore these differences in Chapter 2, and suggest that they complement each other in business in Chapter 6. For the moment, it is enough to note that few would dispute that the sum totals of human ability and talent are distributed evenly between the sexes.

This commonsense assumption is corroborated by higher education statistics in both the US and the UK. In the US women are awarded over 57 percent of bachelors degrees, over 58 percent of masters degrees, 45 percent of doctorates, 47 percent of law degrees,[13] and account for 46 percent of the paid labor force and almost 46 percent of management positions.[14]

In the UK the gender pattern is similar. In the 2003/4 academic year, women accounted for over 56 percent of all first (bachelors) degrees awarded to UK-domiciled full-time students, 55 percent of first class degrees and 49 percent of higher degrees.[15]

There are some signs of acceleration in the adaptation of companies to the gender balance in the talent pool. According to the SSBI, almost a quarter of independent directors appointed to S&P 500 boards in 2004 were women; the largest annual increase in female directors ever recorded. Moreover, the average age of new female directors was 52, compared to 56 for all new directors. There are signs of acceleration in the UK too. Cranfield found that new female board appointments rose sharply in 2004, to 17 percent of all board appointments, although this only brought the number of women directors to 10 percent of the FTSE 100 total. Another sign of acceleration appeared in an interim Cranfield report in April, 2005. This found that another 10 female directors had been appointed to FTSE 100 boards since the beginning of 2005. This increased the number of FTSE 100 companies with one woman or more on their boards from 69 to 77.

Another important trend indicator is the so-called "pipeline" – the number of women who could be candidates for board appointments in the foreseeable future. The pipeline matters, because its current fullness will constrain the potential for the appointment of women as executive directors over the next five to ten years, and impose an upper limit on the rate of increase in the medium term in the gender diversity of boards.

Catalyst's study shows that the proportion of women in the ranks of Fortune 500 senior managers rose from 10 to almost 16 percent between 1996 and 2002.[11] Although this is still way below the proportion of women graduates in the general population, it indicates momentum in the right direction.

Cranfield's study measured the UK's pipeline for women directors by asking FTSE 100 companies to calculate the percentages of women in junior, middle and senior management positions. Only 12 companies supplied the requested information, and some might have done so because they felt they were ahead of the game in this area, so their figures should be taken with a pinch of salt – they might not be representative of FTSE 100 companies as a group. They represent anecdotal evidence, however, which is sometimes all a trend analyst has to work with. For what they are worth, the figures showed that the average proportion of women in the workforces of the 12 companies was 44 percent and women accounted for 29, 28 and 20 percent respectively of junior, middle and senior management positions.

Since this was the first time Cranfield had done the analysis, the figures provide no trend information, but it's reasonable to assume the pattern is similar to that of the US and that all three percentages (which may or may not be representative of large UK companies) are new "highs".

Governance

A crop of corporate scandals in recent years, in both the US and Europe, has led to a tightening of corporate regulation and reporting requirements and more intense public scrutiny of corporate behavior.

The most conspicuous development was the passage of the Sarbanes-Oxley Act by the US Senate in January, 2002. Similar new laws and codes of practice have been introduced elsewhere, such as the Combined Code, issued by the Financial Reporting Council in the UK in 2003, and inspired by Sir Derek Higgs's Report on *The Role and Effectiveness of Non-executive Directors*.[16] These new regimes impose tough new reporting requirements on boards and have made directors more aware of the damage that can be inflicted on their own and their companies' reputations by certain business practices that were previously below the threshold of public awareness.

The institutional framework created by the Higgs and Tyson Reports and the Combined Code is summarized below.

Recommendations for creating more diverse and effective boardrooms

Higgs

- Chairmen of listed companies should encourage and facilitate their executive directors and suitable senior management just below board level to take one non-executive director position on a non-competitor board.

- The nomination committee should evaluate the balance of skills, knowledge and experience on the board and prepare a description of the role and capabilities required for a particular appointment.

- The nomination committee should provide support to the board on succession planning.

- All companies operating in international markets could benefit from having on their board at least one international non-executive director with relevant skills and experience.

- Lawyers, accountants and consultants are used to advising business from the outside – they can bring useful skills as non-executive directors.

- Boards should look to private companies, some of which are of significant scale, as a source of non-executive directors.

- There are individuals in charitable or public sector bodies who have strong commercial and market understanding. Including them on a plc board can increase breadth and diversity, improving effectiveness.

- Boards should draw more actively from groups not traditionally represented on boards – such as human resources, change management and customer care executives – even if they are not yet at board level.

Tyson

- Selection processes for non-executive directors should be rigorous and transparent.

- Boards should have more and better evaluation and training.

- Research and measurement should be implemented to encourage greater board diversity.

Combined Code

1. *The board:* Every company should be headed by an effective board, which is collectively responsible for the success of the company.

2. *Chairman and chief executive:* There should be a clear division of responsibilities at the head of the company between the running of the board and the executive responsibility for the running of the company's business. No one individual should have unfettered powers of decision.

3. *Board balance and independence:* The board should include a balance of executive and non-executive directors (and in particular independent non-executive directors) such that no individual or small group of individuals can dominate the board's decision taking.

4. *Appointments to the board:* There should be a formal, rigorous and transparent procedure for the appointment of new directors to the board.

5. *Information and professional development:* The board should be supplied in a timely manner with information in a form and of a quality appropriate to enable it to discharge its duties. All directors should receive induction on

joining the board and should regularly update and refresh their skills and knowledge.

6. *Performance evaluation:* The board should undertake a formal and rigorous annual evaluation of its own performance and that of its committees and individual directors.

7. *Re-election:* All directors should be submitted for re-election at regular intervals, subject to continued satisfactory performance. The board should ensure planned and progressive refreshing of the board.

Source: Building Better Boards, DTI, 2004

As Michael Cook, retired chairman of Deloitte & Touche, pointed out in the 2004 SSBI, compliance with section 404 of the Sarbanes-Oxley Act, covering the reporting of, and accountability for, financial statements, is so time-consuming now and carries such heavy personal responsibilities that "some highly qualified individuals are questioning whether they want to serve on an audit committee [of a board]".[10]

The impression that the corporate scandals in the US and Europe have given of a new breed of insatiably avaricious, incorrigibly amoral companies has made the thinking public much more interested in financial engineering and so-called "aggressive tax planning", in the same generally censorious way they first became interested two decades ago in the impact of business activity on the environment.

The current debate about how much tax companies should pay exemplifies the new, more critical public perceptions of corporate behavior to which more women directors could help companies become more responsive.

Previously confined to the inside pages of financial sections of the daily press, tax has been making front-page headlines with increasing frequency. The UK's influential *Financial Times* published a series of articles in the summer of 2004 on how "tax planning" (legal tax "avoidance", as opposed to illegal tax "evasion") by large foreign-owned companies was eroding the UK corporate tax base.

A month earlier, a House of Commons motion, tabled by the Labour MP Austin Mitchell, had urged the government to investigate 21 companies that were paying tax at less than the standard rate. When asking "How much [of the sub-standard amounts of tax paid by the 21 companies] is due to tax avoidance, if any, and how much is legitimate?", Mitchell was implying that companies had some kind of undefined moral obligation to pay more tax than the minimum required by law.

But how much more? Where does legitimate tax planning end and the quasi-crime of excessively aggressive tax avoidance begin? Given their duty to maximize shareholder value, how can boards decide the right amount of tax to pay? These are important questions.

Companies play crucial roles in modern economies and societies not only as payers and collectors of the taxes that finance public spending, but also as investors who take taxes into account when deciding where to locate new wealth-creating operations. How we resolve the questions that divide us on the fairness or otherwise of the tax burden, and whether activity that some call tax avoidance and others call tax planning is socially responsible, will affect the health and vigor of our economies and help to define what we mean by the term "good corporate citizen."

Some suggest that boards that include women tend to reach better decisions on tax and other ethical matters, because women have a better sense of what's "right" in a particular set of circumstances (see Chapter 3), because they are more interested than men in ethical and corporate social responsibility issues or because the presence of women on the board limits the power of male "group think" to nod through ostensibly value-creating proposals or policies that are ethically questionable.

It's a contentious suggestion and hard to corroborate. Whether or not one agrees with it will depend more on one's intuition and perceptions of the differences between men and women, than any relevant facts. Writing in the *Independent* at the end of 2004, Jeremy Warner ended a critical review of *The Female FTSE Report*'s attempt to demonstrate a link between women on boards and corporate governance by musing as follows: "one cannot help but think the boardroom that remains womanless is missing out, not just on the talents of half the human race, but also on a ... civilizing and highly practical influence".[17]

The Female FTSE Report 2004 applied 13 governance indicators, derived from the Higgs and Tyson Reports, and found that companies with women directors scored significantly higher than those with all-male boards – the averages were 10.8 and 9.1, respectively. We have sympathy with those who object in principle to this kind of box-ticking approach to corporate governance and we do not regard this as clear evidence that companies with more gender diverse boards are better managed. But it does pass muster as a straw in the wind; as a hint at least that women directors may have an important part to play in the improvement in the standards of corporate governance that the public at large are demanding.

On their own these figures prove nothing, of course, but when combined they paint an impressionistic picture of a corporate species in the early stages of a largely unconscious adaptation to the dominant gender of the marketplace. The puzzle is why it is taking so long. If full adaptation to the queendom of the marketplace confers a competitive advantage, by weaving what George Day calls "pervasive market orientation" into the fabric of a company, and if, as we believe, that adaptation and that "pervasive market orientation" can't be achieved by companies led by all-male boards, why are there still so few women directors? This is the question we now turn to in Chapter 2.

References

1. *The Market Driven Organization*, George S. Day, The Free Press, 1999.
2. Cisco Systems' website; http://newsroom.cisco.com/dlls/tln/exec_team/bios.html.
3. *Re-imagine! Business Excellence in a Disruptive Age*, Tom Peters, Dorling Kindersley, 2003.
4. Think tank: marketing to women – the gender factor, Peter Crush, *Marketing Direct*, December 31, 2004.
5. More than just a pretty face, *Guardian*, September 6, 2004.
6. Liverpool Victoria press release, April 22, 2005.
7. *The Female FTSE Report 2004*, Cranfield University School of Management, 2004.
8. Corporate Governance, Board Diversity and Firm Value, D. A. Carter, B. J. Simkins and V. G. Simpson, *Financial Review*, 38, 2003.
9. Women in management and firm value: An exploratory study, C. B. Shrader, V. B. Blackburn and P. Iles, *Journal of Managerial Issues*, 9, 1997.
10. Spencer Stuart Board Index, 2004, S&P 500 data as of June 30, 2004, obtained from proxies released on or before July 15, 2004.
11. *The bottom line: connecting corporate performance and gender diversity*, Catalyst, sponsored by BMO Financial Group, 2004.
12. Women and Minorities on Fortune 100 Boards, The Alliance for Board Diversity, May 17, 2005.
13. *Digest of Education Statistics*, National Center for Education Statistics, 2002.
14. Current Population Survey, Bureau of Labor Statistics, 2003.
15. Higher Education Statistics Agency.
16. www.dti.gov.uk/cld/non_exec_review.
17. Women directors, Jeremy Warner, The *Independent*, 8.12.04.

CHAPTER 2

Companies are kingdoms

A kind of blindness

A group of 30 middle managers divided roughly equally between the sexes had assembled off-site to discuss their company's new "diversity" program.

"OK!" said the facilitator, loudly enough to be heard above the chatter. "Everyone's here, so let's get started. The first thing I want you to do is spend a minute or two jotting down some thoughts about the company you all work for. Since the subject today is diversity, it would be good to have diverse perspectives, so I want women to describe what it's like being a woman working for the company, and men to describe what it's like being a man working for the company."

There was silence for a few moments, as the 30 participants collected their thoughts. Then they started writing furiously. Or, rather the women started writing furiously. It seemed the men needed longer to gather their thoughts – so long that, eventually, the facilitator asked one of them whether there was a problem. He looked around at the other men and, reassured to see his own puzzlement reflected on their faces, said: "Yes. I'm sorry, but I'm not sure I understand the question."

What we find interesting about this story is not what it reveals about the obtuseness of men, but what it tells us about the nature of organizations. Why are the men bemused by the facilitator's question? What is it about the corporate ecosystem that makes them react to their question as fish might do on being asked to describe water?

Part of the answer is the influence exerted by the disproportionate numbers of men at the top of our largest companies. The fact that the architects of almost all companies were men leads to the tacit assumption that corporate cultures created by men are the only possible corporate cultures. But there must be more to it than that. If it were just a matter of the numbers, there should have been evidence by now of cultural change, because women account, on average, for not far short of half the employees of our large companies. Something, some quality shared by all companies that men are better adapted to than women, is inhibiting change.

Some have suggested that the reason men fare better in companies than women is that companies are the creatures of men; the water of company

COMPANIES ARE KINGDOMS

© Barbara Shore

life is saturated in testosterone, because hierarchical organization itself is a man thing.

Hierarchy is masculine

Matt Ridley, an evolutionary psychologist, noted in his book *The Red Queen* that, although few reasonable people would object to the suggestion that the differences between the bodies of male and female humans evolved to reflect differences in the roles they played in Pleistocene society, all hell would break loose if you suggested the same probably applied to the minds of male and female humans.[1]

Ridley was writing over a decade ago, when sensitivities about such matters were more acute than they are now. Larry Summers, president of Harvard University, caused a furore in early 2005 when he suggested that a study which had found men were disproportionately represented at the top and bottom of science test rankings might help to explain the preponderance of men among top research scientists, but the fuss soon died down.[2] The idea that the minds of men and women are different and this difference must be recognized in any discussion of the role of women in large, hierarchical organizations is, we hope, no longer controversial.

Ridley said that human beings are unique among the apes in having developed a sexual division of labor. In chimpanzee societies, females and males seek the same foods, but in all early human societies, women and men looked for different food. Women gathered food that was "static, close and predictable (usually plants)"; while men looked for food that was "mobile, distant and unpredictable (usually meat)".

Psychological tests have shown that, on average, girls are better at verbal and some visuo-spatial tasks than boys, and boys are better at mathematical and other visuo-spatial tasks than girls. The differences in visuo-spatial skills can be summarized by saying men are better at reading maps and women are better at reading faces – judging character and mood.[3]

Remember the story about a couple in a car getting lost? He reaches for the map; she wants to stop and ask someone the way. According to evolutionary psychologists, both are playing to their strengths. He's relying on the bump of locality inherited from his forefathers, who had to find their way home after long hunting trips. She's relying on the social skills inherited from her foremothers, who had to make allies in their tribes, judge the quality of potential mates and look after the interests of their children by persuading others to help them.

Dr John Gray, author of *Men are from Mars, Women are from Venus*,[4] explains the familiar phenomenon chemically. Women ask for help, because being lost is stressful and asking for help produces oxytocin, which reduces stress in women, but not in men. Being lost doesn't increase stress in a man if he is still relying on his map-reading skills to solve the problem, because being self-reliant produces testosterone, which reduces his stress. The biochemical and evolutionary explanations may both be true, of course.

Whatever their origins, these gender differences transcend cultures. Studies have shown that men in all cultures aspire to be seen as practical, shrewd, assertive, dominant, competitive, critical and self-controlled, while women aspire to be seen as loving, affectionate, impulsive, sympathetic, generous and of service to society.[5] We talk in different ways too, for different reasons. Male conversation is public, competitive, status-seeking, factual and designed to demonstrate knowledge; female conversation is private, cooperative, reassuring, empathetic, egalitarian and meandering – women "talk for talk's sake".[6]

The studies reveal interesting regional variations too, but the differences between European and Asian men, for instance, are not as significant as the differences between men and women within each region.

Ridley says some of these differences stem from differences between hunting and gathering; some come from our ape heritage (women leave their groups on marriage and live with strangers, men live among their kin); and others are attributes of all mammals and many birds (women raise children, men compete for access to women). "It surely cannot be a coincidence", he insists, "that men are obsessed with status ... and that male chimpanzees compete for status in strict hierarchies of dominance."[1]

Straying on to more controversial ground, he suggests that our heritage may also explain why men and women differ in their ambition. In early societies, male reproductive success, which was measured in terms of quantity, depended on status; how far the male climbed up social and political hierarchies. Women had less incentive to learn the art of climbing hierarchies, because their reproductive success was measured in terms of quality, and depended on the status of their mates. The few women who are ambitious do relatively well, but not, Ridley suggests, because "male chauvinism" is a powerful selection mechanism, which only exceptional women overcome. He thinks ambitious women do better than ambitious men because they are more intuitive, better judges of character and less preoccupied with their own status.

Climbing hierarchies is a male pursuit. That is how males attract mates and increase their chances of passing on their genes. Hierarchy is the creature of males. All hierarchies have males climbing up them, and the existence of males is both a necessary and a sufficient condition for the development of a social hierarchy. You could even define a social hierarchy as a structure with males climbing up it.

Ridley argues that, since the bane of nearly all organizations is that they reward ambition, rather than ability, and since men have more ambition, "it is absolutely right that promotion should be biased in favor of women. Not to redress prejudice, but to redress human nature."[1] But there is another way of looking at it.

In a *Harvard Business Review* article, the psychiatrist Anna Fels said that the successful women she talked to hated the very word "ambition", because it implied "egotism, selfishness, self-aggrandizement, or the manipulative use of others for one's own ends", but that successful men regarded ambition as "a necessary and desirable part of their lives." She suggested, however, that this was not, as Ridley had assumed, because women have less appetite for the kind of recognition men desire. She referred to research that shows women compete actively for recognition with other women in sports and all-girl academic settings and are just as aggressive as men when competing for female roles, such as female parts in plays, modeling or music careers. Their distaste for ambition only emerges when they have to compete directly with men.[7]

This is broadly consistent with the results of experimental research by Gneezy et al. In a series of problem-solving experiments, they found that, in mixed sex groups, men perform significantly better in competitive than non-competitive environments, but women in mixed groups perform similarly in both environments. In same sex groups, however, introducing competition (switching from a piece rate, to a winner-takes-all reward system) improves the performance of women as much as it improves the performance of men.[8]

Fels concludes that what makes it hard for women to compete for top jobs in large companies is not a lack of ambition, but a belief that "to be seen as feminine, they must provide or relinquish resources – including recognition – to others [particularly men] … The expectation is so deeply rooted in the culture's ideals of femininity that it is largely unconscious."

In their meta-analysis of 45 studies of leadership styles, Eagly et al. suggest that "incongruity between leader roles and the female gender role could make it … difficult for women to attain leadership roles and produce disapproval when their behavior in these roles fails to … [conform sufficiently] with the communal requirements of the female gender role".[9] Chapter 6 has more on female leadership styles.

To be seen as masculine imposes no such constraints on male ambition. Quite the opposite, in fact – that men will compete aggressively for position and recognition with all comers, male and female, is an expectation rooted just as deeply in the culture's ideals of masculinity. Others have suggested that the root of the problem lies not so much in the culture's ideals of femininity, as in the distinctively masculine culture that has evolved in companies.

In a 1995 review of contemporary research on women in management, Sandi Mann claimed that "all organizations embody a male managerial culture, because when both organizations and management systems were first formed only males were in the workforce … Because it is a culture rather than a formal visible structure that is biasing power it becomes more difficult to change through legislation." She cited "old boy networks" and the uniform of the pinstripe suit as cultural attributes alien to women. She and other commentators also suggest that women have no taste for and decline to engage in the political activity endemic in large organizations, although she acknowledges that, in many respects, they're naturally suited to it. Their intuition, willingness to engage with feelings, sensitivity to mood, greater powers of observation when reading faces and social situations, and their powers of empathy equip women to be formidable political players once they get a taste for it.[10]

We return to the differences between men and women in Chapter 6, when we discuss the qualities women bring to the boardroom. For the moment it is enough to note that these explanations for women's relative lack of success in companies and apparent lack of ambition – that they are the consequences of innate qualities on the one hand, and cultural conditioning on the other – are not mutually exclusive. As Ridley pointed out in a later book, nature and nurture interact in such complex ways, it is impossible to say which is in the driving seat.[11]

Some of Ridley's suggestions are more palatable than others, and there is a strong case for refining his argument and substituting the terms "quality of being feminine" (which men possess, in varying degrees) for "women", and the "quality of being masculine" (which women possess, in varying degrees) for "men". It is also worth pondering an implication of Fels's explanation; women are likely to compete more aggressively for the top jobs when more of their rivals for those jobs are women.

We found the latter prediction intriguing, so we asked some women in senior management positions what they thought of it. Some said they would compete more aggressively for board jobs if more of their rivals were women. Others felt that, because they owed much of their success so far to the support of other women and women's networks, they were likely to see female rivals for senior jobs as allies, and so compete less aggressively with them than with men. One way to reconcile these views is to say that while women's networks remain politically significant in large companies, women will be reluctant to turn on their allies in the war against the masculinity of the corporate culture, but that once the war has been won, the gloves will come off.

Whether one favors the Ridley, Fels or Mann explanation, all can agree that the problem women have working in the modern company is that it is, by and large a "male" institution; innately, according to Ridley, and by virtue of its currently dominant gender, according to Fels and Mann.

There is some evidence for the deterrent effect of the inherent maleness of large modern companies in two aspects of the pipeline for women directors; the relatively low numbers of women who choose to study for MBAs, and the relatively high numbers of women who abandon what appear to be promising business careers.

The GMAT conundrum

Table 2.1 presents details of the gender and scores of those who took the Graduate Management Admission Test (GMAT), the international business schools admission test, in the five years to 2002–03. The headline, for our purposes, is that the proportions of GMAT candidates accounted for by women held steady at two-fifths in the US, and a quarter in the UK throughout the five-year period.

TABLE 2.1　GMAT candidates by sex and mean total scores					
	1998–99	**1999–2000**	**2000–01**	**2001–02**	**2002–03**
US					
Men	58225	58839	62435	74256	70399
%	58.9	58.3	58.4	59.7	59.1
Women	40698	42136	44449	50114	48813
%	41.1	41.7	41.6	40.3	40.9
Total	98923	100975	106884	124370	119212
Mean score	531	526	523	523	524
UK					
Men	1458	1328	1593	2040	1823
%	75.6	73.8	74.2	75.3	76.1
Women	471	472	554	668	574
%	24.4	26.2	25.8	24.7	23.9
Total	1929	1800	2147	2708	2397
Mean score	597	592	584	585	587
World-wide					
Men	111588	115808	129392	146355	137801
%	61.2	60.9	60.9	59.8	60.6
Mean score	546	543	541	543	545
Women	69640	73290	80954	89931	85473
%	38.2	38.5	38.1	36.8	37.6
Mean score	508	505	503	505	504

Source: Profile of Graduate Management Admission Test® Candidates, 1998–99 to 2002–03, Graduate
Management Admission Council

These proportions are of course considerably higher than the proportions of senior executive positions at large companies accounted for by women in the US and UK, but they are low relative to the number of women awarded degrees and higher degrees (see Chapter 1). And they're not increasing. That's both a puzzle and a problem, at a time when the business sector is in desperate need of more managerial talent in general, and more senior managers able to serve as executive and non-executive directors in particular.

One possible explanation for this relative lack of interest women have been showing in business careers in recent years is that the rarity of women at the top of large companies transmits subliminal messages to the bottom that deter women from seeking MBAs, the prime educational qualification for high corporate office, as eagerly as they seek other postgraduate degrees. This idea received corroboration in 2000 when a joint study by Catalyst and the University of Michigan's Center for the Education of Women (CEW) found that a lack of role models was the most important factor discouraging women from pursuing MBAs.[12]

Another possible explanation suggested by the GMAT tables is that women are not as good as men at the GMAT subjects. The mean total GMAT scores for men over the five years averaged 544, compared to 505 for women. Why? Could the GMAT have been indirectly infected in the past by the intrinsic maleness of companies, through the influence that maleness exerts on the curriculums of leading business schools (b-schools) and so biased in favor of males?

A *BusinessWeek Online* survey of female students and teachers suggested that b-school cultures and curriculums have discouraged women from seeking MBAs:

> Until recently the culture at many business schools was a boys' club ... The classroom curriculum also tended to turn off females who [tend to be] ... more interested in using their careers to contribute to the greater good of society ... case studies rarely include women subjects, or women-friendly businesses, which makes it harder for women to relate.[13]

Another deterrent revealed by the survey was timing. Unlike law and medical schools, b-schools require MBA students to have had three to five years' work experience, before embarking on the program. That takes students to their late twenties when many women are planning to start families.

Risk aversion was also a factor. Partly because they earn less, and so save less, women are more anxious than men about their job security and are thus less inclined to invest in an MBA during an economic downturn.

The good news is that people are "on the case". The US not-for-profit Forté Foundation, founded in 2001 in response to the Catalyst/CEW study, is attempting to "increase the number of women business leaders, by increasing the flow of women into key educational gateways and business networks". It uses forums and symposiums to promote awareness of the problem, and offers women scholarships and networking and mentoring opportunities. Sponsored by Crédit Suisse First Boston, Dell, Deloitte Consulting, Ernst & Young, Kraft Foods, Goldman Sachs and JP Morgan Chase, its members include a score of US b-schools (not Harvard's) and the Graduate Management Admission Council.

London Business School, a leading UK b-school which appointed its first female dean, Laura D'Andrea Tyson, in 2002, has two scholarships for women and was the first European b-school to join the Forté Foundation.

It seems likely that as b-schools start to address the deterrents to women mentioned above and offer more courses on corporate social responsibility (CSR), ethics and managing not-for-profits, all of which are of interest to women, but also of more interest to companies (see Chapter 1), the GMAT will adapt in ways that favor female candidates, women's GMAT scores will improve and in due course more women MBAs will enter the board pipeline.

But it is one thing to persuade more women to enter the board pipeline, and quite another to keep them there. The evidence suggests there are two board pipelines, one for men, one for women, and that the women's is much leakier than the men's.

A leakier pipeline

Sylvia Ann Hewlett, founder and president of the New York not-for-profit Center for Work–Life Policy, and Carolyn Buck Luce, head of Ernst & Young's health sciences industry practice, pointed out in a *Harvard Business Review* piece that one in three women with MBAs weren't working full time, compared to one in 20 men with MBAs.[14]

These, and similar figures, inspired the Centre for Work–Life Policy to set up a private sector task force The Hidden Brain Drain: Women and Minorities as Unrealized Assets in 2004 sponsored by Ernst & Young, Goldman Sachs and Lehman Brothers. The task force commissioned a Harris Interactive survey of 2443 highly qualified women (with graduate degrees, professional degrees or high honours undergraduate degrees) in two age groups; 41–55 and 28–40. A control group of 653 highly qualified males was also surveyed.

The survey found that 37 percent of all women and 43 percent of women who had children had left work voluntarily, compared to 24 percent of men.

Luce (co-chair of the Hidden Brain Drain task force) and Hewlett said women were both pulled and pushed from their jobs. Apart from having children, the pull factors included caring for elderly parents and relations (24 percent for all women, 33 percent for women aged 41–55) and health problems (9 percent).

Among push factors, 17 percent of women said they left because their jobs were not satisfying, stimulating or meaningful or they lacked opportunities at work. Only 6 percent left because they found their work too demanding. Push factors were particularly important in business, where they outweighed pull factors.

Only 12 percent of men cited child and elderly care as reasons for leaving compared to 44 percent of women. The wish to switch careers (29 percent), obtain additional training (25 percent) and start a business (12 percent) were all more important reasons for men leaving their jobs than the pull of family commitments. In other words, men leave their jobs to redirect their careers, not to abandon them.

The overwhelming majority (93 percent) of women who leave intend to return to work at some stage for financial reasons (46 percent), because it gives them self-confidence and status and adds shape and structure to their lives (43 percent), or because they want "to give something back to society" (24 percent). After they leave, most highly qualified women still regard their professional identities as their primary identities.

But only 74 percent who want to return to work do so, and of those only 40 percent return to full-time professional jobs. In other words, less than 28 percent of highly qualified women who leave their jobs return to full-time jobs and can, therefore, resume their careers. About 17 percent take part-time work and 6 percent become self-employed.

For those who return, the average period away from work is 2.2 years for all sectors and 1.2 years for business. The penalties for such brief desertions seem very heavy. The average loss of earnings for all women returners is 18 percent; the loss for those returning to business jobs is 28 percent. And the longer the gap, the greater the loss.

The most alarming finding of all for companies is that a mere 5 percent of women returners wanted to rejoin the organizations they'd left and *no women leavers who had worked in business, where the push factors for leaving were highest, wanted to return to the companies they had left.*

In a subsequent article in the *Financial Times,* Alison Maitland wondered why Sari Baldauf of Nokia, Brenda Barnes of PepsiCo, and Penny Hughes of Coca-Cola had recently quit their senior jobs at the height of their careers, and why it was that men and women enter business and the professions in almost equal numbers, but that many more women drop out as they climb their career ladders.[15]

Is it discrimination? Do corporate cultures favor linear career paths? Are women less ambitious than men and less willing to play political games? Are they more susceptible to external demands?

Maitland concluded that the work–life balance was part but only part of it and that another explanation was that women often found themselves increasingly at odds with the management culture as they moved up corporate hierarchies. She quoted Wanda Wallace, CEO of a US consultancy The Leadership Forum, who says senior women are "often troubled by their own sense of isolation".[16]

Wallace interviewed 53 women in jobs no more than four levels below CEO, in global organizations based in the US, the UK and Germany; 26 of their male peers or bosses and 11 women who had quit similarly high-ranking jobs. Only two of the 11 had quit for family reasons. Other reasons included not being promoted, feeling undervalued, being demoted (often following a leadership change), no longer enjoying the job and having achieved what they wanted to achieve.

Becoming weary of corporate politics was another reason for dissatisfaction among senior women executives. "You break so many glass ceilings on the way up", one said, "that you finally come to realize that you have accumulated a lot of shards along the way."

Of the 53, 29 of those still in top jobs had considered or were considering quitting. Why? Wallace says some are frustrated by being held back by their lack of operational experience, some rely too much on one boss for feedback and recognition and others lack the networks of relationships of successful male colleagues that allow them to ask for favors or information, interact easily with peers and hold informal strategic discussions.

Males often perceive their female colleagues as lacking confidence, hard to get to know, or not genuine. "The men are less willing to give women hard feedback, because they are afraid of a lawsuit, or don't know how to handle an emotional response", says Wallace.

Gender bias

We will explore some of the above issues later. The important point here is that the GMAT figures and the relative leakiness of the female half of the board pipeline indicate a basic incompatibility between corporate cultures and modern women. Is it intrinsic and, therefore, incorrigible, or the detritus of the company's masculine origins that will be washed away by time and the exigencies of competition?

And how does the company's inherent masculinity express itself today? If it survives, it is deeply rooted in the company's evolutionary past and largely hidden from view. Because such a bias is politically unacceptable nowadays, it is rarely acknowledged, almost never discussed and usually dismissed as the figment of a paranoid imagination when it is. The common presumption is that, even if the company was once inherently male (many will insist it was always gender neutral) it is no longer, because, in our enlightened age, we can rid ourselves and our institutions of such atavisms.

Large companies have become less obviously hierarchical in recent years, by delayering themselves and adopting more horizontal structures, but it is a difference in degree only – the basic hierarchical shape remains intact. We believe that the survival of hierarchy (or the reluctance of women to climb hierarchies) means that although large companies are overtly and officially gender-neutral now, vestiges of the gender bias survive and alert observers should be able to catch glimpses of it.

We devote the next two chapters to looking at this alleged gender bias problem from two points of view; that of male leaders of large companies in Chapter 3, and in Chapter 4 that of women in the "marzipan layer" (as Laura Tyson, dean of London Business School, calls the management layer below the board), where women are likely to feel the gender bias most acutely.

References

1. *The Red Queen. Sex and the Evolution of Human Nature*, Matt Ridley, Viking, 1993.
2. The truth about men and women is too hot to handle, Andrew Sullivan, The *Sunday Times*, January 23, 2005.
3. *The Psychology of Sex Differences*, E. E. Maccoby and C. N. Jacklin, Stanford University Press, 1974; *Sex Evolution and Behaviour*, M. Daly and M. Wilson, Wadsworth, Belmont, 1983; *Brain Sex: the Real Difference between Men and Women*, A. Moir and D. Jessel, Lyle Stuart, 1991.
4. *Men are from Mars, Women are from Venus*, John Gray, HarperCollins, 1992.
5. *Sex Differences*, K. B. Hoyenga and K. Hoyenga, Little Brown, 1980.
6. *You Just Don't Understand: Women and Men in Conversation*, D. Tannen, William Morrow, 1990.
7. Do women lack ambition?, *Harvard Business Review*, Anna Fels, April 2004.
8. Performance in competitive environments: gender differences, Uri Gneezy, Muriel Niederle and Aldo Ruschini, *The Quarterly Journal of Economics*, 2003, **118**(3), pp. 1049–74.
9. Transformational, transactional and laissez-faire leadership styles: a meta-analysis comparing women and men, A. H. Eagly, M. C. Johannesen-Schmidt and M. L. van Engen, *Psychological Bulletin* 2003, **129**(4).
10. Politics and power in organizations: why women lose out, Sandi Mann, *Leadership & Organizational Development Journal*, 1995, **16**(2).
11. *Nature via Nurture*, Matt Ridley, Fourth Estate, 2003.
12. *Women and the MBA: Gateway to Opportunity*, Catalyst, University of Michigan Business School, June, 2000.

13. Breaking b-school gender barriers, Francesca Di Meglio, *BusinessWeek Online*, December 1, 2004.

14. Off-ramps and on-ramps. Keeping talented women on the road to success, Sylvia Ann Hewlett and Carolyn Buck Luce, *Harvard Business Review*, March 2005.

15. The puzzle of the lost women, Alison Maitland, *Financial Times*, March 1, 2005.

16. *Reaching the Top: Five Factors that impact the Retention and Effectiveness of the Most Talented Senior Women*, W. Wallace, Leadership Forum Inc., 2004.

CHAPTER 3

Conversations with kings

If, as we believe, a gender bias persists in our large companies and it is imposing an opportunity cost on shareholders, its removal is in everyone's interests. But you can't begin to remove a bias before you have acknowledged its existence. For a bias to be remediable, it must first become discussable.

We women have been discussing it for years, of course, but mostly with each other. It has been an intra-gender "supply side" discussion among ambitious women frustrated by glass ceilings; illuminating, even therapeutic, but not very effective. We wanted to widen the discussion and give it more edge, by canvassing the opinions of "demand side" players (male chairmen and CEOs in whose gifts, as individuals or members of nominating committees, most board appointments lie). Following a series of meetings with like-minded women in early 2003 (these led to the formation of Women Directors on Boards – a UK Consortium for Action and Change; see Chapter 5 for a fuller account of its origins), we arranged audiences with some corporate kings, all of whom were CEOs and/or chairmen of FTSE 100 and S&P 500 companies.

We asked them what their reactions were to the latest Cranfield and Spencer Stuart figures for female directors (see Chapter 1); why they thought there were so few women on the boards of big US and UK companies; how comfortable they were about appointing women directors; whether they felt women brought distinctive qualities to boards; what value they saw in diversity itself on their boards and what if anything women and companies could or should do to increase the number of women on boards and executive committees.

In what follows we haven't attributed quotes to individuals, partly because it would clutter up the narrative flow, and partly because the lack of such attributions provides a degree of anonymity some interviewees asked for. We are very grateful to them for giving up some of their valuable time to talk to us. All their names are in the acknowledgements.

To avoid as far as possible imposing our own prejudices on their answers to our questions, we present the views and perceptions of these corporate kings without comment, and leave readers to make of them what they will. We offer some reflections of our own at the end of the chapter.

We don't pretend that the views quoted below are representative, in any rigorous statistical sense, of the leaders of the constituents of the FTSE 100 and S&P 500 indices. The sample is far too small, for one thing, and biased for another, in that the agreement of the kings quoted here to talk to us about women on boards differentiates them from those who didn't agree to talk to us or would not have agreed to talk to us had we asked them (see Note on method).

We do believe, however, that the variety of views and perceptions expressed and the spread of industries covered, from natural resources and transport, to financial services and the media, mean the quotes in the following pages paint a rich, and reasonably accurate picture of what the issue of women on boards looks like from the "demand side"; namely, the current generation of leaders of large US and UK companies.

Reactions to the figures

We asked our US kings how they reacted to the 2003 Catalyst *Census of Women Board Directors*, showing that 13.6 percent of Fortune 500 directors were women, 54 companies had no women on their boards and 208 only had one woman.

We asked our UK kings for their reactions to Cranfield's *Female FTSE Report 2004*, which showed that women accounted for 10 percent of FTSE 100 board positions and 4 percent of executive and 13 percent of non-executive directors.

The chairman of a large UK utility thought the number of women directors at Britain's 100 largest quoted companies (constituents of the FTSE 100 index) was "far too low" and said it reflected "society looking backward and not forward". To demonstrate his credentials as an interested party, he told us he had two very successful daughters – one was about to become a partner at a leading law firm and the other was running her own business.

This declaration of a keenly felt, personal interest in the subject outside work was echoed by an American CEO with a reputation for being particularly enlightened about the gender issue. When we asked why he was such an active supporter of the attack on glass ceilings, he said: "Let's hope it's better for my daughter – she's 21 and I want work to be a different experience for her."

The CEO of a leading media company was "amazed" by the numbers. "I would've said there are no barriers, but subconscious factors come into play. I find it hard to believe people ... [look] for anything other than someone who can contribute. Perhaps it's a gene pool issue, and the balance will shift over a period of time."

The CEO of a major natural resources group admitted that the latest figures were "dreadfully low", but thought that progress was being made.

"I'm not surprised", said the CEO of an influential American not-for-profit, who is also an independent director of several US companies. "UK companies have a large proportion of executives on their boards. If there are few women in the executive population, the overall percentage will be low. In the US, we have a higher proportion of independent directors. The bigger the company, the more likely [it is] that you'll have diversity on the board in terms of gender and ethnicity."

"These figures are too low", said the chairman of a large financial services group. "If chairmen and CEOs put their minds to it, they could appoint more women. We need to name and shame. I can't believe the current generation of chairmen and CEOs has a problem with this."

The former CEO of a major US financial services group said:

I don't know whether this figure is high, or low". What makes you think it is low? The raw statistic doesn't say it's low ... it doesn't say anything. It's lower than the percentage of women in the general population, but the pool of directors doesn't come from the general population. [It comes from] CEOs, senior line and staff executives, lawyers and investment bankers. You need to know the proportion of women in these categories. If the proportion of women CEOs was 50 percent, then the proportion of women directors at 16 percent would be low.

The CEO of the subsidiary of a leading US IT group was not surprised by the dearth of women directors and suggested that most boards that had appointed women had imported them, rather than "grown their own". He believes strongly in developing the pipeline of women. "Women used to account for 25 percent of our graduate intake; that has risen to 47 percent because of our work promoting IT in schools and our computer clubs for girls."

"You need to put this in an historical context" said a retired American CEO and former McKinsey consultant. "As recently as two generations ago, women didn't work outside the home, except as teachers and nurses. Women only got the vote in the US in 1920. The guys had a huge head start. The numbers have gone up a lot over the past 20 years." He pointed out that the SSBI (see Chapter 1) shows an increase of a third, from 12 to 16 percent, in the percentage of women on S&P 500 boards over the past five years.

An American chief operating officer thought the numbers were "probably reasonable; based on what I know. What's more important is that, historically, there have been fewer women on boards. It's not how many women there are on boards now that matters, but how much progress has been made in this area. And we have made progress – when vacancies come up on our board, one factor we look for is more diversity on the board; another woman. I think most boards are trying to do that."

An American CEO suggested that some companies with no women directors were "a product of their entrepreneurial legacies. They are necessarily becoming populated with women. Historically, some [American] companies have played a significant role in changing things. We do have an American way of thinking about things, which includes seeing no reason why women shouldn't succeed."

But a compatriot disagreed: "Americans talk a better game, but our results don't mirror that. Diversity, in general, is a board issue in the US. Women are no exception."

Where to find them, though? "If you look at the population of CEOs and CFOs, the number of women is relatively small" said a US chairman, "and it's hard to put women with less credentials to shareholders."

Another American said that in "today's US board environment, it's difficult to get anyone to join boards. The liabilities are too great."

"We've got loads of women in senior positions," said the former CEO of a UK entertainment organization shortly before he left, "and there are even more in the next layer coming through." He didn't give us chapter and verse, but the impression he gave was of an organization approaching a "tipping point" in the number of women in senior jobs beyond which further progress toward a fully representative gender balance would be self-generating.

He said you had to start by asking whether everybody wanted to do this kind of job, but was surprised that women accounted for only 4 percent of FTSE 100 executive directors and said: "It would be interesting to know what the next layer down are thinking" (see Chapter 4).

Reasons for the figures

If all companies are male, some are more male than others, according to the chairman of a multinational mining and metals group. He said:

> Our top executives have to relocate a lot. That's a big problem for multinationals, because it's so hard to find jobs for both partners in dual career families. It is difficult enough for males, let alone females. The only exception is finance, but we want even financial directors to have broad experience outside finance in operational roles.

> There are no barriers except logistical ones, but the main degree subjects of our directors – engineering and metallurgy – don't attract women, on the whole. In

other companies I have been close to I see an easier onward march of women in the organization, especially in retail. But in our company it's a matter of the woman's choice; whether she wants the sort of international career that's implicit in being a business like this one.

He suggested two other reasons why there were so few women on the boards of FTSE 100 and S&P 500 companies: they are larger companies "where most people don't get on boards until their forties or fifties and there are fewer women coming through in that age group" and they include "a lot of multinationals and the demands of senior jobs are hard to reconcile with having children".

The chairman of a large UK utility gave four reasons for the gender imbalances on the boards of leading companies:

1. *Development* – Twenty years ago, people didn't see this as a major issue, and career patterns open to women, with the required support, didn't exist. So allowing for a natural progression (outstanding people get on a board at about 40), there's a time lag before candidates become available.

2. *Hierarchy* – Industry still tends to be more hierarchical than the service sector, so you're less likely to see women punching holes in the glass ceiling in industry than in the accounting and legal professions.

3. *Attraction* – UK industry has been going through a mega change and I suspect women have weighed up their chances of success, and decided they're greater in the professions where the rewards are higher too.

4. *Work–life balance* – This is the classic reason of course, but it's obviously true that women look at it in a different way from men. And also, in industry, there's a lot of traditional thinking to do with the work–life balance about advancing women.

Another UK chairman said the correlation of age with experience makes it "difficult for women to step out of the workplace for too long". We didn't press the point at the time, but we wonder now what he meant by "too long", given that the average period businesswomen take off to have children in the US is little more than a year (see Chapter 2).

The CEO of a leading international transport company also thought there was a generation issue:

My grandmother was a famous feminist. She had her own radio program when equal pay for equal work was the big issue. So I don't believe the generic problem is as big as you might think. It's a phasing and timing issue. Most chairmen are now in their sixties or seventies. We have one woman on the board and we are about to appoint a female NED with a strong finance background. I look at my team and, apart from the chief medical officer, they're all male. But it's about 20 percent women the next layer down. [The industry] used to be very "male", because [companies] were run by engineers. When their chairmen and CEOs were going through the education system, most people at university were men; women were starting families. That's not prejudice; it's a timing thing. We do succession planning twice a year and there are a lot of women coming through. Gender isn't an issue. I have no doubt that one day a woman will sit in my chair.

Another CEO was less sanguine. "Women have not been recruited and developed for board positions over the past 20 years. These are long-term trends and if you don't recruit and develop, and you have barriers against women being considered for senior jobs, then, surprise, surprise, this is what you get."

The boss of an IT group thought that the leakiness of the pipeline (see Chapter 2) partly explained the low figures: "More women were leaving than joining. So we surveyed all leavers over the past three years. The big issue hitting us in the face was flexibility. This [is now] framed as 'work–life balance' and we found it was as much an issue for men, as women. We now evaluate all jobs for flexibility and work–life balance."

The company's research shows that graduate recruits see no gender imbalance, but this changes at "band nine", when employees are in their early thirties. "This is the time when many women leave", the CEO said. "Is it corporate life that creates that glass ceiling? Is the behavior required to rise to the top at the masculine end of the spectrum? Are we rewarding masculine over feminine competences? This needs a fundamental change of mindset."

The former head of a UK media organization saw the gender imbalance as institutionalized:

Big business is still terribly male – the corporate world is still an old boys' club and the City certainly is. I appointed the first woman director at [a company where he was the group CEO]. The company secretary said to me: "It's not a campaign, you know." I said to him: "It is, you know." Most directors don't think about it. It doesn't even cross their minds.

I think it's a generation thing. I'm 56 and part of that 1970s age group who saw this as a campaigning issue. There is no doubt it's changing, but never underestimate the attitude of NEDs. They're all of a type and they don't see there's any need. The institutions [institutional investors] look for people they feel secure with and, by and large, that's old men. This place was like that. In management roles it's now 40 percent women. The only thing I still see is that, at management conferences, fewer women stand up and talk publicly.

Comfort with women directors

The UK chairman of a mining company said he was perfectly comfortable with the idea of appointing a female executive director. "That wouldn't worry me at all – it's the best person for the job, regardless of sex or nationality. But it's different in our particular business context." The company hadn't yet appointed a female NED when we talked, but the chairman said he would be surprised if it did not do so within 18 months. "It doesn't matter [from the business point of view] what gender they are, but we have to recognize the views of society. We will be seen as insular [if we do not appoint a female NED]. I would say that if we'll be appointing three new NEDs, one should be female. Part of me shrinks from this, because we are looking for contribution."

The "number two" in the company's finance department is a woman. The chairman said:

> We worked out a pragmatic way, over a seven-day week, for her to work at home some of the time. Finance is an area where it's possible to do that. The most senior woman in head office is head of IT. She spends most of her time on planes. We used to send men abroad on their own, but we're loath to do that now because of the risk of breaking families.
>
> I've been on boards where the table was tilted [in favor of women]. There is a certain amount of political correctness and companies are increasingly being forced down that path by corporate governance issues. On other boards it's different. I was an NED at [a UK retailer]. When I joined, there was a female NED and she was later replaced by another. A retailer without female representation on the board would be odd, and it would be bizarre for there to be no female directors in some other business sectors. But in a business like ours it's not an issue one way or the other.

The company appointed its first female NED in early 2005.

Another CEO said he was "totally comfortable" about appointing women to the board. His company already had female executive and non-executive directors and was busy recruiting more when we talked. "As an outward-facing utility meeting the needs of ordinary people, with a very ordinary product, it was just the smart thing to have women on the board. We are looking for two US women to join the board at the moment. America is ahead of Britain. I think women have come further, faster there over the past 10 years."

Although another king was "perfectly comfortable" with the idea of women on the board, he was finding it a real challenge "to find women of the quality and experience you need. You don't want token women or token anything. They [directors] must all be there on merit. But you have to be very careful how you judge merit so that it isn't biased."

An American CEO said:

People want people from large prestige companies. There are still some old boys who aren't comfortable [with the idea of females on their boards], but this has changed – the guys have seen the women perform. Younger guys are much more comfortable with it. Some CEOs are aggressively looking for women. They believe the board should represent shareholders and customers. Other guys do it out of commitment to change and equality. Carly Fiorina's failure was very high profile, but plenty of guys have failed!

At McKinseys I worked with plenty of women. At [an HR consultancy where he was CEO and chairman] a third of the partners were women. The ratio went up and down in both companies. My view was that we would be idiots not to have someone who was capable regardless of color or gender. I actively tried to help women. I hired the first black employee [at the HR consultancy]. When I joined in 1984, the directors (all guys) were a clubby partnership. I also saw it as an ethical issue – half the people on the planet are women and we didn't have any on the board.

According to another American CEO:

When I came here about 10 years ago, there was only one woman out of 26 board members and only three non-US directors. Now it's an entirely different picture. We have seven women on the board and people of eight nationalities and five ethnic groups. All were CEOs of well-known companies. I didn't go out of the orbit of stature to get the diversity. It is a myth that you have to compromise to get diversity.

Yet another American chairman said:

To me it makes no difference. It's who is going to make the best contribution that matters. But we also try to bring on people from different walks of life. We get different perspectives from people with different types of experience. If we didn't have a woman on the board we would probably feel compelled to appoint one – women make up half of society and in terms of consumer, social and environmental trends, their perspectives are important.

We have one woman on our board and I'd love to recruit more. I'm currently recruiting and we've got three promising candidates who are all women. Once you have one woman, the experience usually drives you to hire another. With the current selection of candidates it has partly been about networking and working a bit with headhunters. I told the headhunter that for the first 60–90 days of the search I only want to see diversity candidates. It forces the recruiters to do their job. I don't think I'm unique – I've heard about other people doing that for senior management positions too.

A US CEO said:

You know, we haven't used headhunters. Some people think we should, but we haven't felt a need to. We have a nominating and governance committee of the board that is responsible for looking for potential board members. We have a retirement age of 75 on the board; someone's going to be coming off in the next few years, and we will be looking for a replacement. But we are always looking for new board members. In general, we are able to find high-quality people from our own networks. If someone thinks someone's good and the nominating and governance committee like them, they'll have the chairman meet with them to make sure and to get our input.

Another American chairman said:

Acting as a champion of women can be a problem [for a senior man]. I've always believed that the formation of women's groups, for example, can institutionalize solutions and give a framework to help to deal with some of the awkward career management situations that can arise. If a woman approaches a senior man and asks him to act as her mentor or if she tries to network without such a framework, other male peers might think there's a different motivation.

We spoke in March 2005 on the day US aircraft manufacturer Boeing announced that its CEO, Harry Stonecipher, had resigned because of what Boeing called an "improper relationship" with a female executive. The chairman thought an important benefit of our Cross-Company Mentoring Programme (see Chapter 5) was that it provided a formal framework that helped to minimize the risk of such accusations of impropriety. The same is true, in his view, of women's networks: "At [the chairman's previous company], I met with the Women's Network twice a year. I heard that after I left, the incoming chairman removed the women's group meetings from his diary saying, 'what did [I] have this in here for?'"

Women's contribution

"My perception is that women are more sensitive to people-related issues at board meetings than most males", said the former chairman of a mining group. "That's important in companies with a lot of women employees and customers. In our industry it is more likely that a woman director would bring a focus on the so-called 'soft' agenda – the environment and social issues."

Another UK CEO laughed when we asked what special qualities women brought to a board:

Men will hate this! Women are better lateral thinkers; they're less structured and see things more in the round. They're also more aware of the human issues, be it customers or employees. They're acutely aware of social dynamics in a group, and will worry about them. Men are pragmatists – women are more ... [he hesitated] idealistic. They want to be clear they've reached the *right* solution. And they also want to be sure that practical things are being accommodated: when people have babies, go sick.

"I think women are wired differently from men", said a UK chairman. "Men often get stuck on transmit. Women pick up nuances in conversation men miss, so it's best to have a mixture at the table. But I'd never have a woman on my board sponsoring "women's issues" or an environmentalist sponsoring environmental issues. They can speak to them, but not out of the mainstream."

He went on:

Anyone impartial and observant can see that some women are showing them-selves to be superior to men educationally and there's a certain female dogged-ness that I like. Women can be dogged in a far less offensive way. We men have been playing the game for a very long time and we've been rumbled! Younger women simply won't understand they might be discriminated against. My 12-year-old daughter will go straight through. In the end the only thing that will slow down the increase in women's participation on company boards is the number of women available, because women do make decisions to go off and have families.

He is all in favor of women on the board because "it brings a freshness, a difference." But he thinks it is less important for them to be on the board than to be on the operating team (executive committee). He appointed his HR director to the main board. "She was great; so good. Hard as nails, but she does it with grace and decency. We appointed her because she was good. She was promoted from within. We didn't interview her, we elevated her."

Another UK CEO doubted whether women bring anything to the board per se and he would not go out of his way to "balance" a board:

It's possible women bring different perspectives, but I seek particular expertise. I've never really faced this issue. There's a certain liveliness, an intuition that is needed in business and that a woman's more likely to have than a man. There's also a feel; women say "why don't we do that?" And they're often very intuitive about other people. A bit less ego? Either that, or they conceal it better. There's less ego around – less positioning. We're all bloody kids. Boys are boys. Women bring calmness and objectivity; not all the time, but generally they're calmer and there's less jostling for position.

THEY WERE AT EACH OTHER'S THROATS
BEFORE WE GOT A WOMAN DIRECTOR

A former UK CEO saw a strong, commercial case for more women directors: "We need people with different backgrounds, perspectives and ideas." He thought women also had a better feel for people: "Many of the women I know are more sensitive than men, more skillful negotiators, less prone to bore everybody to death at meetings, as men do. And better judges of character."

Another chairman found it difficult to say what distinctive qualities women brought to boards "without sounding patronizing and politically incorrect", but, in his view, women are "perfectly capable of bringing the intellectual rigor men bring, and they also bring a sort of intuition, a sensitivity – especially on the more difficult soft issues of relationships and that sort of thing."

The former chairman of a major UK energy company saw no differences in the way women operate: "The women on our board speak their minds and do a good job. It's different in an oil company. In a service-oriented environment women may be more confident, because they've had more women round them as they've risen to the top."

Another disagreed and saw significant differences in the ways men and women operate:

> Men are better at pulling off the quick deal. Women are better at creating long-term, project relationships with clients. I prefer the latter [because it leads to] "win–win" relationships and long-term contracts. Male behaviors have driven the business. We've lost the coaching element. It's not that people are bigoted about diversity. They just don't care – they're simply choosing the horse that will run.

An American CEO saw no difference in how men and women operate, but interesting differences in how men perceive women:

> There are two types of response: if the woman is reticent, but very pleasant, she's a "lovely lady", but if she feels the pressure of being a woman in a man's group and loses her sense of humor over it, she's "a pain in the ass".

> But I don't buy the style difference – a couple of women on our board have been aggressive, some have been more "nuanced".

The former CEO of an American financial services group said there were only two possible reasons for having women, qua women, on a board: "they might improve the quality of board discussions and might serve as role models for others in the organization." He was not persuaded by the "customer is queen" argument:

Directors don't represent customers on boards, they represent shareholders – all of them, not distinct groups. I don't believe women bring a different voice about customers, or a different perspective. I'm not convinced. I've never asked board directors to review our advertising! There were two women on the board when I was chairman – I didn't expect them to have a different view because they were women and I didn't see a different style in them.

I don't doubt that women and men view cars differently, but you don't need that difference on your board – you can use market testing to get different input into product design.

You want women in a company because it doubles your pool. You need to have the best people at all levels. I know that if an organization does a better job of hiring and developing women, it's undoubtedly also doing a better job with the men too. If I am looking at the women in my succession plan and my competitors are not, I know I'll kill them. There are women who can make an identical contribution, their gender is irrelevant.

A fellow American CEO thought there was more to it than that:

Women have a different train of thought from men. I recognize that and respect it. I think women bring a different perspective on social and environmental issues. Men don't see things in the same way. We read different magazines; watch different media and our areas of knowledge are different. My wife has perspectives and sensitivity to certain issues that I, with my business background, would not necessarily share. We as a company need to understand changes in consumer behavior; what appeals to men, what appeals to women.

The value of diversity

One chairman suggested that "in the society emerging in the UK, with a much broader culture than simply white Anglo-Saxon, diversity, in terms of age, background, geography, skills and experience, is essential on a board. Each diversity dimension leads to more debate. The ages of our directors range from 40 to 65. Women see things differently – I'm a fan of that, but you've got to have very talented people."

He has three criteria for the perfect board – that directors look at things differently, debate the differences honestly and recognize their collective accountability. "An ability critically to analyze events, circumstances and information from different points of view is invaluable, because it reduces the chances of you rushing, lemming-like, over cliffs and leads to robust and sensible decision-making."

"We all felt that we should look for women directors and we did over a long period", said the former chairman of one of the few large UK companies to have made a deliberate effort to get more women on their boards. "It turned out it was a good decision. We looked at the way we recruited for the same reason – you disadvantage yourself, as a company, when you neglect half the world's talent pool."

He told us that for every senior job he asks five questions:

1. Where's the woman on this list?
2. Where's the top woman who didn't make it to the list?
3. Where's the young candidate?
4. Where's the candidate of another nationality?
5. Where's the candidate from another business?

He said: "A diverse board is critically important for a global company. That is why we began to increase diversity on the board five years ago; not just gender and nationality, but also different backgrounds. Nationality is important for a global company, and one thing that is often neglected is diversity of thinking. That brings an intellectual questioning and a challenging of perspective."

Another chairman said that it was "important to have a diverse board," because a company needs "different perspectives, from different backgrounds". One of his female NEDs is an economist: "She has given us a new view from outside. We now look outside the company for every senior position. Half our top 32 people are from outside. Our board is very diverse in terms of nationality and we're still predominantly a UK company. It matters even more for global companies."

A major challenge, according to one CEO, is to get women and men to take on board diversity in their leadership roles. He is convinced of the business case for diversity and women on boards, and sees many bottom line benefits:

> People have to believe that support for diversity is genuine. I want this to be the number one company from a business perspective and the number one employer of choice.

> We need mechanisms for hearing the views of those who don't believe in the need for it [diversity] and consequences for not encouraging it. We need to fight for the corporate reputation to the death – we have to get management buy-in for diversity. We have to measure it of course, and we allow targets to

be set, but I don't think counting matters. If you focus too much on the number of women on boards, you encourage companies to shop around for women rather than tackle their own pipeline challenges.

"American companies began appointing non-Americans to their boards about 20 years ago", an American chairman recalled. "It was a 'best practice' to have foreign nationals on your board. Boards need people from countries they are trying to do business with – people who will bring a different perspective. We've also seen a rise in activist groups who try to convince people not to invest in companies that don't have women on their boards. But if there are only 12 board places, women are competing for places with other minorities."

The CEO of a New York not-for-profit said:

Getting from one woman to seven wasn't easy. We had to work at it. It's more difficult to get women and non-white males – they have so many options, they are in great demand. Once you have a diverse board it's easier to get others; it's one of the selling points. We had to convince people about their value and that we didn't just want tokens.

I believe workplace diversity is a strategic issue. It is in the interests of shareholders and the workforce to have a diverse board. If that was the case for companies in general, we had to look at ourselves first. There are five people who report to me and only one is a man. It's not about finding women – it's about finding people who ought to be promoted, irrespective of gender. We've been able to carry out "gender-blind" recruitment.

Diversity's one of five things that we say are essential for businesses. I have never got any push-back from other board members. People know from our strategy that one of our planks is workforce diversity.

Another US CEO said:

Half our employees are women. Why wouldn't a board reflect the [gender mix in the] workforce? If you believe in a meritocracy, you have to demonstrate that the best talent gets to the top. When I joined McKinsey, 40 percent of hires were women, but the election rate for [women] partners was a lot less. At my previous company, there were over 20,000 employees in the workforce and over half were women.

It is vital to bring in more women at board and senior management level to create critical mass. I'm trying to do that here. But, in corporate America at large, diversity is always a lower priority than financial results.

BRING YOUR FAMILY TO WORK DAY

© Barbara Shore

Another US CEO said:

All aspects of diversity are important. You need men who are different, too. A lot of boards have annual golf days; I don't play golf!

I served on one board with Sally Ride [the first American woman to go into space]. She was a science professor at San Diego, California, and as good a board member as you could find. Another female director I've worked with has never run a business and is also one of the best board members I've ever served with. I can point to an equal number of men who have been in science or academia and not had bottom line experience. Nobody questions this.

It's good to have people who can deal with a range of issues. On one board I served on, three people came from private equity and I have an investment banker on my board now. You need a mix.

Advice

"There's a minimum threshold of achievement at the top end of companies and not-for-profits", said an American CEO, when asked what advice he would give to aspiring women directors. "If you're not at that threshold, no one takes you seriously. You need to be the 'chief' scientist, economist or whatever, not the 'deputy' economist. Whatever your specialism, you have to be at the top. Accomplishment and achievement are what counts."

A UK chairman made the same point in another way. When we asked him what women should do to increase their chances of getting to the top, he said: "Don't worry about it – spend the energy being twice as good. Women own the future every bit as much as men."

He insisted the government should not try to correct the imbalance, because "there's a risk of artificiality". In his view, it is all about confidence: "My daughter will have that confidence. Younger women aren't going to think in those terms. It will wash itself through. My advice would be that women should be themselves, and not push their femininity – the fact is that they have the skills. Be confident and do what is expected of you really, really well."

Another chairman urged women to network more:

American women are very good networkers. In Britain women are still outsiders. Despite all the policies, our society is still essentially a male-dominated culture, and the practice in companies often doesn't match the commitments. It is not because leaders don't want it to happen, it's down in the guts of organizations. We'll have to get more prescriptive to crack this. I really do believe that."

What did he mean by "more prescriptive"?

Build women's networks. Encourage the right social policies. Introduce mentoring for talented women by other women and by leaders. Try to make industry attractive and exciting. Has the CBI [the Confederation of British Industry] played any role in this? Should Patricia Hewitt [the then UK secretary of state for trade and industry] ask Digby Jones [director-general of the CBI] what he's doing about it? We need to build a pipeline.

He saw the lack of women on boards as a real problem and had some trenchant views on what should be done about it:

It's all very well concentrating on the tip of the iceberg. It's certainly crucial that we have diversity on boards, so that there are role models for younger women to admire and aspire to follow. But the number one problem is the shortage of supply [of women] from lower down the iceberg, and that has to be addressed structurally. The reason why the first woman on our [board] was an American is that 25 years ago there were many more American women at university. They had more opportunity in the US. They weren't discriminated against so much in the rush to the top. You need to get the university side sorted out, the recruitment side sorted out and the development sorted out and then make sure jobs are allocated fairly. The way to get more women on boards is to get more women up through the regular business route. The big shortage is the shortage of women CEOs and you don't solve that by bringing them in from outside. They should get there because they're good. We have a load coming through. Nearly 10 percent of our senior people are women. A bit lower down it is 17 percent. And women are 35 percent of our graduate recruits. The answer is in the pipeline, and whether women get a fair share of that.

He believes that, by publishing the numbers regularly, the Cranfield School of Management in the UK, and Spencer Stuart and Catalyst in the US make the position transparent:

CEOs look at what other companies are doing and ask themselves: "Is this important? Are we off the pace? Ought we to be doing more?" In the war for talented young people you do yourself no favors when you bias your selection against a serious number of candidates.

He thought more naming and shaming of companies that were not taking action to appoint women directors would help to get the message across. Then an idea seemed to occur to him while we were talking:

We could arrange a series of meetings between five or six women below board level, and five or six CEOs to discuss the issues, and get the CEOs' agreement to support the women and encourage them to put their names forward to head-hunters for non-executive board positions. This way we could form a pool of women for potential board positions, executive and non-executive. Some companies don't like directors being on other boards, because of the time commitments, but they allow them to do voluntary work and become local councillors, and so on, so why couldn't we allow people time in outside director roles? It's good development.

When asked what women should do to improve their chances of being appointed to boards, he said the real issue was:

about how women manage their careers and the amount of time they take off for maternity, and how often ... There's no doubt that it does affect the rate at which they progress and the number of different experiences they have. Women need to be given proper operating experiences. They would be able to contribute even better at board level if they had run operating units. Companies must take more risks with women. We only have one woman area director in our retail network – perhaps we should take some risks and appoint some more and give them the support.

Another UK chairman said:

It is not my role to appoint executive directors, that's up to the CEO. I approve his appointments. It's easier for me to demand the removal of an executive director who isn't delivering, than to tell the CEO who he should appoint. He must be free to appoint people he wants. I can't risk inhibiting his delivery of shareholder value, by insisting he appoints someone he doesn't want. He lives and dies by the results of his executive committee. We're about to appoint a second woman to the executive committee from outside the company – there wasn't anyone, male or female, inside who was suitable for the position.

I knew a woman from another company I'm on the board of. I took her out to lunch and invited her to join the board. The other woman was already on the board of a company we acquired. I knew her from there and I approached her. We can't limit our search to the women we know, because we don't know many women. Most of those I come across are either from government or regulatory bodies and we can't appoint them. I know some women on other boards I serve on, but most companies only allow executive directors to serve on one other board. We could go down a level and look for women below the board in these other companies. We need to take some risks.

Another CEO suggested:

Women and men need to think about the Venus and Mars differences.[1] When women make contributions in meetings, it's often in a visceral or tentative way. So if a man builds on her suggestion later, it could be because he didn't think it was a definite suggestion. Guys need to be aware that a woman may say things in a more flowery way and not discount them for that reason.

It's a culture thing. We need to listen to people who are different. It is incumbent on us all to think, before leaping to conclusions, when people do things differently.

Groups and group leaders should question more – if they look around a table in a board meeting and see 12 white men, they should ask themselves, "Is this right? Does it make sense? Does it match our shareholders and customers?"

An American chairman suggested that companies should give their headhunters more inclusive briefs:

Increasingly, companies use search firms. They should put out specifications welcoming non-traditional candidates. They should define things broadly.

Y'SEE, THERE'RE JUST NO WOMEN AROUND TO CHOOSE FROM

Instead of saying they are looking for "a CEO", they should make the defini-tions functionally broad. What is it we want – an economist, lawyer, scientist, marketing person, or someone who has served on the board of another Fortune 500 company?

I'd suggest that, if you've been ambassador to Germany, dean of Wharton or a member of the Federal Reserve Board, you have executive experience. These are demanding roles. Active CEOs can only be on a limited number of boards now, so companies have to widen their search criteria. When I started, it was the norm to be on four or five boards.

A former British CEO he said he didn't know what women could do to increase their chances of getting to the top:

Maybe they'll have to play more men's games. But they have to want it and some may decide they do not. It's still early in the process – 20 years ago women's horizons were so restricted and narrow. It's changing pretty rapidly, but there clearly is a glass ceiling below executive directors and women need to see other women breaking it. It matters what your peer group thinks. If, when the board turns up, they're all old white men in shirts and ties, it's discouraging.

Until a generation has moved on, it will continue to be quite tough. First of all you have to have more women NEDs; women who are not "posh".

In the past women here who got to the top had to be like men; by and large they gave up on families. But the role models are there now. It happened in 10 years, because my predecessor started it.

"There's nothing women need to do differently", an American CEO said:

It is no different from appointing women to senior management jobs. At [a company where he was a CEO previously] I set up a women's council and met with them twice a year. In the morning, we would cover the business issues and in the afternoon, the career issues. It became a very visible group and two of the women became division presidents. I'd brought one of them in from outside. If you've got less than 10 percent women at the top, in my view, something is wrong. You need to bring in or promote enough women to create a critical mass at both board and senior management level for things to change.

Reflections

Readers will draw various conclusions from the above comments, but it seems to us that seven distinct themes emerge.

The first is that, although this imbalance is evident in all industries, it is more "natural" in some than others, because some industries are more "male" than others, they need skills in areas, such as geology and engineering, that attract more men than women, or their customers or clients are mostly men.

There is some evidence for this. An analysis of Cranfield's figures reveals a tendency for retailing and healthcare companies to appoint more women directors than food and drink manufacturers and other industrial companies (see Table 3.1).

TABLE 3.1 Average sector diversity		
Sector	**Number of companies**	**Women on boards %**
Consumer retail	10	14.17
Healthcare/pharma	7	10.10
Financials	20	9.55
Utilities	10	8.80
Technology, media and telecoms	14	5.98
Service industry	13	4.87
Leisure	5	4.60
Food and drink	7	4.38
Industrials	14	3.12

Source: The Female FTSE Report 2004

There is also anecdotal evidence that some industries develop cultures that are distinctly "macho" and tend to reject women. If the arguments presented in a number of multi-million dollar sex discrimination cases in Wall Street in the summer of 2004 are anything to go by, investment banking is one such industry. Frank Partnoy, professor of law at the University of San Diego and a former derivatives trader, believes it is the character of Wall Street rather than the character of men that discriminates against women. Partnoy says:

> Investment banking is dominated by men, for some of the same reasons the Mafia and other gangs are dominated by men ... [it] attracts and rewards people with certain skills and predispositions – appetite for risk, willingness to bend the law, knack of cultivating clients while fleecing them – that are, or at least are perceived to be, more prevalent among men ... During the past decade women have held 20 to 40 percent of positions on Wall Street, but all the high-profile prosecutions for financial wrongdoing have involved male defendants.[2]

A second theme is that most large, multinational companies require their board candidates to earn their spurs so to speak by traveling a lot, accepting overseas assignments, or gaining operational experience, and that women are less mobile in this sense than men.

The third theme is that the gender imbalance in boardrooms, which all the kings we spoke to saw as a problem that should be corrected, was essentially a pipeline issue; a failure, not on the demand side where merit is the only criterion for a board appointment, but on the supply side. There are simply not enough suitably qualified women available for appointment to boards. It clearly follows from this explanation that once gender balance in the board candidate pipeline is achieved, it is only a matter of time before it feeds through to boards.

The fourth theme is that one of the reasons there are so few women in boardrooms, is that there are so few women in boardrooms – that there is some "tipping point" out there in the future when the number of women on boards will exceed a critical quantity and progress toward gender balance will accelerate dramatically. One variation on this theme is that the network effect (the number of connections in a network increases geometrically with its size) will become apparent as the number of women directors rises.

The fifth theme is that women bring valuable qualities to a board: a better feel for social dynamics, relationships and the "soft", people issues; more intuition, sensitivity and objectivity; less ego; a greater willingness to listen; a "certain female doggedness"; the ability to think more laterally than men; and a tendency to be more idealistic and more determined to reach the "right" decision.

Not all our corporate kings shared this view, however, and it was not clear from what those who do share it told us, how and to what extent this female value could be or was being traded off against other qualities desirable in directors. The insistence that "merit" was the only criterion for promotion begs questions about the definition of "merit" and where the line is drawn between minimum "qualification criteria", without which candidates can't be considered, and "differentiation criteria" used to choose between qualified candidates.

Could *being female* ever be a "qualification criterion" that could be traded for mobility, for example, in certain circumstances, or can it only ever be a tie breaker for choosing between equally qualified candidates? More to the point, perhaps, to what extent does *being male* still act, despite universal protestations to the contrary, as an unofficial, subconscious qualification criterion and how often does it break ties in favor of male candidates?

We ask these questions in the knowledge that they can't be answered, but in the belief that they should at least be put.

The sixth theme is babies. All the corporate kings we interviewed mentioned what is usually assumed to be the principal reason for the lack of women on boards, but none of them made a meal of it. Perhaps they felt that it would be indelicate to do so, given the gender of their interviewers. Perhaps, if we had been men, the babies thing would have featured more. We do not think so. Our impression was that they saw childbearing and child rearing as an issue, but not a major one and that, insofar as it was a problem, it was as much a problem for companies as it was for women.

The final and arguably the most important theme of all is the only argument for more women on boards that our most skeptical interviewee subscribed to: "You want women ... because it doubles your pool ... If I'm looking at the women in my succession plan and my competitors are not, I know I'll kill them." Several other kings agreed: "half the people on the planet are women [so it is inappropriate not to] have any on the board"; "you disadvantage yourself as a company when you neglect half the world's talent pool".

If we had to choose one argument when making the business case for women on boards, this would probably be the one. But it's a gross oversimplification and, moreover, we find the suggestion that one needs a "business case" for more women on boards rather odd. No one says you need a "business case" for appointing more men to boards. It seems to us that if talent is distributed equally between the sexes and women currently account for 10–15 percent of board members, it's a "no-brainer" that boards need more women.

One last point about our conversations with kings. One king said: "You need to put this in an historical context … As recently as two generations ago, women didn't work outside the home, except as teachers and nurses. Women only got the vote in the US in 1920." It is a fair point. Britain's Married Women's Property Act only elevated women from the status of their husbands' chattels in 1882, women only got the vote in the UK in 1918 (the age of male majority of 21 wasn't extended to women until 1928) and at two of Britain's "big four" clearing banks, and probably many other British companies, women still came under pressure to resign on marriage as recently as the 1950s.

It is always interesting to look at trends in a historical context, but it would be folly for companies to see the recent origins of women's political and economic rights as reason to delay a reform in the composition of their boards that offers competitive advantage.

These then are the views of a small, but we believe indicative, sample of US and UK business leaders about the gender imbalance in boardrooms. In the next chapter we look at the phenomenon from the other side of the fence, so to speak – from the point of view of the women already in senior management positions who want to be appointed to their main boards.

References

1. *Men are from Mars, Women are from Venus*, John Gray, HarperCollins, 1992.
2. A man's game in need of women, *Financial Times*, July 26, 2004.

CHAPTER 4

The view from marzipan

In Chapter 1 we looked at the mismatch between the gender balance of boards and the gender balance of the marketplace and new graduates, and presented some evidence of a positive link between the proportion of women on a board and financial performance.

We suggested in Chapter 2 that one possible explanation for the persistence of this mismatch, despite the evidence that it reduces performance, is the persistence of the deep-seated maleness of hierarchical organizations and business organizations in particular.

To test this suggestion and gain an impression of what this gender bias, if it exists, looks like from the demand side of the market for directors, we talked to several corporate kings – current and former chairmen and CEOs of large US and UK companies.

We derived seven themes from our interviews:

1. The gender imbalance on boards is easier to understand in some industries than others.

2. Most multinational companies expect executive board candidates to have overseas and operating experience, and women tend to be less mobile than men.

3. The gender imbalance on boards is a supply, rather than a demand problem – companies want more women on their boards, but cannot find enough suitably qualified female candidates.

4. One reason why there are so few women on boards is that there are so few women on boards; after the number passes a "tipping point", progress toward gender-balanced boards will accelerate.

5. Women bring some distinctive qualities to boards that most corporate kings value.

6. Childbearing and rearing is an issue, but not a major one, and is a problem as much for companies as for women.

7. The most persuasive argument for increasing the proportion of women on boards is the fact that women account for half the workforce and half the talent.

This, then, is how the males, in whose gifts most board appointments lie, see the gender issue.

To get a feel of how accurate these perceptions are, we asked several senior women in the US and the UK who were close to the board (in what Laura Tyson calls the "marzipan layer") how they saw the problem from the supply side. As in the previous chapter, we haven't attributed quotes to individuals, but all their names are in the acknowledgements.

Reactions to the figures

We began by asking them how they reacted to the latest figures showing that women accounted for 13.6 percent of Fortune 500 directors in 2003 and 9.7 percent FTSE 100 directors in 2004.

None of the women was particularly surprised by the headline numbers, but all felt they were much too low. "It's a very big problem" said one. "Having done quite a lot of work on diversity within my company, and being a strong advocate of diversity, I find it completely unacceptable that we have such a tiny representation of women. But I am not surprised by these numbers, considering where the development of women in UK business has got to so far."

Another said:

I'm not surprised. Twenty years ago I was one of only 3 percent of women taking an engineering degree. It takes 25–30 years to get through the pipeline. In marketing, we talk about the "purchase funnel"; if 1000 people hear about a product, the numbers who enquire are fewer and the numbers who actually buy are much fewer. So it's a similar problem. The group of women I began my career with 25 years ago was much larger, but a lot of women have dropped out. We are living with the sins of the past. We need to look at who's coming into the funnel now.

I'm not sure this percentage is the whole picture. At large international groups there are women below main board level running large businesses; in a smaller company they'd be on the main board. Also, many UK women choose to join US companies that are not listed on the London Stock Exchange, because they have reputations for being more progressive in this area. Professional organizations [accountancy and law firms] also attract more women, because they also have reputations for being more progressive.

An American VP of a major multinational didn't see it that way:

It's very tough as a woman to go beyond being VP to president or CEO in the US. On the outside it looks as though we've got our act together in the US. On the inside, it's not the case. To get to the top level, you need a killer instinct. I don't want to be so aggressive that I leave dead bodies along the way. I don't want to lose my values. This shouldn't be the only way. We still have a lot to work on in US corporate life.

A senior American executive working in London was "surprised at how low the figures are" and said:

I think the percentages are better, the further down an organization you go. The demographics of my own team are 80 percent men and 20 percent women, although on reflection, my team is probably higher on women than others at this level.

Despite the figures being lower, I think there is more openness about this issue here [in the UK]. There's a lot of talk about equality in the US, but it doesn't happen. It's the same with customer service; the US talks a good game! Maybe US women find it easier to get on boards in the UK.

Maybe, indeed! A UK marzipan woman thought the situation was worse than the figures suggested in terms of the pipeline: "There are no home-grown senior women executives at my company", she said. "They've all been brought in from the outside."

A woman who had recently resigned from a "marzipan layer" job was concerned by the disparity in *The Female FTSE 2004* report between the figures for executive directors and NEDs (see Table 4.1). "The problem is in the executive director numbers. The pipeline table is very disheartening. There won't be much change if there are so few women just below the board. Has BP really only got four women and United Utilities only one woman at that level?".

Another woman didn't find those pipeline figures surprising either:

I knew the figure was low. You just have to have been around business and industry – I've been on several management programs at business schools, and women didn't account for more than 2 percent of the intake at any of them. So if that's a reflection of what's coming through, and these are all aspiring board members, you wouldn't be surprised to see that played out in real life. If you stop people in the street, they can name the women who are at the top of organizations because there are so few of them.

Others also read more positive messages into the NED figures than into the executive director figures:

The fact that the NED figures are a little better than the executive director figures shows that boards are waking up. That's encouraging. One has to take

TABLE 4.1 Female talent pipeline in FTSE 100 companies

Company	Women in workforce	Women in junior management	Women in middle management	Women in senior management	Women just below board	Women executive directors	Women NEDs
Aviva	UK 53% Global 53%	UK 40% Global 42%	UK 37% Global 36%	UK 19% Global 19% (15% of "snr mgt group")	2 women	0	2
BP	27%	21%	UK 11% Global 13%	UK 8% Global 15%	4 women	0	1
British Airways	43%	50%	36%	26%	18% direct reports to leadership team	0	3
BSkyB	45%	N/A	27%	25%	2 on exec bd, 26 in tier below	0	1
Centrica	UK 34% Global 34%	UK 25% Global 27%	UK 28% Global 27%	UK 24% Global 23%	UK 16% Global 18% (13 women)	0	3
GUS	53%	N/A	N/A	25%	4 women	0	1
Intercontinental Hotels	N/A	N/A	35% middle and senior management group		2 UK, 2 US women	0	0
ITV	47%	43%	44%	36%	35%	0	0
J Sainsbury	60%	11% store managers	25%	23%	3	0	2
O₂	53%	38%	25%	23%	19 women	0	0
Shell	UK 29%	UK 26% Global 20%	UK 17% Global 11%	UK 13% Global 10%	12 with global excom remit	1 (Global)	2 (UK board) 1 (NL board)
United Utilities	42%	21%	23%	14%	1	0	1

Source: The Female FTSE Report 2004 p. 28

heart. But I'm not sure what the figure should be. I'm not in the 50 percent camp – if women had 20 percent appointments that were serious, not token, that would be good. The figures for executive directors are more disappointing. There just hasn't been enough progress in the last 20 years.

"I'm not surprised, really", said another. "In some ways, it's very positive that we're seeing any female directors. But it's slow and there's a certain degree of anxiety amongst senior managers. They don't know how to deal with women at that level. It causes men to look at their own behavior."

Reasons for the figures

Next we asked our "marzipan" women why they thought that the percentage was still so low and why progress was so slow.
Said one:

I always find it striking that in the US, the progress of women to senior positions is ahead of the UK [not by much, see Chapter 1]. It's a relatively new development in the UK. It's over the last decade or so that we've started to see women coming through to senior positions here. I think that, to a large extent and for a long time, although people said it was a "good thing" women came through into senior positions, nothing much was done about it. It was left to happen, and it doesn't happen without some sort of intervention. So, in terms of culture, many organizations were effectively, if not consciously, certainly subconsciously, making it very difficult for a woman to progress to the top level.

We were interested by this mention of culture, because so often the problem is said to be the role of women as the childbearers, and the solutions are therefore more maternity provision, flexible working, and so on. We asked her to expand:

Well, certainly over the last few years, I see more and more women who are prepared to take on the challenges of very senior roles and manage families – people who've continued to work, despite having children. But it is still a real rarity for women to be appointed to very high positions. I've almost never met anyone who has talked about active discrimination, so I think, in general, companies have gone through the process of understanding that they must treat women fairly and ensure that all their processes are fair. But there's still something in the culture that makes it easier for men – maybe the way people get known in the company and are earmarked to progress.

... AND THIS IS WHERE WE ALL HANG OUR HATS

I think there are often unwritten codes of conduct that make it easier for men to shine through, and to be seen as being very high performers and high potential people.

An "unwritten code of conduct"?

Yes. I haven't really thought about this, but I must say that, having been involved in the Women Directors on Boards programme [see Chapter 5], I am getting more and more messages that reinforce the view that board selection is a rather special process. It's about who you know, so women not being in senior positions and not being widely networked into the business community have an enormous hurdle to get across before they even get considered.

Another interviewee echoed the sentiment:

From my own experience there are issues of culture and behavior that many women just don't want to put up with. In that sense, you have to wonder if women, who certainly have the potential to rise to board level, really have the ambition.

I suspect part of the problem is that there haven't been many men who have seen it as part of their remit, as CEOs, to nurture women into the role. So it has been a bit of a closed shop. It's like the trade unions – for me it brings to mind Fleet Street, where you had the big print unions, all closed shops, and you were either a member of the club, or you weren't. "The club" happens to be a different club, but it's still a club. I don't know why but men are not really that "new-mannish" when it comes to work; even those who are quite liberated at home don't necessarily bring that attitude to work. And I've always been surprised that even younger men, my generation, who you would expect to have a broader view about women in the workplace, carry the same baggage. I wonder if it's partly because they've learned what you have to do to get on. They mimic the behavior of the people who they aspire to be, so it's a self-perpetuating situation. I think it's something about not being members of the club, and about it being very hard for women to join the club.

There are few female role models and some aren't very good models, because they have compromised so much. If you scratch the surface, you find they are not like the rest of us – they don't have the responsibilities, because they've made different life choices.

I've actually watched senior women create cultures that make it impossible for other women to get on. They get to a point in the organization and look at where they're aspiring to be, and work out that it's a club and to be in the club you have to play by certain rules. So they forget. I have actually seen women who get there and almost shut the door behind them, as if to say: "Well, I've done it, but it was terribly difficult, and I'm now in the club and …

But I've also worked for some men who, without singling you out and giving you special treatment, wanted you to be recognized as just as capable as your male peers. And I've worked for some men who were fantastic at just making it a level playing field. I've also worked for some men who promoted women at the expense of men in the team when, actually, the women shouldn't have been promoted.

Another suggested:

Some female characteristics sometimes let us down. For example, we don't take enough risks. But women can also be rejected by the culture. It happened to me, when I took my last big role. During the first six months, it turned out that several of my male colleagues had not agreed with my appointment and they sat there, with their arms folded, to see if I would sink or swim. They weren't going to help me. I thought "I'm not going to let them get to me."

There was no collegiate feel; no attempt to welcome me to the team or offer me mentoring or coaching. I was very much on my own and you can't do a job in these large companies without the support of your peers.

After six months I spoke to my boss about it. I said I didn't want to work in this environment where you are constantly being challenged and tested in this way. I like the challenge of the work. It's not about that. It's about the challenge and undermining from colleagues. He said he was glad I hadn't made the comment earlier, or he would have had concerns about my ability to handle the job. By then he knew I was capable of delivering performance.

Women shouldn't have to put up with that. I don't want to be cosseted, but I should be treated as an equal member of the team. Unfortunately, this kind of treatment is not uncommon and there are also still too many Queen Bees in organizations – other women can also be a big barrier to diversity. They can have a seriously negative effect.

We found this story particularly poignant, because we knew this woman was a leader of the company's women's network and a role model for other women. She left the company she had joined as a new graduate 20 years earlier soon after we spoke to her. She's only 42. What a waste!
She continued:

It's not just business. It's society. Earlier in my career in customer-facing, commercial roles, some customers would ask to deal with my boss rather than me. I had to tell them "I am the boss" and then work to gain their credibility. It's an extra hurdle men don't face. It is the same on our parish council. Women have to prove their value. At a recent meeting, the men seemed amazed that I was challenging and asking questions. I guess they're not used to women like me.

People in smaller companies probably behave differently. I wouldn't remain in a role if the environment got as bad again. I've realized that you can't change things as an individual. The plus side is that, as a woman, you can get offered some really good jobs and you do get noticed. A lot of women do want good challenges.

Another suggested:

It's a combination of things. There is the attitude of existing boards; men of about 50 in grey suits with closed minds. Even here that's true. They don't have an internal pool of women to choose from. It's manufacturing and they seem to think men do manufacturing so this is a male-dominated company. And then there's the women themselves – we tend to undersell ourselves. We don't do boasting. We don't promote ourselves. We're not political. We don't tend to exaggerate our good points. We just quietly get on with it and do more and more work!

I realized five years ago I'd never get anywhere if I hid my light under a bushel.

The former HR director of an investment bank identified two reasons for the low figures for women directors; male misconceptions and female reluctance:

There's a set of assumptions going on largely among men. For example, that women won't want to travel. That may be true but they've not tested it out. And, if you're not visible on those big deals, you don't get on. So the big enemies are the thought patterns.

Life in very senior positions in a large organization can be pretty damned unpleasant in terms of the inroads it makes upon your life. Some women are just not interested in making the sacrifices, because they don't value what they get for it. Men value status and position much more.

"I've climbed the ladder by hard work and understanding this business", said a US executive. "The road isn't easy. You have to really, really want it. I insist on giving my two kids the attention they need. They've had au pairs, but the kids know I'm their mother! I've had to turn two jobs down, because I couldn't move. I've put my foot down about moving so that I don't disrupt the children."

"In a large company like ours, jobs are not always posted", said another American woman. "There was an article in the *New York Times* a couple of years ago about how women in the class of 1985 should have been in the boardroom by now. A lot of educated women give up on the bureaucracy and game playing, because they can afford to. They tend to marry bright guys, with good jobs. So lots of bright women are now overprogramming their kids!"

Another interviewee echoed the point: "A lot of women choose not to compete at that level. They take themselves out of the workforce, or decide not to press their candidacies." She thought it was partly "the macho culture that makes women opt out" and partly a perception problem:

Men misinterpret the signs. They mistake a lack of confidence as a lack of ambition. They don't think enough about encouraging women to come to the table. In a discussion about a job move or a promotion, a woman might say:

"I'm not sure I want it, really." Her male boss interprets that as a sign of incompetence: "If she's not hungry enough, she couldn't possibly manage the role."

I don't see as many absolutely driven women as men. Rather than take what people say about their ambitions for granted, I watch their behavior when they don't get the jobs they go for. It's very interesting; women don't get as consumed by disappointment as men; they don't tend to get as suicidal if they don't get jobs.

There are women around who are simply not good enough – they don't network enough especially if they have family commitments. You have to know as many people as the men. You need strategies for dealing with the discussions men have in the loo!

A former consultant thought:

Senior people have ingrained notions of talent that are not necessarily what the business needs. On the whole, they choose people to run yesterday's business. You do have to have some research about yesterday's success, but you also need a very big aspirational element. Our model is based on both aspiration and past success. One important aspect is how well you can adapt your style. Command and control leadership has been used, and been effective in the core business, but managing joint ventures requires a different style. Today there's more need to manage ambiguity and support people who come to the company from different ventures. Many women are better at managing some of these things. Success in the future will be less about warlike and sporting behavior, and more about multitasking and managing complexity and ambiguity [see Chapter 6].

Another woman felt it was partly to do with the less favored routes to the top often taken by women, and partly to do with the reluctance of women to "sell" themselves:

People are more comfortable promoting someone who's had the same experiences they've had. Sometimes women have got to senior jobs via different routes and experience. And they're not very good at marketing themselves. GE Capital's women's network says individual branding of PIE is essential for favorable promotion decisions:

Performance – counts for 10 percent, because everyone performs

Image – for example, being known to be capable counts for 30 percent

Exposure – that is, being known counts for 60 percent

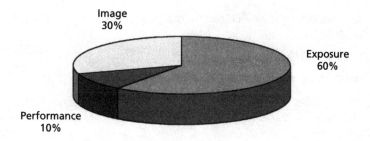

Figure 4.1 Getting the balance right

Women are not good at the E. We tend to undersell ourselves, whereas the guys brag, and tend to oversell. We're not that confident. And we sometimes develop coping strategies early in our careers for being a woman in a man's world that can backfire on us as we get more senior. When I was younger and had older men reporting to me, I would deliberately put myself down so that I didn't come across as threatening. I still find myself pandering to older guys' egos when I'm sitting next to them at business dinners; we talk about what they want to talk about. We are not like this at university, but we've learned behaviors to adapt as we've climbed the ladder that stay with us.

Another made a distinction between executive and non-executive directors: "It's been easier to get a non-executive director role, particularly if you have no public profile. For executive director jobs you're always on a more competitive arc. It's easier to move companies. I've done it."

"It's a combination of some men not letting women in, and women discounting themselves", said another interviewee. "Men are more choosy – they do things that are high profile, rather than things that need doing. Women seem to do a lot of menial tasks. They pick up so many low-level tasks they don't have enough time for the higher level tasks. And women don't extract the maximum public relations from their achievements."

The point about women taking on the menial, but necessary tasks that men tend to avoid brings to mind a tale Stephen Covey told years ago about a lecture on time management (see box).

Is it full?

The lecturer puts a wide-mouthed gallon jar on a table, alongside a pile of fist-sized rocks and asks the class how many rocks they think he can get in the jar.

Some guesses are made. "Let's see", he says, and puts as many rocks as he can in the jar.

"Is the jar full?", he asks.

"Yes!", shouts the class.

"Ahh", he says, reaching down and lifting up a bucketful of gravel. He pours some gravel in, shakes the jar and the gravel fills up the gaps between the rocks.

"Is the jar full?", he asks again.

"Probably not", someone mutters.

"Good!", says the lecturer, producing a bucket of sand. With the help of some shaking, the sand fills up the spaces between the rocks and the gravel.

"Is the jar full?", he asks a third time.

"No!", shouts the class.

The lecturer grins and produces a bucket of water. With the jar brimming over, the lecturer says, "What's the point?"

"You can always get more into your life?", someone suggests.

"No", says the lecturer. "The point is that if I hadn't put the rocks [those higher level tasks] in first, I wouldn't have got any of them in."

Adapted from *First Things First*, Stephen Covey, Simon & Schuster, 1994

On being appointed to a major company's board

We then asked our marzipan women how comfortable they were with the idea of being appointed to the board of a major company.

"I'd welcome it with open arms", said one. "I'd love it. I'm not sure I know enough about what would be expected of me, though. I have a lot of personal power, but not much positional power, because of being in HR. I've got to a stage where positional power is what I need."

Another woman was equally positive, but did not feel she was typical:

I would be pretty comfortable about that, but I have been raised in a male environment. In my first job I was the only woman. I was a junior member of an otherwise all-male team in a male environment – newspapers, you can't get more macho than that. Then I went into radio and television, which are also predominantly male. So I would have no problem with it, but that is more to do with my training than it is to do with what makes me comfortable.

So I'm not really a very good example. I am atypical. I've had to learn to thrive in that environment. If you go on the road for a week or two and go somewhere difficult and dangerous and you are with a crew who are all men, they don't care whether you've got a change of knickers with you or not. It isn't their problem. They just expect you to cope and you learn to cope. So putting myself into a situation I perceive to be male wouldn't bother me.

The former marzipan woman who was about to resign was less sanguine:

I am not sure I want to do that now. I was earmarked as having high enough potential – I was in the top level talent pool and I suppose I thought that if I progressed at the predicted rate, I would have a good chance of getting there. But it didn't turn out like that.

I haven't been approached about an NED role, but I have put myself forward for some public appointments. I've put myself on a database to get notified about public appointments. I've applied for two, but wasn't interviewed for either. I haven't worked in the public sector, but [the organizations] both stressed they were looking for commercial experience of which I have loads. But the feedback was that I hadn't got public sector experience! If that is a prerequisite, then of course I'm out.

So I'm now a foundation governor of a school. They seem keen to take me on for my commercial experience and they listen to my views and learning. They value the diversity, in other words, whereas the civil service just seems to want more of the same. At a seminar I went to about public appointments, the speaker used behavioral examples of why people were rejected at interview. To my mind, they were issues of style. She seemed to be saying that there is a game to play in the way you come across and the language you use. There's a set of rules, in other words, which you need to know.

I've also decided to make myself known to organizations and people working with SMEs [small and medium-sized enterprises]. I think I have a lot to add to people building businesses. Maybe that's where to focus.

"I think I would feel very similar to how I've felt when being appointed to all completely new positions, which has happened quite often in my career", said another; "tremendously excited, I'm sure I'll cope with it, but I know there's a huge learning curve."

"If I was appointed an executive director, my only concern would be my lack of financial experience", another woman admitted. "I've been a lawyer for 20 years, so I've loads to offer in areas like risk analysis, risk management, legal, property and insurance. Having sat on boards since 1997, when I was company secretary at my previous employer, and being secretary to the audit committee here, I'm comfortable in the board setting. But I would need some extra training."

That last point was echoed by another woman. "I'd be relatively comfortable being appointed a director. The thing that is lacking is any sort of proper training for people, men and women, assuming board positions."

Another woman also said she would feel differently about being an executive and a non-executive director. "I would be very comfortable about becoming a non-executive, but not an executive director in a large organization." We asked why not.

"I don't think I'm confident enough." She paused for a moment, gathering her thoughts. "I've seen a lot of incompetent people in very big jobs … I think women tend to be more competent than confident. With men, it's the reverse. They're often more confident, than competent."

"I am relatively comfortable about being appointed an executive director to a company at the bottom end of the FTSE 100 or in the 250", another marzipan woman said. "I would be comfortable about becoming a non-executive director at any company, but they usually want 'branded women' – a dame or baroness, for example. I think I would make a good chairman or CEO, because I look at the bigger picture and don't get bogged down in the detail."

Board experience

Having established a general hunger for board appointments among the senior women we spoke to, we asked them whether they'd ever been approached or had put themselves forward for executive or non-executive board positions, what their experience had been and how they had gone about it.

None had been approached to become a member of a FTSE 100 or a Fortune 500/ S&P 500 board. One had been invited by her CEO to sit on the holding company board for two subsidiaries and another had been on her company's European board for three years:

> I knew the board was being formed, but I didn't do any lobbying – I thought I'd wait and see. We had a new CEO in the US and he appointed me. I am head of HR in a male-dominated environment. I'm the first and only woman who has ever been appointed to one of our boards. It caused a ruckus on the

SORRY MADAM, THE ICING IS RESERVED FOR THEM OVER THERE © Barbara Shore

investment management board – one director resigned. My membership has been a challenge for everyone, but it was great for me, because I had the people there I needed to make certain decisions. But they didn't communicate. Few of them acted as I had expected directors to act. They didn't put their own interests second. There was more fighting for your own corner than for the good of the European firm.

Several of the women we talked to were interested in becoming NEDs. Two had talked to colleagues about the training they would need to become NEDs; one had had some dealings with headhunters indirectly; another had put her name forward with headhunters:

I've emailed my CV to, and had meetings with, a couple. One advised me that coming from a bank could be a disadvantage, and that I might have to market myself differently, to show that I am more of a general manager than a banker.

Our deputy CEO helped – I put the idea on my development plan. He "gave me permission" to talk to a headhunter, and introduced me to one. The chairman also supported my involvement in the Cross-Company Mentoring Programme [see Chapter 5], and offered to give me a reference, if I'm offered an NED role. The problem is getting that first role – the same people are approached and once you have one [board position] it seems easier. I've talked to our NEDs at board lunches about how they set about getting their first NED roles.

The importance of a diverse board

All the marzipan women we spoke to thought companies needed to have diverse boards.

Said one:

> I think it is extremely important, for the same reasons it is important in all management teams at all levels in an organization. The world of business is getting tougher, more challenging and more multifaceted. So an ever wider range of risks and challenges needs to be considered, and the more different approaches, views and mindsets that you bring to address the issues, the more likely you are first of all to identify all the key issues and then to have a balanced discussion and a lot of different views to come to a robust conclusion.

"You do need to see things from different angles", echoed another. She continued:

> Women do have different views of things. I do think it's very important. I was the only female on that board and it was quite lonely. The men always accepted

WHAT PROBLEM?

my views, but we might have had a slightly different approach to the people-related stuff if there had been more women on the board. Women operate to different values. The point about an "employee franchise" [the need to get employee buy-in to a decision or course of action that affects employees] is sometimes lost on men. It was a key tenet of the global CEO, but some of the others had to be dragged there kicking and screaming.

"Diversity is very important, both from the sex and the nationality point of view", said a woman who sat on a subsidiary board. "Our board has improved a lot, but on the group board we see a lot of traditional male behaviors – a lot of power play. I have found women more prepared to put their own status aside and more willing to address conflict – men won't tackle the difficult issues."

We asked them what dimensions of diversity they thought were important. Said one:

There are two main things, diversity of experience, which means being able to see things from different angles, and different approaches to problems, which is in your genetic make-up. I know people from very similar backgrounds some-times see the same problem in completely different ways. To make this prac-tical that means reflecting the headline dimensions, such as gender and nationality, to bring in diverse experience and backgrounds, and having different types of people.

When you have a diverse group of people working on issues, the value comes through at different levels. Sometimes it comes through at a very practical level. I've had to deal with teams working on acquisitions where having people who can relate easily, in terms of style, to the people they are dealing with is a tremendous benefit. I'm also convinced that, in businesses with customers, having people on the management team and board who reflect the customers in some way is important, because you are much more likely to understand what customers are looking for and make the right decisions. I also think, and I have seen this, that if you have different types of people, you get a lot of strength in discussions. It makes life more difficult, of course – it often makes it quite difficult to reach conclusions!

It's not just having women – having more diverse backgrounds in general is important. Academics, for example, see things in a different way. But women do stand back a bit; think for themselves; have their own views – men often seem to want to agree with each other in a clubby sort of way.

Few senior women I know in business have children, because it's so hard to combine working in a senior role for a multinational with having children. But women do think about the work–life balance much more than men. Men have lots of help; usually a wife, for a start. They eat out with clients every night and other people (usually their wives) put the children to bed. Women want to put their children to bed themselves.

Women also tend to be more inclusive, of men as well as women. Men include people who are like them (mostly other men). Women also have many more ways of skinning cats than men.

"Diversity's very important", said another interviewee. "You have to reflect your employees and your customers. Half of our customers are women, 60 percent of our staff are female, 10 percent of our customers are from ethnic minorities. We do have a diverse board – the chairman has been instrumental in bringing new people in."
Another said:

It's not just gender. It's also race and I also think there is a need for diverse experiences. When you sit round the table with people who have always been in the City, they all have the same view and it's hard to challenge that view.

Women are more willing to address conflict. They're more collaborative and they have better interpersonal skills. They've learned different approaches and have a wider variety of styles than men, perhaps because they've had to struggle more to get to the top. I have relationships with people that help me to get things done.

"It depends on your business", another suggested. "If it's a UK retail chain, you would need to be worried about the gender and ethnic mix, but you don't necessarily need a global board. You need to reflect the main stakeholders. For global companies, a global mix on the board is critical. I think gender also matters, because women bring characteristics that suit future business requirements. We've deliberately headed that way with our board."
Said another:

Oh yes! Absolutely! Diversity is vital. Why? Because … well, it's glaringly obvious. If everyone's the same, there's never any challenge; there's no innovation; there's no questioning of the direction you're going in. It can be successful in a stable environment, but what happens when the environment changes? You put together a board for one environment and then the environment changes and you have no voice saying: "I know we're marching over here, but actually …".

And because there's no voice there to say "the outside is changing", or "I don't agree", or "hang on a minute, what about …?", by the time you realize, you've gone over the edge of the precipice; by the time you've woken up to the fact that actually you might need somebody else's view, the closed group is so self-enforcing and endorsing that you've marched over the edge of the cliff before anyone says "hang on a minute, there's a cliff!"

Variety of voice, variety of background, variety of cultures. [X] is a very good example. It's full of people from Oxford and Cambridge, all with a particular view of life. They may have different backgrounds; they may have been born in different parts of the country or been brought up by different sorts of parents, but they are quite self-selecting.

If you need a very close relationship with the consumer, it doesn't matter whether you sell them toothpaste or television programs, it's no good if the people setting your strategic direction only understand the perceptions of five percent of that consumer base.

How women change boards

Next, we asked our interviewees what differences they thought women made to boards.

"I think women, typically, have a very different experience of life through their education, groups they become members of, their friendships and their very different networks", said one interviewee. "I hate generalizations, but one of the key jobs of a board is to understand societal issues and I think women have a different "take" on that. There is a lot of overlap, but women tend to think about community and family as well as all the other issues."

"They bring different viewpoints and experience", said another. "There are experiences women have, which men don't. It dampens down the testosterone. Any team with a mix is better, because it stops the "testosterone high". All female teams are not good either."

"I don't think that it's breadth of experience so much", another suggested. "Women often bring a different view of business and of the community within a business. It goes back to the differences in the management styles of men and women. I think women bring a totality of life experience to a board. On the whole men will just bring their work to the board."

Another thought a woman on a board often modified male behavior:

Men tend to compete when they get together – act macho. Women say "that's very interesting, but let's consider …". They have more finely tuned interpersonal skills.

© Barbara Shore

GOOD GRIEF — WE'VE NEVER CONSIDERED THAT

Business is all about problem solving, and women tend to approach problems differently, because they have been socialized differently – multiple views give a more interesting range of solutions to a problem.

Another felt one woman on the board wasn't enough: "If your culture is very male, it's difficult for one woman to have an impact that's more than a fly on an arm. Numbers make a difference. If you have women, they're good and you let them contribute, it changes the nature of conversation. The challenge for women is to change the conversation, but not so much that the men stop listening."

Another spoke of courage:

Part of the value women bring to a board is that different voice, but they have to feel safe enough to do that.

Safe enough?

Yes. I think there's a danger that having got there, having broken through and won their place with so much courage and so much self-belief, women are so, kind of – not relieved, that's not the right word – they're so proud of themselves for having got there, they are really at risk then of playing by the rules of the club they've joined. It's hard, particularly if you're the only woman, to be as courageous sitting at the table as you were getting to the table.

Sometimes women are their own worst enemies. Sometimes women get there and they kind of feel that they exceeded their rights just to be there and they certainly don't have the right to have a position and voice that position. The bravest of them do, but I think it's quite hard. I do think it's really difficult, having fought your way to that place, to muster enough energy to carry on fighting.

We told her one of the chairmen we had spoken to said he liked to have more than one woman on his board.

"He's right" she said. "It's the point we've just made. I wonder, I have no evidence for this, if a woman remains courageous after getting there, could that make men more courageous too and make them brave enough to join her?'

Getting on the board

We then asked interviewees what they thought women needed to do differently to achieve executive and non-executive board positions.

"Network more; get known" said one. "This comes up again and again. You see it in a company like ours. Women don't build networks in their organization as easily or as naturally as some men do."

She's right. It does come up again and again and we find it puzzling. Women are generally said to have better social skills than men, to have more of a sense of community, family and inclusiveness, and to be more eager than men to avoid conflict and smooth ruffled feathers. One would have thought that with their innate communication skills and their interest in people, women would make better networkers than men (see Chapter 2). We asked her why she thought they did not.

She agreed that women were capable of networking well, but said they lacked courage:

Women need to be braver. They need the self-confidence to say, "I can definitely go the next step, and the next and the next"; to push for it and not to look for external reinforcement; to believe they can do it.

Part of it is to behave with more confidence – with more stature, gravitas and poise. Act as if you are equal with the men and they will regard you as equal. Also, don't speak shrilly, getting higher and higher, and faster and faster, which women often do.

During the interview she said:

> It's good to have the opportunity to speak like this. This sort of thing really helps, because you realize there are other people out there with the same aspirations.

Others echoed this idea: "We need to market ourselves more. People who move around between companies get better known. Women don't tend to move as much as men, so they aren't noticed. We're OK on performance and image, but poor on exposure. We can't do that weekend "exposure stuff" on the golf course."

Some have suggested that one reason why women don't change jobs as much as men is that they feel grateful to their employers when they come back from career breaks and tend to be more loyal as a consequence. See Chapter 2 for a summary of a US study of women returners.

> Women need to be more confident – far too many women don't think highly of themselves. Women generally aren't very self-confident or assertive enough. It's almost as if they need permission to do something. I feel like that. I think: "If they need me, they'll call me." I don't put myself forward.

> It's about raising visibility, but also ambition, networking and using the skills you've got in different ways. Women do their jobs, they hopefully do them well, but they tend to leave it at that. They stay in their own, small environments. Men tend to network more.

An American VP said:

> There are two women at the top but they're not in hard-hitting roles. I took my current role for marketability purposes, because it has an operational element. You need to get support from all those round your boss, so that if he's going to do you in, you will have enough support elsewhere for your career.

> I'm learning how to balance what I say and when I say it. We're not taught these things early enough in the game. I have one-to-ones with the CEO even though I'm not in the "kitchen cabinet". He listens to me but I choose when and how I give him information.

> I've made mistakes along the way. I was a steamroller at first – it didn't work. You must keep your integrity. I don't have to get to the top quickly, but I do want to get there. It may take longer this way, but it's a case of the tortoise and hare. Everybody was going right, when I was going left. My friends were having kids while I kept going with my career. I have two kids now, but I'm slightly older.

Another interviewee advised women not to expect too much too soon: "We have to accept that organizations aren't going to change as much as we want them to, and give us the home life, as well as the work life we want. That means we face some pretty stark choices."

One interviewee gave this advice:

Take as a baseline that you develop yourself well (as you would expect any executive to do). This includes being prepared to do the loneliness and take those tough decisions. Then you have to "play the game" a bit, but not so much that you lose your authenticity. Playing the game is marketing yourself. You can't always tell the entire truth. You have to be careful where you express concerns – things can be misinterpreted as a lack of ambition, for example.

Women also generally need to be more confident and think about things they can do. You have to initiate things to achieve change – it can be difficult when you're the only one. Women need to help other women more.

Another woman suggested women should be "less emotional":

"I don't mean that in a derogatory way but I think it's about discipline. I think women need to learn the art of disciplining their emotions. They have to harness emotion; to use it rather than treat it as a kind of free spirit that you sometimes keep the lid on and sometimes don't. Women are not great at that. They need to learn how to harness emotion.

They also need to be more rigorous and pay more attention to the detail. I am not talking about women with financial backgrounds; they do pay a lot of attention to detail; they're trained to. But I've seen women at very senior levels who seem to think a flutter of the eyelashes and a giggle will cover up the fact that they don't know how their budget is spent. I have actually heard a very senior woman, when quizzed about a £350 million issue say: "Oh, I don't do money".

I sense a kind of lack of rigor, almost as if they're saying: "I'm a woman and I've got here. That's been a slog and that's enough. I do everything by instinct, you know, I'm very instinctive." You hear women say "oh I'm great with people" – as though that excuses them from being rigorous about things that require you to pay attention to the detail.

She'd applied for non-executive jobs in the public and private sectors, but had found "a lot more prejudice in the public sector. The culture change is slower there."

We asked her to say more about this, because it is usually assumed that the public sector is forced, by its political masters, to be more advanced than the private sector in promoting diversity and inclusion:

> The difference is that, in the public sector, your survival doesn't depend on it. Increasingly in the commercial world the face you present is part of your competitive advantage, and women are such a large part of the customer base that it is hard, even for CEOs who are uncomfortable about appointing women to their boards, to carry on ignoring it. There isn't that driver in the public sector. It's a very comfortable environment so the women you see progressing through in the public sector are mostly very good. But they are still playing predominantly by the old rules.

We asked her how she had gone about finding senior jobs and if she had used headhunters:

> My experience of headhunters is that I found them pretty poor at asking what I think is a pretty good question: "What sort of profile have you got"; and at explaining "What sort of person are you looking for?" They'll look at your CV, but they don't seem to be very focused. I had quite an interesting conversation with a headhunter last week. He said really good women for board jobs were like gold dust. So, what has my experience been? One of the things I was kind of raised on is that if you're interested in a job and you've applied for it, do your homework. One of the things you do is find people who will talk to you, perhaps even the CEO, and you go and talk to them. That's fascinating because, without exception, the conversation is always about how brilliant they are; never about what they are looking for or how you can improve the dynamics of their board or their environment. It is always about: "Well, of course, it's a fantastic team, because I lead it so well – I've been really brilliant at this." And that's just the informal conversation!

> There's loads of ego and then you're fobbed off on somebody else: "Oh I've kind of run out of steam now. I've got other things to do." It's a very odd situation when you're really interested in working for a company and you're there to try to glean enough information for yourself and what you get is a 20-minute press release. Another thing that's interesting is that I've also talked to lots of women about working for them and they don't do that; they talk to you about what a good team we would be and about your skills. It's quite an interesting difference.

> They say: "I'm like this – together we would make a great team." They don't always follow it all through if you end up working for them, but it's their starting position.

Bringing women forward

Next, we asked our interviewees what FTSE 100 and Fortune/S&P 500 companies could do to increase the number of women on their boards.

First of all they need to think what they're doing at all their management levels to try to bring more women through the organization. That is important as well. It isn't just boards. It's a pipeline, isn't it – how you manage talent? Then they need to review the mechanisms they use to make appointments to boards, and ask "is that women-friendly?" If they're simply going through a network and asking who the chairman or CEO knows and so on, is that stacking the odds against finding a woman right from the beginning? Health checks on processes are crucial, to ensure they're not inadvertently excluding women.

One of the things we have done for appointments internally is to put in a diversity check on the decision, which asks: "why did I chose this candidate and not another?". It's to ensure that there aren't a lot of prejudices and assumptions that effectively say: "I think this person's a better candidate because he or she is more like me; more like the normal model".

Several women mentioned the pipeline issue. "Make sure the funnel's as wide as possible and the reasons women leave are dealt with" and "make sure they have a broader range of people on their slate" were typical suggestions.

Another suggested cultivating more awareness about how to get on boards. "A course on aspiring women directors, for example. Men are in the pool. Women are excluded from that. They don't know how to go about it."

An American interviewee urged companies to "identify capability and provide help around confidence and assertiveness. Help women build self-esteem."

Another marzipan woman suggested:

We have to tackle some of the questions much more openly. We're playing around with networks – that's great, but it will take time. We have to move on a number of fronts at once. There's been this debate about whether you need special development for women directors. I believe you do. You must give the right women the skills and confidence they need; treat them like top-track talent, but give them senior mentors – men and women – outside the organization; provide them with broader, higher level experience and support them while they're doing it.

Another woman echoed the point: "I'd like to see more mentoring by women or men who are already there of people who have the potential to get there."

"Companies need to develop women", said another, "the processes and access to positions must be fair. Chairmen/CEOs should take women under their wings."

"Marketing and exposure" was also emphasized. "We need to do something with headhunters and chairmen, to help them understand the female talent that is available. Socially, we relate in a different way. Women Directors on Boards [see Chapter 5] has a role to play in marketing to headhunters."

Another felt the need for more evidence of the value that women add to boards:

It would be better if senior executives were more convinced that there was a correlation between women on a board and performance and more evidence of better connections with customers, because then you could set targets. This kind of cultural change needs to be led from the top, but women should also be encouraged to apply more for senior jobs.

Most important, there should be much more focus on the pipeline. Companies need to do more to get women to just below board level so there are more to choose from. What's being done to ask chairmen who don't have any women on their boards what they're doing about it? Have you interviewed any of them for your book?

Another woman said:

That's funny. I was talking about "squeezing both ends of a problem" this morning. In an ideal world you'd do two things, wouldn't you? Instil in women a kind of belief that they have the right to be there, and persuade men that there are huge, commercial advantages in creating the climate. I'm not massively in favor of simply saying: "OK, I want you to get three women on your top team …". You kind of need them to do that, but I'm much more interested in how you create a climate in which it seems cool and sharp and business focused to want to do it.

I'm interested in how you appeal to the male ego in ways that say: "You'll be head of the pack if you do this." Then they promote women automatically, because it's part of the culture of the place. Meanwhile, you give women the belief that they can do it if they go at it properly in the way men do, with all their attention, rather than saying: "Oh, I don't know. I don't do that, I have somebody to do that for me."

I don't think companies are very good at painting a picture for women that makes them want to do it – I can't think of lots and lots of women who want to do this.

We told her of a seminar one of us had gone to a couple of weeks previously about the liabilities of directors at which a speaker had said: "We all know people whose lives have been wrecked by being on a board." She replied:

Yes, that's right. Because of the changes in the law. I think women aren't sure what's in it for them, really. They want to be on the board of course, because you can see the tangible success of that, but I'm not sure they see the point. We're back to this figure of 13 percent NEDs. That's the 13 percent who've left industry and landed a few NED roles that keep them ticking over. They're usually senior older women. Of the two figures, it's much less worrying than the 4 percent of executive directors, because that means you're not getting a pipeline.

Ambitions

None of the marzipan women we talked to had ever been in the running for an appointment to the board of a FTSE 100 or Fortune/S&P 500 company, but some had served or were serving on the boards of subsidiaries or associates.

"I was on the board of our associated company in Pakistan", said one. "I pushed to get on that board, to get some experience – it was a deliberate decision to equip myself with that experience."

Almost all said they wanted to be appointed to a main board, although a few were aiming for non-executive appointments.

"I've made it clear I want my boss's job", said an American VP, "and I've let my boss's boss know that too! Women need to be graciously firm, when stating what they want."

By and large, British women haven't yet learned to do "graciously firm". As a North American woman put it, tongue in cheek, at the launch of the *2004 Female FTSE Report* at 11 Downing Street (official residence of Britain's Chancellor of the Exchequer): "We New World women are inadequately socialized. We just don't realize what our place is in the social fabric!"

We asked our interviewees what they would do if they were not appointed to the board in the next few years and whether they were planning their careers.

"Absolutely!" said one. "As well as working actively internally, to promote myself and make myself as credible a candidate as possible for the board, I am networking actively externally, including contacting head-hunters, to try to find opportunities for non-executive positions initially."

Being appointed to the board "is in my portfolio of ambitions", said another woman. "It's an ambition, but not the overriding one" said a third. "I want to make a difference and add value. I would consider a senior position in a large company which was not on the board if it was a position of influence. I don't want it for the stripes, as some men do. I would leave this company for the right job, not for the status. Egos and land grabs are important to the guys, but I don't judge achievement that way. What's important to me is what I'm delivering."

"If I'm still doing the same job in three years' time, I would probably move on", said another. "Or I might stay on and do a non-executive job at another company." Others felt the same: "If I'm not appointed to the main board in the next five years, I would think that was a failure"; "If I can't get what I need from corporate life, I'll go back to running my own business."

Most said they would leave their current employers for a chance to become a director of another company, "in the right circumstances", or "if something really right for me comes along".

A word of warning: our sample may not be representative of the ambitions of senior women. Our work in this area over several years, including work with the Female FTSE rankings, the Women Directors on Boards consortium and most recently the FTSE 100 Cross-Company Mentoring Programme (see Chapter 5), may have led us to a group of women who care more than most about these issues.

As one of our interviewees said: "There is a lot of noise about women being on boards, but no one's asked women if they want to be on boards. There are lots of women in very senior jobs who have chosen not to take that step."

Matters arising

We learned a lot from our conversations with these marzipan women from both sides of the Atlantic. We hope you have too. We learned, for instance, that despite the widespread belief that the US is "more advanced" than the UK in the pursuit of the gender-balanced board, senior female executives see the issue in much the same way and seem equally frustrated on both sides of the Atlantic.

Their prescriptions were similar too; network more, be more confident, play the game, increase your "exposure". We conclude from this that the position in the US should not be seen as a target for UK companies. There's still "a lot to work on in the US", as an American marzipan woman put it.

There was even a suggestion that the UK was more advanced in this area than the US, in that the issue was being debated more openly here.

One of our hopes when we embarked on these interviews was that by comparing and contrasting the demand side views of the corporate kings we summarized in Chapter 3 with the supply side views summarized above, we could reach a deeper, three-dimensional picture of any institutionalized bias, barrier or glass ceiling that may be inhibiting the appointment of women to board positions.

It seems to us that there is a considerable amount of common ground between the views of the corporate kings and the marzipan women. Both groups regard the pipeline issue as crucial. Both recognize the importance of role models for aspiring female board members, although the corporate kings appeared to be less concerned than the marzipan women about the de-motivating effect of so-called Queen Bees (of whom more in Chapter 8). Neither group seemed to regard childbearing and child rearing as a major issue at this level.

There were also some interesting differences. Despite the general agreement on the need to get more women into the board pipeline, marzipan women don't see the current scarcity of female directors as essentially a supply side problem. "Well they wouldn't, would they?", we hear some readers say. "They are the supply." True, but if there are able and highly qualified women who want to become directors, but haven't so far been offered board jobs, it is hard to argue that inadequate demand is not implicated in some way.

The marzipan women were more aware of cultural barriers than the corporate kings. They talked of the upper executive echelon as being a "closed shop" or a "club", and some came close to suggesting that male-dominated cultures at the top of companies had some kind of immune system that rejected women.

They also suggested that many men in whose gifts board appointments lie may be guided by unconscious prejudices when choosing between board candidates that favor men. They misread the signs. They mistake a lack of confidence for a lack of ability, and a lack of hunger for a lack of competence. Some women felt that these failures of mutual understanding were partly their fault, and they should keep their emotions under tight control, be less tentative, more ready to "sell" themselves, and (although none of them put it quite as baldly as this) be less frank about their weaknesses and reservations.

Some pointed out that a disproportionate number of senior female executives worked in areas, such as HR, that were, for most companies and for the time being, "less favored routes to the top" – the so-called "pink-collar" jobs (see Chapter 7).

Several suggested that women did not put themselves forward for board jobs, because they didn't find them as attractive as men did – they did not value high-status jobs as much as men and were more conscious of the growing personal risks that directors ran as a consequence of recent legislative changes. It wasn't always clear, however, whether women's relative lack of appetite for board positions was caused mainly by their distaste for the job itself, or their perceptions of the cultural environment it would take them into.

Many marzipan women we talked to emphasized the need for training for board positions and for mentoring relationships with men or women who are already on boards. We devote the next chapter to the origins and experience so far of just such a mentoring program.

CHAPTER 5

Bridging the gap

Most of the time being joint authors poses no problems. We are friends, and we both believe passionately that major companies need more women on their boards. We have the same outlook on most matters connected with the subject and, although we argue and debate with each other, we usually end up seeing things in much the same way, certainly as far as this book is concerned. In other words, most of the time, the first person plural suits us just fine.

In this chapter, we switch temporarily to the third person singular, because we want to set the scene for our discussion later in the chapter of the FTSE 100 Cross-Company Mentoring Programme we launched in 2004 by describing the routes each of us took to it. It seems to us that, in a small way, the tale of the origins of the program (and our journeys toward it) is an example of the kind of thinking and action that can promote change in an area where discussion and debate have often generated more heat than light.

So, for the next few pages "we" will split up into Peninah and Jacey.

Peninah's interest in the distinctive qualities of women leaders stems from her earlier career at NATO, where she worked with the NATO Board of National Delegates and as a director at PricewaterhouseCoopers, where she worked in Government Services and Economics and Corporate Transformation. She operated at board or Cabinet Office level in both roles, in both the public and private sectors, with ambassadors, ministers, cabinet secretaries, CEOs and chairmen in the UK and most countries in western Europe, Hong Kong, Singapore, India, West Africa, Kuwait, Malaysia and the US. She observed, at close quarters, how senior men and women lead, and became increasingly aware of significant differences between their styles. This awareness was sharpened further when she joined The Change Partnership in 1998 as a director and began coaching senior civil servants, CEOs and board members of FTSE 100 companies. Her growing curiosity about the nature and origins of the differences led her to undertake, with two collaborators, a research project into the educational and family backgrounds and work and life experiences of 52 women leaders in the UK public and private sectors. The results were published in 1999, under the title *The Changing Culture of Leadership: Women Leaders' Voices*.[1]

Although a modest volume, the book attracted a lot of attention, because it was the first substantial piece of research into the views of senior women conducted in the UK since 1992. There had been (and continues to be) much published on the topic from a pop psychology perspective. You know the kind of thing: "the 100 Most Powerful Women in Britain", and its ilk. This book was seen as a serious attempt to describe the predicament of able and ambitious women in a man's world. Peninah and her colleagues were taken aback by the newspaper, magazine, radio and television coverage the book attracted, and Peninah realized that the interest had important implications for her work as an executive coach.

A series of lunches at London's Reform Club followed, at which senior women executives met to discuss issues of importance to them as leaders. Peninah recalled:

> We were invited to present a paper on our research at the UK Coaching and Mentoring Conference, and asked to talk to various groups, ranging from women in asset management to women leaders in post-16 learning, and in organizations ranging from the BBC to the Bank of England.

> From these experiences we learned a huge amount about the issues currently facing senior women executives in the UK. We now understand something about the challenges they face; the support they do (or don't) receive from their organizations; their perceptions of their strengths and areas where they need development. We also gained a good understanding of how UK public and private sector organizations manage and deploy the skills of senior female employees, and the extent to which they understand, and respond to, women's career development needs.

Peninah was asked to contribute to the Commission for Judicial Appointments and the *Tyson Report on The Recruitment and Development of Non-executive Directors*[2] commissioned by Laura Tyson, the then new dean of London Business School. This followed the Higgs Report on *The Role and Effectiveness of Non-executive Directors*, which was itself a response to the widespread public and political concern about standards of corporate governance that arose after the Enron scandal in the US. Among the Tyson recommendations were initiatives to "disseminate best-practice examples of how … companies build more diverse and meritocratic boards and … [assess] the impact of board diversity on board and company performance".

Since joining Praesta Partners Peninah has been asked to craft a leadership development programme for senior women academics at one of the Russell Group of universities.

Jacey's interest in women's leadership, and "difference" generally, was born partly out of her own experience of climbing up male-dominated hierarchies (as we refer to them in Chapter 2), but also from her experience of working as a practitioner over many years in the area of management and leadership development. Her interest in diversity intensified, however, in 1997, after the merger of Lloyds Bank in the UK, with the Trustee Savings Bank (TSB) to form Lloyds TSB. The combined board of the new company contained two women non-executive directors, but in the course of the merger it transpired that several senior women (from what we would now call the "marzipan layer") had left the company. The first time the board looked at the new group succession plan, one of the women NEDs asked where the women were. "In short, the merger proved a catalyst for action", said Jacey. "To its great credit, the company recognized that something systemic was wrong which had to be addressed."

The board's response was to advertise for a new position, head of executive succession, with a remit to bring more women into the succession pipeline. Jacey felt ambivalent about the new position, because she was not sure how far she wanted to be associated with such a specific "women's issue". After all, so far she had built her own career without making an issue of her gender. But, out of curiosity, she decided to look at the numbers. "The gender stats were my wake-up call", she says. "I knew that about two-thirds of our staff were women. What I hadn't realized was how sharply the numbers fell at each step up the hierarchy until they reached zero at the executive committee level."

She applied for the job, got it and started to look at the world inside and outside the bank through a gender lens. It was more or less inevitable that her newly gender-sensitized eye would be caught by *The Changing Culture of Leadership: Women Leaders' Voices*. She read it, liked it and called Peninah to talk about it. They met, got on very well and became collaborators in addressing a market failure they were both becoming increasingly concerned about. As a result of her research and learning, over a three-year period, Jacey devised and led a strategy which resulted in a substantial increase of senior women in the bank's pipeline. When she moved to Shell to take up a global diversity role, Peninah and Jacey kept in touch. Jacey continues the story:

In late 2002, while I was head of diversity strategy at Shell, Peninah and I met at a conference at the Institute of Directors (IOD) in London for the launch of Cranfield's *Female FTSE Report*. I had agreed on Shell's behalf to sponsor the event on the understanding that the organizers would try to get chairmen, CEOs and senior male executives to attend. I had attended the launch of the

© Barbara Shore

WE REALLY NEED TO DO SOMETHING ABOUT THIS LACK OF WOMEN
— DON'T YOU WOMEN ALL AGREE ?

Female FTSE Report 2001 when I was still working at Lloyds TSB and had arranged for the bank's chairman, Maarten van den Bergh, to address the conference on the business case for appointing more women to boards. He made a fine speech, but Maarten was preaching to the converted – a room full of professional women. I didn't want that to happen again.

Unfortunately, it did. Despite the organizers' best efforts, the attendees were, in the main, women (many aspiring to be directors) and HR people – an important group of influencers, but not the movers and shakers who had the power to change the boardroom status quo. Part way through the conference, disillusioned (as one is!) by the absence of men, Peninah, Sue Vinnicombe [professor of organisational behaviour and diversity management at Cranfield and joint author of the Female FTSE Report], Sarah Churchman [of Pricewaterhouse-Coopers], Hilary Samson-Barry [of the Women and Equality Unit at the DTI] and I adjourned to the IOD wine bar, cracked open a bottle of champagne and got talking about the need to do something different.

Fast forward to that dead period between Christmas and New Year, 2002. For some reason Peninah and I were both nursing dreadful colds and we seemed to be the only people in London at work! We met in the Shell Centre coffee bar looking out over a grey skyline dominated by the London Eye and returned to our discussion at the IOD. We decided that 2003 should be the year for action! Our first step was to invite the IOD group to a formal session with some other interested people. Leslie Mays, head of global diversity at Shell, was keen for Shell to take a lead and hosted a breakfast meeting, to which we also invited Laura Tyson, dean of London Business School, Clara Freeman, the then chair of Opportunity Now, Deborah Lincoln, then political adviser to the UK secretary of state for trade and industry and minister for women, and a representative from the IOD.

Peninah and I prepared a paper in advance of the meeting, which positioned the absence of women directors as a supply and demand issue. We argued that most attention had until then been focused on the supply side (women who aspired to be directors), and very little attention had been paid to the demand side (chairmen and CEOs of FTSE 100 companies in whose gifts board appointments lay). What did they think about appointing women to their boards? What were they looking for in directors? Did they recognize the value of diversity on a board? Were they, and if so how, searching for women directors? What were they doing at their companies to "grow their own" women directors?

That first meeting in January 2003 confirmed that there was plenty of work to be done and plenty of enthusiasm to do it. We were all frustrated by the lack of activity by "UK plc" to solve what we saw as a critically important problem for business. We formed ourselves into a group, assumed the working title "the women directors project" and drew up a plan of action, including research on the hitherto neglected demand side.

Over the next few months the group met several times and Peninah and I had conversations with a number of chairmen and CEOs, to try to find answers to some of the questions posed above [see Chapter 3]. We used the opportunity of the launch of Cranfield's *Female FTSE Report 2003* to test the demand side theories we had developed. Our group secured the commitment of the then chairman of Shell, Sir Philip Watts and Patricia Hewitt, then secretary of state for trade and industry and minister for women, to issue personal invitations to FTSE 100 chairmen to an off-the-record breakfast meeting at Shell Centre. The 17 chairmen who attended that November 2003 meeting told us how they too were concerned about the lack of women in UK boardrooms and how they wanted to play a part in correcting that imbalance. This helped to shape the agenda of the project, which was renamed Women Directors on Boards – a UK Consortium for Action and Change (WDoB).

We felt we were getting somewhere. The members of WDoB[3] were united in the belief that increasing the proportion of women on the boards of large UK companies would improve their performance. And our demand side research had revealed considerable interest in the problem among male CEOs and chairmen, a willingness – almost an eagerness – to debate the issue and, by implication at any rate, a readiness to help.

It was from the surprising warmth of the welcome we received from the kings of industry during our research on the demand side of the market for women directors, and the acknowledgement of the 17 corporate kings who attended the Shell Centre meeting that there was a problem that needed to be solved, that the idea of forging a mentoring alliance between the supply and demand sides emerged.

The FTSE 100 Cross-Company Mentoring Programme

When Odysseus went to war against Troy, he entrusted his family to the care of his friend, Mentor. The goddess Athena assumed Mentor's shape from time to time and became the counsellor of Odysseus's son, Telemachus. Goddesses rarely masquerade as male mentors nowadays, but the idea of putting a young high-flying executive under the wing of an experienced colleague who "knows the ropes" of corporate life, has the right connections and is willing to make this wisdom and knowledge available to his or her protégé(e) is as valid today as it was in Homer's time.

In what the *Financial Times*[4] called "a ground-breaking programme to increase female representation in the boardroom", 20 chairmen and CEOs of some of the UK's largest companies agreed to act as mentors for senior women at other companies in what has come to be called the FTSE 100 Cross-Company Mentoring Programme. By the end of June 2005 (the time of writing) 26 chairmen had signed up to mentor (see Table 5.1).

The aim of the Programme is to help women from the "marzipan layer" nominated by their chairmen to manage their careers in ways designed to secure appointments as executive or non-executive directors of FTSE 100 companies or equivalent positions in the public sector.

For example, the chairman of Anglo American is mentoring a woman from HBOS and the chairman of HBOS is mentoring a woman from United Utilities.

The pioneering Ruter Dam (Queen of Diamonds) program for women managers in Sweden includes an external cross-company mentoring component, alongside seminars, internal mentoring, company visits and networking in its one-year program (see Chapter 10), but we know of no other comparable initiatives.[5] Since the launch of the UK program, however, we have been consulted by groups in France, the US, the Netherlands and Canada who are interested in launching similar schemes.

The Change Partnership issued some general guidelines for participants.[6] Mairi Eastwood, the then managing partner, commented: "We see this as a marvellous opportunity to build the capability of executive women with the ambition and potential to become company directors in the UK."

TABLE 5.1	FTSE 100 Cross-Company Mentoring Programme: mentors	
	Name	Title	Company
1	Maarten van den Bergh	Chairman	Lloyds TSB Group plc
2	Peter Erskine	Chief Executive	O2 plc
3	Paul Skinner	Chairman	Rio Tinto plc
4	Stephen Green	Group CEO	HSBC Holdings plc
5	Baroness Sarah Hogg	Chairman	3i Group plc
6	Sir John Parker FrEng	Chairman	National Grid plc
7	Lord Dennis Stevenson	Chairman	HBOS plc
8	Sir Gerry Robinson	Former Chairman	Allied Domecq plc
9	Sir Mark Moody-Stuart KCMG	Chairman	Anglo American plc
10	Sir Tom McKillop	Chief Executive	AstraZeneca plc
11	Rob Margetts CBE	Chairman	BOC plc and Legal & General Group plc
12	Sir Richard Evans CBE	Chairman	United Utilities plc
13	Sir Roy Gardner	CEO	Centrica plc
14	Charles Miller Smith	Chairman	ScottishPower plc
15	Donald Brydon	Chairman	Smiths Group plc
16	Dick Olver	Chairman	BAE Systems plc
17	Bryan Sanderson CBE	Chairman	Standard Chartered plc
18	James Smith	Chairman	Shell UK
19	Roger Carr	Chairman	Mitchells & Butlers plc and Centrica plc
20	Niall Fitzgerald	Chairman	Reuters plc
21	Patrick Cescau	CEO	Unilever plc
22	David Reid	Chairman	Tesco plc
23	John Allan	CEO	Exel plc
24	Peter Sutherland KCMG	Chairman	BP plc
25	Iain Ferguson CBE	Chief Executive	Tate & Lyle plc
26	Tom Glocer	Chief Executive	Reuters plc
27	Anthony Habgood	Chairman	Whitbread plc and Bunzl plc
28	Matt Ridley	Chairman	Northern Rock plc

Cross-Company Mentoring Programme: Other Mentors as at 15 December 2005

	Name	Title	Company
1	Lord David Currie	Chairman/Dean	Ofcom/Cass Business School
2	Dominic Casserley	CEO	McKinsey & Company inc. UK

In the guidelines, we said that mentoring relationships work best when they're based on mutual respect, candour and trust; when the mentee gives the mentor a clear idea of what she is hoping to get from the relationship; when the parties commit to devoting a certain amount of time to the mentoring relationship and then honor their commitments; and when mentors give their mentees the benefit of all their experiences, the good, the bad and the ugly.

At an early meeting, the mentor and mentee should agree an informal contract setting out the basis of the relationship and each party's role in it. This might include a description by the mentor of the preparations he wants the mentee to make, such as preparing a summary of her ambitions and goals, the barriers she sees to her success, her priorities and the criteria she would use to judge the success of the mentoring process afterwards.

These mentee judgements are provisional, of course. They will change during the mentoring process. The mentor might disagree with them and persuade the mentee to adopt different goals or priorities. The relationship requires an initial direction, however, and the personal needs that the mentee perceives at the outset are the proper basis for that direction.

As part of the contracting process, the parties should agree how often they aim to meet, who is responsible for setting up meetings, at what point they intend to review the effectiveness of the relationship, and so on.

Confidentiality and trust are the two foundations of fruitful mentoring and a willingness to listen and empathize is its driving force. It is a strange type of meeting for most mentors, because they're not expected to solve any problems, or provide any answers. They must be willing to challenge mentees strongly, with tact and understanding; give constructive feedback, when appropriate; and act as sounding boards on private and personal matters, when necessary. Above all, they should encourage their mentees to become the authors of their own stories and find the courage and confidence to realize their potential.

The essence of mentoring is conversation. As the senior partner, the mentor must take the initiative, at least in the early stages. As the relationship develops, the personal narratives merge into one and the undertaking, which is the realization of the mentee's ambitions and potential, becomes a joint venture in which both parties are investors.

When we tell potential mentors it's a two-way street and that, although the balance of benefits is heavily weighted in favor of the mentee (that's the objective, after all), they too should benefit from the process, we are not simply "selling" the Programme.

Mentors usually derive enormous satisfaction from knowing that their wisdom and experience are being put to good use by a member of the next generation of leaders. It feels like repaying a debt; like "putting something back". Mentors may also gain insights into themselves and their own organizations and the friendship that often emerges from the process may prove a valuable cross-generation extension of the mentor's own network, particularly if the mentoring process is successful and the mentee realizes her ambitions.

In this particular mentoring Programme mentors may also derive satisfaction from knowing that they've contributed to solving the problem that inspired most of them to agree to be mentors in the first place; the lamentable lack of women at the top of UK industry, banking and commerce.

It's still early days for the Programme, but feedback so far is encouraging from both sides; mentors and mentees.

Progress report – mentors

In our roles as directors of the Programme, we interviewed several mentors in early 2005 and asked each the same questions. For the reasons given previously, we have not attributed quotes to individual mentors. The FTSE 100 chairmen and chief executives involved in the Programme are listed in Table 5.1. The names of those who talked to us are mentioned in the acknowledgements.

PUTTING SOMETHING BACK

© *Barbara Shore*

Motivation

We first asked the mentors why they had agreed to participate in the Cross-Company Mentoring Programme.

"I think the main thing was, I've been lucky enough to have some reasonable mentors myself", said one, "and I wanted to give something back by mentoring someone else."

Another mentor said he wanted to get involved because "it's a huge waste of talent if women are not making it to the top. Organizations are losing out. Women make up a large proportion of the workforce so it's wasteful in terms of resources and contribution."

Although he had never had a mentor, as such, himself, he valued the support he'd received from various people, at various times. His two daughters were both working for large organizations, so he knew the difficulties women faced in advancing their careers. He thought it was important for people like him to help to change things.

"I've been in line management for donkey's years", said another mentor. He continued:

> I'm in my fourth decade. I came up from the bottom of the management structure. I have lots of experience and had a long-term interest in developing

people and getting women into senior jobs. It's bloody tough to find them and will remain so for a decade or more, because it must be on merit. There are lots of able women in finance, law, academia, social science, politics, science and engineering, but very few with operational experience and they're to be treasured, because there are so few of them.

I've been headhunting for [a FTSE 100 company of which he is an NED] right from the start. I found one woman recently, but lost her because she and her husband went back to America. I've found an excellent woman who runs a division of [a major oil company]. I found another woman, after a lot of searching, who ran a steel company and I think I've just found another American woman.

At my own company, I have two NEDs and we are about to appoint a third, who happens to be female. I like to have two women on a board, because then you get a behavior shift. There's only one on the board of [a company where he is an NED] and she struggles. It's very difficult to find good senior women with enough operational experience.

So, in answer to your question, I know there's a problem. I have something to give. I wanted to help.

Another mentor also mentioned the duty of the current generation of company leaders to help to address the shortage of female board candidates, by helping to nurture the next generation:

Well, I think you have a responsibility if you lead a company, particularly a large company, to help create some new seed corn for the boardroom. There are people below the board, who won't necessarily get through in their own companies, but will make excellent NEDs outside if they're groomed, advised and pointed in the right direction. It's about investment really; investing in a new layer of people who have the potential to come through.

I think that, if you want to break through to that next layer, you have to look for people who are not on the radar screens of the big headhunters. To my mind that's what this mentoring process is about; to get these people to a stage where you can put them forward [as candidates] with recommendations based on the fact that you've spent some time with them. You've effectively done some shadow interviews and, hopefully, in your dialogue with them, you have learned a lot more about them and where they might do a good job.

I'm very interested in the management of boardrooms and the composition of the board. Companies with six or more NEDs can certainly start to take a chance by bringing someone through who may not have all the qualities your other ranking NEDS have, but who if you see the potential there would be an investment for the future. You obviously can't have too many passengers on a board (not that I'm suggesting women in the marzipan layer are passengers by any means), but they would not be the fully groomed and experienced NEDs you would consider for most FTSE 100 boards. You're identifying this talent line. You're helping to bring it forward and give it exposure. And there is some self-interest in this really, if you take a holistic, plc view. I also think you're addressing a mismatch in the plc circuit – the lack of female NEDs in the "soup". We have to help accelerate them through.

"The idea of getting more women into boardrooms is a good one", said another chairman mentor, "and getting them from current executives is an even better one. There's a shortage of executives so we should maximize the take-up. It seemed a worthy experiment to me. I wasn't quite sure what it would involve or lead to. Boards are trying to fill slots at the same time. If they want their new directors to bring commercial skills, as well as experience from overseas or from the regions they're from, it is very difficult to find any women. So expanding the pool is the answer."

Another king of industry echoed the *noblesse oblige* point and talked of the value of board experience in career development:

I don't think any of us would do this simply because of our position. It's much wider than that. It's not philanthropy, exactly, but it's close. I see it as part of doing the right thing by the people in that layer. There's no point in moaning that "we can't find any high quality women" without trying to do something to help. I've done it here with our people. The development process never stops, of course, but serving on another board, particularly in the early days, gives you an experience no business school can model. You're there every month, often more frequently, dealing with live business.

It isn't case studies, it's real – the balance sheet's real, the gearing's real, the bank covenants are real, the acquisition is real, the bottom line is real each month, the cash is real each month. Until you have gone inside another company like that you couldn't experience it anywhere else.

Three of our people have joined other boards over the past two years since our merger. One woman is on the board at [X], our FD is on the board at [Y] and another of our directors has gone on the board at [Z]. So we have got two of our people on the boards of FTSE companies and a couple more who should be ready to do the same in the next 18 months. Sure it costs us a couple of days a month of their time, but we'll get an executive who will mature faster as a result of that experience. These are very, very highly qualified people who will add a lot of value.

Relationships

Our chairman said:

> I've met my mentee three times now. I guess there is one small link; we have both worked for [X]. We are different generations, but we talk the same language. It's hard to come out of a tough, but cloistered environment in a private company into the world of a plc – to a large listed company with a lot of challenges. I think it's been useful. I told her I was meeting you to discuss the Programme and asked her if she had found it useful so far. I think she feels it has been. She said she'd certainly come away from the first two sessions with a sense of benefit.

> At the beginning I talked very frankly with her, and said everything would be in confidence, but that I wouldn't pull my punches. She brings to our conversations real-life business situations and challenges as a relative newcomer to a big machine. Her thinking was that she wanted to bring specific issues. I wasn't sure if I added value, but she certainly seemed to go away with something: she said she'd had a hard think and wanted to come back again. I have also obviously encouraged her to. We must have met every three months, but I've encouraged her to call me in-between times if she needs to.

> I've enjoyed it. It's interesting, because some of the business issues are common and, when talking about them, you think about your own business. And I'm learning a bit about a different sector through her and about some of the individuals in it; that's useful and interesting. So it's time well spent from my point of view and I said to her we won't do it unless she is getting something out of it. I think she has decided that bringing tangible things to discuss is best. I try to do no telling, though that's hard, and more giving.

We asked him whether he thought she realized he was taking that stance. "I suspect so. She's a bright woman."

Another mentor had also had two meetings with his mentee so far. He thought that it would take time to build the sort of relationship where they can be completely open with each other, but felt they were "on the way". He asks her to think about two or three things she wants to discuss and to give him the headlines ahead of each meeting so he can think about them. She is in the driving seat in arranging meetings. She had to cancel one, because of a business trip. He was very understanding about that; "these things happen". He gives his mentee a few things to ponder and follow up at the end of each meeting.

They have agreed to review the relationship after a year. If either of them thinks it isn't working or isn't needed any more, they will end it. He has said he is prepared to tell his mentee when they review the relationship at the end of the year if he doesn't think she's quite ready. If she wants to continue the mentoring relationship nevertheless, he is happy to do so.

Another mentor said of his mentee:

She's very decent, very conscientious and very loyal and committed – a person of high integrity. She's trapped in a way of life she must try to extricate herself from. She works too hard, and a year passes and then the next. She's traveling, but has no clear destination in mind. She's absorbed in her job – it's not surprising at her stage of life, work is all-absorbing – but it's not providing options for later. She needs to do things that could lead to something in future.

She needs to be creating more breadth and width for the future. Why is she in this pickle? Is she driven by the circumstances of the job? I'm not so sure – she is such a committed person that I suspect she doesn't delegate enough. I've taught her approaches and now I've given her homework.

I asked her to summarize what she did last month. She must think about how she delegates. She needs to hire the best people and give the work to them. She seems receptive, but I won't know until she's out of driven mode. She's not blessed with bosses who coach her about management, training people up, delegation and having clear objectives. She's not in a good environment. We talked about how she could manage her boss better, and get more out of him. If he does something wrong, don't tell him so; don't email him; put nothing on paper. People make the most basic mistakes.

Another mentor thought women should "get themselves about a bit more. You don't bump into them at seminars, talks in the evenings, or dinners. Why is that?" He realized it was difficult for some women, because of their family commitments, but not all women. It puzzled him.

"I think that is an issue", another mentor agreed. "One possible reason, but maybe it's just my experience, is that women don't like networking as much as men. Does that sound desperately patronizing? I think there is some substance to it, but it may be rubbish – that women don't network automatically. I do think it's necessary though, if they want to progress. Is it worth getting the mentees together on this? Then they'll create their own network."

We told him this was part of the plan – that PwC were sponsoring a mentee network, and there had been one dinner so far – and asked him whether there was anything else he thought we should be doing. We told him that another mentor had said he thought his mentee should get her CV in front of the half-dozen or so leading headhunters. He replied:

I think he is dead right about CVs. One of the leading headhunters runs an annual event for people who aren't yet on boards or who are, but want to get on more. It runs for two-and-a-half days and there are a series of role plays. They ask an existing CEO, a chairman and a finance director of a plc to act out their roles in a fictional company. A couple of years ago I was asked to play the CEO and [two other well-known UK business leaders] played the chairman and the CFO.

You go through various role plays. You're on a remuneration committee, and then you're chairman of the audit committee. We [the real chairman, CEO and CFO] don't just sit there like dummies! We're sometimes asked to be part of the group for a session as well and people who played our roles in previous years are asked to the dinner. I mention it because it's awesome networking – you seem to get the best there. I recommended it to one woman I knew. She went along, loved it and has since been appointed to a board. It was great networking for me too. I still talk to fellow actors in the role play. It's just damned useful.

I must be awfully careful here, but I did say to my mentee: "do you want to go on a board because of your own worth, or because people want a woman for other reasons?" It should be because "this lady is great" not because she's a she; because there's some tokenism.

We asked him how she reacted to that.

She said she had thought about that. I am sure some boards say "we have to have a female" and, to be blunt, although of course I've seen boards where some males are useless, some women have been useless. The thing is, do you want to play that card? You could get three or four non-executive jobs, you can be "plural" and all the rest of it, but you should think it through. Do you want to be a good contributor to a board? It was a difficult area to go into, but I think she [his mentee] faced up to it. She didn't seem to get upset. I think she's thinking more about how she does the job well. I don't think she's in a rush.

Another mentor also told his mentee not to be "in too much of a hurry". She already had a lot of access to her board and a lot of visibility. Although she was not on the board yet, she was getting called in to various meetings to give presentations and contribute.

Another mentor was pleased with how his company was handling things. A very successful, experienced, high-powered female director had recently left for a senior job at the European Commission and, when we spoke, the company was planning to appoint two more women to the board:

> It will be a first board for [one of them] and I think that's great, because what we're saying is we want to go down a level (for want of a better word) and get all the freshness of that rather than appoint a seasoned well-known woman. So I think we are putting our money where our mouths are.

> I think if you rang a headhunter today and said: "Look, I want to appoint a non-exec, and I would prefer a woman" (well you don't exactly say that, but you know what I mean), I think you would get 15 names and that is not good; that's a problem. And if you are only looking for real performers, the list gets even shorter. There may be some real sizzlers, but the problem is they are often on four boards already so you have to break out. Headhunters find it hard, but that's partly because they can't or won't, but certainly don't go one level down. There are also a lot of boards who won't take a risk, so headhunters only put the same people forward. When we announced we would be looking for a chairman, one of our directors said we needed someone who had experience. In the end, I eyeballed him and said: "But what you're saying is that unless someone's been a chairman, we don't want them. That's twaddle." If you say people can't be chairmen unless they've been chairmen, you would never get any breakthrough, would you?

> But it's true it's getting harder to find non-execs, because more and more people are realizing that the risk/reward ratio is horrible. You don't know if the company's OK and a catastrophic failure at board level is on your CV forever. So you need to be pretty familiar with the business, because being a non-executive is becoming deeply challenging.

We asked him what the solution was to this shortage of qualified candidates for non-executive director roles.

"The only trick, and it's happening, is to pay them more", he said.

We told him that another mentor had said he didn't want anyone on his board who just wanted the money, and asked him to respond to that:

> He has a point, but it narrows the gene pool, doesn't it? I think you have to see the risk/reward point, because an executive can just about spare the time for one non-exec post. I was approached by a headhunter about becoming a non-exec of a major company that is very well run, but very vulnerable to events – oil crises, terrorism and so on – that are outside your control. A job that looks as if it will take you a few days a month could suddenly eat the whole damn

month. You could be up to your arm-pits in meetings. I couldn't do this job if that happened. You want a life.

Another area I'm sure that other mentors talk about is whether our mentees are practically up to going on a board if things get rocky, or it gets into an acquisition. A friend of mine was a non-executive director of a company when it was bought by private equity. The way he tells it is that the first two years were great; the right amount of time, lots of interest. But once it came into play it was a year of very intensive work. You have to be prepared for that.

"I think for me", said another mentor, "it's been very rewarding to find that I can add any value at all. You come at these things and you think: 'Will I really be able to add value?'"
Why such diffidence, we wondered.

When you are dealing with people, you must never have an overrated view of the contribution you can make. I think that you have to perform the role of a headhunter to some extent. If I was a headhunter sifting through hundreds of names and doing 25 interviews a week, I could probably do it standing on my head. But I'm chairing a plc! I don't interview all that many people and I know precisely the slots I want to put NEDs into. So I have no difficulty interviewing for slots in this company or another company I am involved in. But I'm not dealing with a slot here – I'm dealing with a young woman. I have to understand her talent and her skill set (which I would have to do if she was coming on our board), but then I have to give her advice about what she should do and where she should head – that's what I don't do every day. You have to be careful not to give bad advice so I have to think very carefully about all the advice I give. I don't regard this as "turn the handle" stuff at all.

With [his mentee] what I was able to do was to say: "Look, you really have to structure your CV much better; you have to bring out your skill sets and your experience in the business world, and then you have to start to think very hard about where you could add value and in what sector. Take the FT prices pages, go down the sectors and then decide which do you think, first of all, you would enjoy going into, that you would feel comfortable in, and where you really believe you could add value." I'm trying to get her to a point where she can market herself very effectively, because you don't just go along and say you're looking for a non-executive role.

Heavens above, good headhunters must hear that 20 times a day. Instead, you go along and say: "Look I'm in this layer, I've actually had some mentoring, I've been through the following process, here's my CV, here's an analysis of what I think my strengths are and the areas where I contribute and these are the sectors I would be very interested in." I think that has helped her to focus on herself and her potential match with a company. That is a very important linkage. It sounds simplistic but it's vital. It's the difference between saying where you are now, and saying: "I am marketing myself to the following sectors."

I've also given her a list of headhunters so she can get her name on their radar screens. And I said: "If you have gone through this structured process to focus yourself on given sectors, that's much better for getting onto the headhunters' radar screens than if you go in as yourself with the following background, because you've done part of their work for them as well."

We asked him whether he had noticed any diffidence in his mentee.
"No. She's a self-assured and experienced lady. She's very "grown up" as it were, takes advice well and asks highly intelligent questions. She probes a bit when you give a piece of advice, so it's been a very mature dialogue."
We asked him what he had got out of the process:

I always say that even when you visit a poorly run manufacturing operation and you walk around, you can always pick out something good. If you talk to any professional manager of this calibre, you're going to pick up a lot of things, and it just so happens that her chairman is now the chairman of one of our biggest customers. We chatted about that and other little connections.

It is always interesting to talk through another person's business. How do they see it? What have they been through? She has been through a demerger. That's an area that interests me very much too. What are the implications for the business? How did it go after the demerger? So lots of things that we've talked about are of interest to me.

When asked how it was going, another mentor laughed and said:

Ask my mentee! … Well, I think. We've only had a couple of sessions, partly because she's in a period of significant change in her organization. We get on quite well so it's an entertaining conversation. She hasn't given me any feedback – we haven't been terribly structured about it. She has a list of questions that very broadly relate to the background of where she is in the company; what the opportunities are. The first time I saw her she had had a career offer from the CEO, which had pros and cons. We walked through them. She actually took the job and we talked about what to do in it.

She was extremely busy. I told her there was no hurry to do the outside director thing [NED]; that she was getting lots of exposure to the board and was learning a lot. She attends most board meetings for something or other and she's getting a lot of visibility. It's also exposing her to an essential area of professional development. So the promotion was probably a very good thing. I'm sure it's going to add to her. It's a good job to have taken.

We asked him what he had learned so far, and what he thought his mentee was learning:

To me, it's a useful exposure to the sorts of things women are or might be concerned about, and it also helps me when thinking about people in our own organization.

I think it is useful for her to have someone outside the organization with whom she can kick around ideas. For example, we've talked about what having an impact in a process job actually means in practice, and how to make sure the team is working well and happily and how to make them feel valued. I've suggested she could think more about risk and how it fits into strategy. We have both quite enjoyed it.

I did tell her that if I were her I wouldn't rush into running for outside director posts. At our company, we set out to find a woman – we needed someone with different geographical experience and background – Latin America, Asia, someone who was commercial. We're very happy with the woman we've found for our board. She has a financial background and process experience. But she worries that she is not contributing enough – I don't know what to do about that.

Surprises

We asked our mentors whether there had been any surprises:

To be honest I've been a bit surprised by how valuable she has found it. I don't think she's just saying it. I felt afterwards that what I'd done had been OK, but pretty inadequate, so that was a nice surprise. I know nothing about her business, after all.

I felt what I said was pretty bland, perhaps a statement of the blindingly obvious. I was very motivated, I suppose, and I wanted to do more. I'm just glad she found it useful. I think that's what mentoring is about: you don't actually come in with the great silver bullet and incisiveness, but you get her talking.

Another said:

By her age I would have expected her to have a much firmer view on the way things ought to be; to be more networked and to be engaged in more activities outside work. All top managers are engaged in life and all its riches, because they need to be, *and* they enjoy it! She's not enjoying her job, either. She told me that – she is not getting as much fun out of it as she should be.

My guidance to her is geared toward her operational role so there's still a long way to go before we get to the more difficult things, such as how to create an environment, set a context, craft a culture. There are three things you need to be a top manager: a fine and broad intellect; great interpersonal skills; and drive.

Another chairman said of his mentee:

It all fell into place easily. She is mature in the professional sense. I wasn't dealing with someone I had to guide through the undergrowth of corporate life, so to speak. She understands corporate life. People from purely operational roles often do not fully appreciate what goes on in the corporate world, so you are asking them to make the leap. I suppose I would get more surprises dealing with some of those types of candidates about the gap. And there really is a gap there. One of our guys went on another board about 18 months ago. We still put quite a bit of support behind him, and in one of my one-on-ones with him recently, he said, "it is only in the last few months that I've really started to get comfortable. It has taken me a year to work my way into what it's all about, because so much of it is new."

Said another:

I can't think of many surprises. I think we both felt quite comfortable together, from the outset. We began by introducing ourselves in quite some detail, which allows you to get to know someone. She's unusual – she had this thing about around the world sailing. I sail too, so there was common water, so to speak. We got on quite well together. No, there haven't been any surprises. One of the nice things is that you get to know someone. It is extremely interesting talking to someone about his or her aspirations and goals.

Progress report – mentees

Once again no names here, but the mentees who talked to us are mentioned in the acknowledgements. We didn't use a list of questions for these interviews – we just asked mentees to talk freely about their overall impressions.

One mentee said:

I did some soul searching. I read the mentoring document and got ready. He just got on with it. I worried that I was being railroaded, but the second session was much more about my interests; what motivated me. I've found the conversation broadening – it hasn't just been about applying my experience. Talking things through and having affirmation has been good.

He was thinking about the best headhunters for me to talk to and suggested someone. I called her, used his name and got an appointment straightaway. We have met twice. The first meeting was just a chat; the second was a more detailed discussion. She explained how the NED recruitment process differed from the executive recruitment process. It is a longer process, and people have their networks in mind. They make initial contacts and then there is a system of referral. It's not a linear process like executive recruitment.

She had also recruited our non-exec board, so I could take her through how they've bedded down.

After I met her [the headhunter] I talked with my mentor about the process used by recruitment people. He asked me what experience I'd had interacting with boards. I told him that I had been an NED of a development agency with a fully non-executive board.

Both my mentor and the headhunter explained the importance of the impression, the contribution and the impact/influence you have.

It is different from an executive role, because, as an executive, you have a much clearer picture of what you're accountable for. They both talked of how you slowly earn the respect of your peers, start to contribute and work out what role you can play – input on the marketing side, or providing some consumer insight, for example.

The headhunter asked me: "Do you have the ability to bite your tongue, and make sure your contribution is constructive?" She knows our board.

Then I went to meet the other headhunter my mentor had recommended. He was totally different! He's chairman of the firm. It was a bit of a surprise! I hadn't expected to get the chairman. He told me that FTSE 100 chairmen were still very … that there was still a lot of discrimination; along the lines of "I've got my one" [woman]. So I need to be mindful of that. He was much more into giving me feedback right away. He asked whether I would be happy to work for a US company over here (because Americans often struggled with the British culture). He also told me that it takes a long time. He said he would brief his non-executive *and* executive team members.

The thing that's so pleasing is that he genuinely believes in all this. He uses NED roles to develop his own executives. If more company chairmen felt like that, it would really start to change things. Our CEO sits on another board but he's the only executive director who does. There is a layer of us who are "developable" as NEDs. My mentor isn't simply paying lip service to that – he's doing it. Is he unique? Is this unusual? One of his messages to me is: "Don't wait for the sake of waiting, but don't take too many risks."

It is invaluable having access to someone who's totally objective, but who wants to help. This opportunity to talk about how you position yourself and what your skills are worth is really invaluable.

Another was not sure she wanted a board position now:

My thinking has been affected by the changing nature of board responsibilities. When I began the Programme, I hadn't given much thought to being on a board. Then I began to think I could make a contribution to a board. Now I am wondering whether I really want to do this.

My mentor's great. We've had two meetings and scheduled a third. He's very straight talking. He challenged me about being in a "dead-end role". He has helped me think through how to position myself for a director role. But I wouldn't share my concern with him [about the risks of being a director]. He is the type of man who would see this as a sign of lack of ambition. So I'm using a headhunter to help me think my concerns through and will use my mentor to help me get there.

Another mentee had only had one meeting with her mentor, because he was not sure if a role with her functional specialism ought to be in the Programme in the first place, in view of the limited board opportunities for specialists.

She told him she couldn't fix her background, but wanted to broaden out, so they also talked about opportunities in the private equity and the not-for-profit markets. He talked a lot about corporate governance changes and how they made it harder to take on non-executive commitments. He thought a FTSE 250 role may be a more realistic aim. He told her what he looks for in NEDs and emphasized the importance of being a team player.

Another mentee said her mentor had been very positive about her aspirations and advised her to think very hard about what she wanted:

We agreed to run the relationship for a year then review it. I asked him about a fast-track route to understanding the corporate world. He suggested that I attend his AGM. I said I would. He will brief me beforehand about what he's looking for out of the meeting.

He emphasized the importance of "good fit" and networking. We talked about the FTSE 100 Cross-Company Mentoring Programme. He thought headhunters have a role to play. He thinks the role of mentors is to engage with headhunters about the Programme.

He's in his 60s, grey hair, grey suit. Quite a good listener. He didn't strike me as a person who dominated a meeting. He asked me what I thought: did I want to continue? He was quite modest. He didn't assume I'd be falling over backward to go on. I sent him my CV before the meeting and a summary of where I thought we'd got to after the meeting. Someone like him is so busy – if I were him I'd want a simple folder with a few sheets of paper. Also, if he refers me to others, it would be useful for him to have something on paper about me.

He made an observation about his own career being with large companies and this having had an impact on his skills, which made me think. I've just got a new role that will last about three years. If I do a good job there, I should be in a position to feel there's a real alternative to [her company].

Another mentee said her mentor had said he thought that she was good:

What was it I did to make him say that? Can I replicate it? The question for me is how to hook into this value. I'm broadly sceptical about the Programme – none of us [mentees] know what will happen. Some of us will succeed and for some of us it will be "so what?" I don't want to be one of the "so what's"!

One's conversation with one's mentor is private, but risky. I don't really know what to take to my sessions with him. He said that instead of thinking only about what I need to do for [her company], I should think more about my opportunities. He was challenging me to raise my game.

We can name one mentee, because she mentioned her involvement in an article in the *New Statesman*. She is Lorraine Heggessey, former controller of BBC 1 and now CEO of Talkback Thames. "I'm part of a cross-company mentoring scheme that aims to get more women on to the boards of FTSE 100 companies" she said. "I have my first meeting this week with my mentor, the impressive Roger Carr. Not a household name maybe, but well known in the City as chair of Centrica and Mitchells & Butlers. He and I hit it off immediately. I have found the older I get, the more prepared I am to learn from other people."[7]

Matters arising

We became aware during the mentoring process that there was some concern at one company that the chairman's mentoring of an external woman might have a negative effect on prospects for the promotion and development of internal women. The company's women's network was interested in the Programme and conscious of the fact that all three women on the group's main board had been external appointments.

We recognize the need for participants in this mentoring scheme to be aware of and take into account the reactions of internal audiences, but as far as we can see there are no losers in the process. For one thing, participating CEOs and chairmen reciprocate, when agreeing to act as mentors, by putting forward mentees from their own companies. By obliging them to search their own marzipan layers for candidates, this increases the visibility of senior women generally in their organizations. The CEO's or chairman's involvement in the scheme also makes it easier to start new or expand existing internal mentoring programs and, moreover, the scheme's basic cross-company nature is more widely applicable. At the time of writing, for example, the women's network at one participating company was actively exploring the possibility of starting a similar cross-company scheme for female middle managers.

One or two mentors wondered whether we had "got the level right". As one of them put it: "You do need to have women who will be top of major companies, because chairmen are at their best with one or two levels down, not three." We recognize that level is important and chairmen should not be obliged to waste their valuable time mentoring women who have no hope of making it to the top. But we also value the scheme's reciprocity principle that requires mentors to judge the suitability of mentees.

We also suggest, tentatively, that the mentors have something to learn about the suitability or otherwise of women mentees – that when judging the quality and potential of their mentees, they may sometimes unconsciously be applying male-biased criteria. As we suggest in Chapter 6, women bring distinctive qualities to leadership, and what a man might see as "a lack of drive" might actually be a manifestation of the characteristic preference of women to explore all options before deciding on a course of action and, having chosen the course of action, to gather support for it before pushing it through.

One of the insights we gleaned from our feedback interviews is that there is a significant gap between the place where some of the mentees are, and the place they want to get to.

"The boardroom's a riskier and more complex place than it was a decade ago", was how one of our mentors put it:

So the gap between what goes on in the boardroom and what goes on in operations is much wider now and you have to prepare people in the businesses to take that very important step.

I would be looking for the gap all the time, because I've seen it so often in my life. There's probably a need to distinguish between mentees who need coaching across the gap dividing functional roles from the group board, and those who are already in that climate or work in corporate centers and are not as remote from it as those who are still in the businesses. I suspect I had one of the easier candidates; I didn't have to bridge that gap.

Another made a suggestion directed at the big four accountancy firms that we hope will be taken up. "These accountancy firms all have business breakfasts, but the invitations usually go to directors, because they are easy to identify. I think the accountancy firms could be encouraged to include a few marzipan women on their invitation lists. That would get them into a good networking environment. They might be sitting at a table and chat to somebody, and who knows where that might lead."

Several mentors emphasized the need for patience.

"Success is a journey, not a destination. I've told my mentee it's going to take time – you have to get yourself on the headhunters' lists. Patience is an important point to stress. I guess, for them, the value we add will only be finally judged useful if we can direct them in ways that lead to a board appointment. As a mentor, you can only go so far to prepare your mentee for that. You can't leap the chasm with her."

References

1. *The Changing Culture of Leadership; Women Leaders'* Voices, Elizabeth Coffey, Clare Huffington and Peninah Thomson, The Change Partnership, 1999.
2. The Tyson Report on the Recruitment and Development of Non-executive Directors, June 2003, London Business School.
3. www.womendirectorsonboards.co.uk.
4. Mentors to help women on to boards, Alison Maitland, *Financial Times*, Oct 21, 2004.
5. www.ruterdam.se.
6. *FTSE 100 Cross-Company Mentoring Programme, Mentoring Guidelines*, John Coleman, The Change Partnership, 2004.
7. NS diary, Lorraine Heggessey, *New Statesman*, February 28, 2005.

CHAPTER 6

A woman's touch

The John Lewis Partnership (JLP), one of the UK's largest, oldest and most durably successful retailing groups, is an oddity. It is so different from its rivals (see box) that it seems very likely that its success is because of, rather than despite, its many distinctive features.

The John Lewis Partnership

In an age when mega-retailers are exporting their business models all over the world, the JLP confines itself to its domestic market. In an age of "niche" non-food retail concepts, it continues to open supposedly uneconomic department stores. In an age in which ownership and control are wholly divorced in practically every other large company, it is owned and effectively controlled through democratic institutions operating in accordance with a written constitution, by its "partners", who are also its employees. In an age in which the maximization of shareholder value is the universally acknowledged *raison d'être* of management, its constitution declares the JLP's ultimate purpose to be "the happiness of its members".

To 21st-century eyes, all this seems absurdly utopian, almost naive, and very old-fashioned. It brings to mind those philanthropic companies of the mid-19th century (many owned by Quakers) that were the principal providers of social services until the advent of the modern welfare state. A company governed by such archaic principles and purposes couldn't possibly survive in the tougher business environment of today, and surely not in one of the most competitive of today's industries, could it?

It can and it does.

The 140-year-old company that time seems to have passed by has over 60,000 employees, running 26 department stores and 163 Waitrose food shops, and a total annual turnover of over £5 billion. In the five years to 2003/04, JLP sales increased by 35 percent during a period of significant deflation in many of its department store lines and increasingly competitive conditions for Waitrose in the food sector. Gross margins improved in both divisions. Profits in 2003/04 rose 19 percent, compared to 2002/03, to £174 million pre-tax and the partnership bonus was 12 percent of partners' pay against 10 percent the previous year.[1]

There are two distinctive features of the JLP, which incorporates the John Lewis department stores chain and the Waitrose supermarket chain, that are of particular interest to us.

The first is that four of the 11 members of the John Lewis board and three of the nine members of the Waitrose board are women, and that with women accounting for 52 percent of John Lewis managers (department managers and above) and 40 percent of Waitrose managers, there's a well-balanced blend of the genders in the board pipeline.

As we saw in Chapter 3, retailers tend to appoint more women directors than non-retailers, but the average proportion of women on the boards of the 10 retailers in the FTSE 100 was 14 percent, compared to the combined 35 percent on the John Lewis and Waitrose boards.

The second distinctive feature of JLP that is of particular interest to us is a special position called the "registrar".

The latest edition of JLP's constitution says that registrars

> have independent status within the Partnership, and are responsible ... for ensuring that the Partnership's principles and policies are applied consistently ... [they must have] a thorough knowledge and understanding of the Constitution ... [and are obliged to] tell the Partner's Counsellor [who appoints registrars] of any matter that seems to them contrary to the Partnership's Constitution or policies ... [they must also] encourage understanding about the Partnership and [act as] channels of communication between Partners in the branches ... and other Partnership authorities.[2]

An important historical feature of this office is that it was laid down in tablets of stone sculpted by the partnership's founder, John Spedan Lewis, that the registrar should always be a woman. The founder's gender rule was never part of the constitution and is no longer obeyed, but the principle lives on. At the time of writing (early 2005), both divisional registrars, 10 of the 14 John Lewis registrars, and 9 of the 11 Waitrose registrars were women.

There's no mystery about the idea behind it. Spedan Lewis saw companies as families, writ large. As Pauline Graham put it, in her book *Integrative Management*[3]:

> Just as in the family, the husband was the go-getter and aggressive breadwinner and the wife the peacemaker and the upholder of the family's conscience so, Spedan Lewis deduced, it had to be in business. The general manager was there to make the profits but the registrar had to ensure that these were achieved fairly and justly.

Pauline Graham was a JLP store manager. She says that her registrar "was a tremendous support and comfort ... [and] more than a 'conscience'. Being in a way outside the hurly-burly of the business side, she was an impartial and disinterested observer ... whose business judgement I valued highly."

The idea of "the company as a family" seems dated now, and the division of roles by gender seems politically dubious, if not illegal. But we believe that whether it is because of our genes or our cultural conditioning (see Chapter 2), men and women have different aptitudes and priorities. When raising a family, for instance, mother and father rarely agree on how soon and to what extent their children should be weaned from parental care and allowed to go out on their own, watch more adult material on television or at the cinema and generally assume more control of their own lives.

Mothers want to protect their children from a world full of dangers, while fathers want to prepare their children for a world full of dangers. The tension between the two parenting styles is usually constructive. Each constrains the other. From the tension a sensible compromise emerges, which acknowledges and gives due weight to both the need to protect and the need to prepare. One doesn't have to subscribe to the company as a family idea to believe that tension between male and female attitudes can be equally constructive in business and that the differences themselves are inherently creative.

Graham exhorts women managers:

> Please keep your differences; do not push them under the carpet or work at doing away with them. Our contribution which is unique to us as women is to bring, at every managerial level, our different perceptions ... ways of looking at the world, of doing things. The large corporation, especially, needs the new and different to weave them into the fabric of its history and culture and thus make them anew ... Not only do I hold that women should be at the highest levels ... I also hold that business and other organizations would be better run if more women were actively involved in their decision making."[3]

Graham was deeply influenced by the ideas of the American social scientist Mary Parker Follett (1868–1933), who demonstrated in her life and work how the feminine approach to management differs from, but also complements, the masculine approach.

She wrote about the importance of groups and group dynamics; what she called the "law of the situation", according to which conflicts should be resolved; the reconciliation of competition and cooperation; and the importance of what she called "power-with", rather than "power-over". Like Spedan Lewis, she saw companies as social institutions. She advocated the removal from the business vocabulary of all negative words, such as "grievance" and "complaints". Some claim that she anticipated many if not most of the themes of modern management thinking, from total quality management and the idea of "empowerment", to the networked organization and corporate social responsibility (CSR).

Like Sergeant Pepper's Lonely Hearts Club Band, Follett goes in and out of style, but her position in the pantheon of management gurus grows stronger each time. A collection of her management writings and lectures, edited by Pauline Graham, was published in 2003: *Mary Parker Follett, Prophet of Management: A Celebration of Writings from the 1920s.*[4] Today's management luminaries gathered round to acknowledge their debt to Follett. Rosabeth Moss Kanter wrote a preface, Peter Drucker wrote the introduction and there were commentaries on the 11 pieces Graham had selected by Warren Bennis, Nitin Nohria and Henry Mintzberg, amongst others.

Although Follett never addressed the gender issue directly, her ideas have a very feminine ring to them and her prescriptions have a strong appeal to women. It is easy to detect her influence, for instance, in an article by Carlotta Tyler in *OD* (organization development) *Practitioner* published in 2002.[5]

The arrow and the spiral

According to the website of her OD consulting business, odc, Tyler was, at the time of writing, herself writing a book based on research between 1981 and 1997 with over 1500 women leaders. We don't want to pre-empt her book, but the ideas she outlined in her article relate directly to the argument we are making in this chapter; that companies run by men *and* women will be better run than companies run by men *or* women.

Tyler's research leads her to three main conclusions:

1. Women's ways of conceptualizing and organizing work are different from, but complementary to, men's

2. By combining the best of both women's and men's models, "an entirely new paradigm can be created" that could help organizations trying to adapt to the challenges of change achieve "wholeness and balance"

3. To achieve such fusion, we must examine "the core beliefs we bring to, and find reflected in, the design and operation of our organizations".

She found that working environments designed by women reflect a preference for organic structures and collaborative working in which the flow of work defines the form of organization and information is shared freely "without attachment to functional position". A commitment to values defines context and informs processes. There is an emphasis on building relationships "to establish the trust needed to accomplish complex tasks". As much attention is paid to processes as to outcomes, and – echoing Follett's emphasis on language – the words, symbols and metaphors used in organizations designed and run by women are often very different from those used in organizations designed and run by men.

In one female-run organization Tyler studied, for instance, biological and botanic metaphors were *de rigueur*, because managers disliked the way that the analytical language traditionally used in strategic planning distanced their planners from the system:

- They called strategic planning "midwifing" the new organization.

- Surveying stakeholder inputs was "tilling the soil".

- Efforts to improve the organization's effectiveness were "nurturing".

- New investment was "watering".

- Marketing was "seeding".

- New programs were "buds".

- Existing programs were "flowers".

- Initiatives within existing programs were "petals".

Sounds flaky? To some maybe, but evolutionary and biological metaphors for business have become more popular in recent years and it is worth thinking about your organization in these terms for a while, to see where it leads.

Greg Dyke, possibly the most admired broadcasting executive of his generation, used some botanical words of this kind when he was restructuring the BBC during what many people at the BBC regarded as a regrettably brief stint as director-general.

The male business lexicon has a military, mechanical flavor reflecting the organizational model that the modern company inherited when it emerged as a distinct corporate species in the mid-19th century. The traditional hierarchical structure (see Chapter 2) in which orders come down from the top and reports move up from the bottom, information rights are attached to position, rather than interest or involvement, and the main emphasis is on outcomes rather than processes, is also reflected in the language.

Tyler says men and women also pursue ideas and targets in different ways. Citing Carol Frenier's book, *Business and The Feminine Principle*,[6] she says that men employ "a focused consciousness, notice content and seek a finite solution" when solving problems, whereas "women use a diffuse lens, notice context and remain open to multiple potential resolutions". Their objective is not to find a unique solution, "but to allow a multiplicity of ideas to emerge and expand, providing space for viable ideas to embed and grow."

Tyler contrasts the shapes of these male and female approaches. Men favor the "arrow" – a linear, sequential and direct progression from conception to completion, where each step is deliberate and quantifiable and attention is focused on the outcome. Women favor the "spiral" – a circuitous, more wide-ranging route that moves from idea generation to attracting interest and involvement, by sharing ideas. Once attracted, members move in and out of collaborations, according to their circumstances and responsibilities, which may include family care. Tyler found that periodic detachment from a group did not seem to preclude subsequent reattachment.

Both models have strengths and weaknesses. The male "arrow" model has a beginning, a middle and an end. The beginning is an idea; for solving a problem, providing a service, satisfying a need. The middle is a process aimed at realizing a target derived from the idea, with milestones, measurement systems and feedback loops. The end is the achievement of the goal and praise for the individual or team who came up with the idea. Tyler describes the model as essentially "mechanistic". She believes its weaknesses are that "it can miss emerging factors critical to operations" and "is proving too rigid for the requirements of rapid change and increased uncertainty that characterize today's marketplace".

The female "spiral" model is less rigid, but also less clear. It relies on collaboration, the free flow of information, experimentation and tolerance of and a willingness to learn from error, by sharing information on what's working and what's not. It is essentially organic. Tyler suggests that its weakness is that its focus on means, rather than ends, and its emphasis on inclusion and emergence can make it indecisive, at times when decisiveness is necessary.

She regards these two models as manifestations of the "complementarity" of the sexes in nature. There is "a functional fit" between them. They're yin and yang; two parts of a whole, rather than opposites. Tyler believes that combining the models will lead to completeness. "If the arrow represents a direct route to effect an idea, the spiral represents a diffuse process of generating and refining a multiplicity of ideas." Tyler sees the spiral as an ideas incubator, and the arrow as a process for transforming ideas into products and services. Combining the two, she suggests, ensures that ideas "are successfully grown and launched into the system".

It's an intriguing notion, but it will take many years and many more women directors before the spiral claims its rightful place alongside the arrow in formulating and implementing strategy. We believe that, in the meantime, other valuable benefits will emerge as the proportion of women directors approaches parity with that of men.

Hunting and gathering

In Chapter 2 we noted (quoting Matt Ridley) that early women gathered food that was "static, close and predictable", and men hunted for food that was "mobile, distant and unpredictable".[7]

If, as Ridley and others suggest, male map-reading skills reflect the fact that Pleistocene men were hunters and needed such skills to find their way home after long hunts, what distinctive skills would women gatherers need? Silverman and Eals conjectured that they would need to notice things; to spot roots, mushrooms, berries and plants and remember landmarks, so that they knew where to look each season. They asked students to memorize pictures full of objects, and recall them later. On every test of object and location memory, females performed 60–70 percent better than males.[8]

The use of the word "husbandry" in the English language, to mean "domestic economy" or "the management of a household" is thus a mistake, because the original sexual division of labor assigned this task to women.

Ridley suggests that farming, which is another meaning of "husbandry", became a male activity when its early mechanization required male musculature, but that it was, and remains, a job better suited to the female mind, with its local focus and superior pattern recognition ability.

Husbandry in business is careful and constant attention to the domestic or operational details. While some hunt for business and develop new products and services, others must "mind the shop", "keep the home fires burning", feed the livestock, weed and water the crops, gather and store the produce and generally ensure that domestic matters are "spick and span".

This suggests that women may be naturally (by their natures) more adept at corporate husbandry than men. It is quite possible that had husbandry-type roles been assigned to women in the past, companies would not have been so surprised by the shoddy state of corporate husbandry revealed in the 1990s by the activity-based costing (ABC) concept developed by Robert Kaplan and Robin Cooper[9] and what Mike Hammer and James Champy called business process re-engineering.[10]

ABC says:

Pay attention! The method you're using to assign costs to your products and customers is completely outdated. It might have been OK 70 years ago, but things have changed a lot since then and if you look closely, you will find you've been losing money on some customers and some products for years.

BPR says:

Pay attention! Your business processes might have worked OK on the Ark, but a lot has changed since then. New technology offers enormous potential for increasing the efficiency of your processes. If you look closely, you will find that some of your processes are superfluous and many of the rest are extremely inefficient.

It is the clear responsibility of managers to ensure the accuracy of their costing systems, which guide their resource allocation, and the efficiency of business processes, which determine their cost competitiveness, at the highest possible level. Unlike some aspects of management, both variables are controllable. Managers who allowed their costing systems and processes to drift out of line with changing customer needs and the growing power of IT were making avoidable errors and thus failing in their duty to maximize shareholder value.

Companies must have been making these errors for decades; how else can one explain the shock with which the revelations of ABC and BPR were greeted? Managers had been letting things slip. They had not been paying sufficient attention to internal, "domestic" affairs. They were so preoccupied with external matters that they failed to notice their cost allocation systems and business processes had become increasingly antiquated.

The huge improvements in profitability some firms achieved by applying ABC and BPR attest to the delinquency of managers in the domestic sphere over the previous 50 years or so. Could it be that substantial costs associated with this delinquency might not have been incurred, or at any rate, not to the same extent, if companies had been in the habit of appointing women to the position of chief operating officer?

Some will point out that many of the huge efficiency improvements that BPR delivered came from the application of IT, and go on to argue that women tend not to be as interested in technology as men, and might not, therefore, have seen the potential of IT as clearly. Maybe so, but it's also possible that some of the horrendous sums of money companies wasted on badly designed IT systems would not have been denied to shareholders if women's sensitivity to the subtleties of group dynamics and relationships and their preference for free access to information had exerted more influence on the design of IT systems.

There are many other ways in which the appointment of more women to senior executive positions is likely to improve the quality of management.

The way we do things

That women are naturally suited to some top jobs, such as finance (because of their superior pattern recognition) and HR (because of their superior social skills) is already reflected in the patterns of female appointments to boards and executive committees. Operations – for the reasons indicated above – should also be recognized as peculiarly suited to the aptitudes of women. The appointment of more women to boards, in whatever capacity, will also produce more general benefits in terms of style, culture and the ways organizations go about their day-to-day business.

In 2004, TNT appointed a woman to the board. Peter Bakker, CEO, said in early 2005: "Marie Christine has been on the board for over a year now and the egos have left the room. Board meetings have a much better tone and feel about them now." As we saw in Chapter 3, other kings of industry echo the sentiment. Having women on a board "brings a freshness, a difference", said one. "There's a certain liveliness; an intuition that's needed in business that a woman is more likely to have than a man. They're often very intuitive, particularly about other people. Women bring calmness and objectivity … and there's less jostling for position."

Board and other face-to-face meetings often play a role in companies that women find surprising and hard to get used to. They are not always, as one might suppose, occasions when important decisions are made. Although competitive pressures, more regulatory scrutiny and the new legal responsibilities of directors are changing board meetings, some retain a theatrical element. In some cases, by the time items appear on the agendas of such meetings, they have been settled in informal discussions or prepresentations.

Face-to-face meetings are expensive in terms of the opportunity costs of the time they take (in the meetings themselves and preparation for them) and should not be wasted on ego-tripping and jostling for position. If the appointment of a woman to a board drives egos from the room, that's almost reason enough for appointing her. She will give board meetings a chance to be what they should be; high-level discussions that culminate in decisions about important issues.

As well as redeeming board meetings in this way, female directors also help to ensure that enough high-level attention is paid to the so-called "soft" management issues that all-male boards often dispatch with indecent haste. "Women are more sensitive to people-related issues at board meetings", said one chairman we spoke to. "That is very important in businesses focused on women as employees and customers."

Other kings we talked to agreed. Women are "more aware of the human issues … they're acutely aware of social dynamics … and will worry about them … women are more idealistic. They want to be clear they've reached the right solution."

The suggestion that women are more idealistic than men, or at any rate are more inclined to keep ideals in mind when discussing practical matters and making difficult business decisions, is hard to prove. Many people of both sexes believe it, however, and if it is true, the presence of women at the top of companies should reduce the risks of reputational damage that large businesses have become increasingly sensitive to in recent years, and thus improve the quality of corporate governance (see Chapter 1 for evidence of a link between women on boards and standards of corporate governance).

Another valuable quality women bring to boards and executive committees is difference itself. Several male leaders we talked to stressed the need for different perspectives on boards. "Women are better lateral thinkers [than men]" said one. "They're less structured and see things more in the round. There's a certain female doggedness." Another said: "An ability critically to analyse events, circumstances and information from different points of view is invaluable, because it reduces the chances of rushing lemming-like over cliffs and leads to robust and sensible decision-making."

Female leadership

To acknowledge that women bring different and valuable qualities to boards and executive committees is one thing; to accept that these qualities add up to a distinctive style of leadership that may, in some ways and in some situations, be more value-creating than male leadership is quite another. Beverly Alimo-Metcalfe, professor of leadership studies at the University of Leeds, suggests that one reason for "women's lack of access to power in organizations" is that all leadership research has been "the study of men, by men" and has, therefore, failed to acknowledge the existence, let alone recognize the value, of the female style of leadership.[11]

Through its influence on such assessment processes as selection, promotion and performance measurement, the "received wisdom" of leadership research stands guard at the gateway to high office in most organizations, applying its largely unacknowledged male bias to all-comers.

It's not just theory, either. Male leadership models have been perpetuated in the past by the practice of asking existing leaders what qualities they attribute their success and effectiveness to, and then using their answers to construct "competence frameworks" for recruiting and developing future leaders. This methodology was widely used by companies to build competence frameworks in the 1980s.

The economist John Maynard Keynes mused at the end of his *General Theory* that men "who believe themselves to be quite exempt from any intellectual influences are usually the slaves of some defunct economist".[12] It may still be true that people responsible for making senior appointments, who believe themselves to be, and are widely seen to be, exempt from gender prejudice, are the slaves of some defunct builder of competence frameworks.

Alimo-Metcalfe summarized the history of formal leadership research in her paper. It began in the 1930s with the "great man" or trait approach, which saw leaders as exceptional men who possessed innate characteristics, such as intelligence, energy and dominance in unusual abundance. When it became clear that personality traits were poor predictors of business success, the focus switched in the 1950s to the behavior of individuals who influenced followers, and subordinates were asked questions about their bosses. This led to a model of business leadership based on consideration for employees and the design and introduction of efficient structural features.

The failure of these behavioral theories to take context into account led to the emergence of new models of leadership in the 1960s and 70s, known as "situational" or "contingency" theories of leadership. They were useful in dealing with complexity and improving efficiency, but provided aspiring leaders with no guidance on coping with continuous change.

Thanks partly to the scorn heaped on leadership studies during this period by maverick management guru Henry Mintzberg,[13] so-called "new paradigm" views of leadership began emerging in the 1980s, incorporating "visionary", "charismatic" and "transformational" models. These were then combined with older situational, or "transactional", models to create an integrated model on which the Multifactor Leadership Questionnaire (MLQ; now widely used in academic studies) is based.

Transformational leaders are very different from transactional leaders who simply reward and punish appropriate and inappropriate behavior. They are admired, respected and trusted, and motivate and inspire those around them by providing meaning, optimism and vision. They encourage their followers to question assumptions, reframe problems and be generally creative and innovative. They try to understand followers' needs and desires and see it as their duty to help their followers realize their potential.

In a meta-analysis of 45 studies of leadership styles, Eagly et al. found wide agreement that female leaders were more transformational than male leaders. They also found that transformational was more effective than transactional leadership and that all aspects of leadership style where women are better than men correlated positively to a leader's effectiveness, whereas all aspects of leadership style where men are better than women had either no impact or a negative impact on effectiveness.[14] In other words, women are better than men at the things leaders do that have the most impact on performance.

The following summarizes their definitions of leadership styles:

Transformational

Idealized influence	personal and behavioral role models
Inspirational motivation	optimistic and excited about goals
Intellectual stimulation	encourages novelty
Individualized consideration	develops and mentors followers

Transactional

Contingent reward	rewards good performance
Management by exception	attends to mistakes and poor performance

Laissez-faire   hardly ever there

Studies of anonymous, 360° feedback from followers have consistently rated women significantly more transformational than men. One study which used the MLQ found "women leaders were rated by both their female and male direct reports as displaying ... key aspects of transformational leadership more frequently than men" and "female leaders were generally rated higher ... on leadership factors that have been shown to predict individual, group and organizational performance".[15]

Management Research Group (MRG) reached similar conclusions when analyzing 1800 questionnaires, completed by 900 male and 900 female managers in the US and Canada.[16] All 1800 managers were also evaluated on a 360° basis by (on average) a boss, four peers and four direct reports. The analysis of what MRG believes was the largest ever controlled quantitative study of gender differences and leadership revealed:

- Women scored higher on leadership scales relating to setting high standards and achieving results.

- Men scored higher on scales relating to strategic planning and business orientation.

- Women were seen as more energetic, intense and emotional, and having greater capacity to keep others enthused and involved. Men were more seen as low-key, understated, quiet and controlling their emotions.

- Women were rated higher on people-oriented skills. Men were rated higher on business-oriented skills by bosses, but not by direct reports.

- Bosses saw men and women as equally effective overall. Peers and direct reports rated women as slightly more effective than men.

As well as being very large, MRG's study is interesting in another way. It did not use the MLQ and its analysis was not influenced by the distinction between transactional and transformational leadership styles.

Authors Robert Kabacoff and Helen Peters acknowledged the possibility that women score lower in strategic areas because they "feel more vulnerable in their positions and consequently focus on achieving results to prove their worth. They may have a strong need to ensure that the job gets done." They suggested that men "may feel freer to engage in the 'luxury' of visioning and strategic thinking, which are riskier endeavours".[16]

Eagly et al. made a similar point about context when admitting that their meta-analysis only included seven studies of business executives, and two of these found male leaders more transformational than female leaders:

> Perhaps some organizations, especially some corporations, do not provide a congenial culture [for] women to display transformational leadership. Although these studies of executives are informative, they provide a limited amount of data for drawing general conclusions about the effects of hierarchical levels of leadership on male and female leadership style.[14]

Although no quantitative conclusions can be drawn from the qualitative research we present in Chapters 3, 4, 5 and 7, it contributes to the general understanding of gender and leadership.

When planning her own research[11] Alimo-Metcalfe was mindful of the distinction between "distant" and "close" leaders. (Distant leaders are seen as ideologically oriented, and having a strong sense of mission, which they express eloquently and courageously. Close leaders are seen as sociable, considerate, expert, dynamic, intelligent, wise, setting high standards for themselves and followers, being original, and having a sense of humor.) She focused on the latter, partly because she disliked the tenor of the charismatic models of leadership popular in the US, which she felt harked back to the discredited "great man" theories of the 1930s and 40s.

In two parallel gender-inclusive UK public and private sector studies, they found concepts of leadership were similar in both (the public sector model had more concepts relating to "integrity" and its concepts about the needs of stakeholders were broader and more complex), but differed significantly from US models derived largely from male samples.

UK models were more complex, and where US models rated vision and charisma the most important leadership qualities, both UK models rated "concern for others' well-being and development" the most important quality. Vision and charisma came much lower.

There was also more emphasis in UK models on collaboration and elements of "humility" absent from the US models. And whereas US models saw leaders as role models for followers, the 4000 or so participants in Alimo-Metcalfe's study saw leaders more as servants of followers. In the UK model, leaders engage their followers as partners in developing and realizing their shared visions, empower others to lead, create environments that are conducive to creative thinking, challenge assumptions, are sensitive to the needs of all stakeholders and are "connected". Alimo-Metcalfe says it's "essentially more 'feminine' than existing ... models of leadership" and that her research shows "a more feminine model is desired at all levels of organization".

Other studies suggested that women are more realistic than men about their leadership abilities, and are particularly good at communicating, standing up for principle, inspiring and "empowering" others, encouraging new ideas and reacting appropriately to poor performance.

Alimo-Metcalfe's research, the 44 studies covered in the Eagly et al. meta-analysis and MRG's analysis, are about as conclusive as things get in this area, but the conclusion doesn't always "feel" right, even to many women. It is counterintuitive, because the qualities most of us associate with women, such as friendliness, kindness and unselfishness, are at odds with those we associate with leaders, such as assertiveness, dominance, decisiveness and competence. As Eagly et al. put it: "People's beliefs about leadership are more similar to their beliefs about men than women." This was amply demonstrated by Schein, in her "think manager, think male" study.[17]

One possible explanation for the contradiction is that popular conceptions of leadership have yet to catch up with the qualities an effective leader requires in today's more complex, poly-cultural business world. As one of our marzipan women said: "Today there's more need to manage ambiguity and support people who come to the company from different ventures. Many women are better at managing some of these things. Success in the future will be less about warlike and sporting behavior and more about multitasking and managing complexity and ambiguity" (see Chapter 4).

In their book *The Partnering Imperative*,[18] Anne Deering and Anne Murphy argued that a new kind of leadership was needed in a business world where an explosion of joint ventures, collaborations and strategic alliances was heralding what the consultants Booz Allen & Hamilton called "a new chapter in the evolution of free enterprise".[19] Partnerships in which power and information are distributed equally cannot be managed in the traditional "command and control" ways. They require a lighter and we would say more "feminine" touch if they are not to break up amid mutual recrimination and the shards of wasted opportunities.

Hybrid vigor

Some of the most widely used psychological assessment and evaluation tools in business are based on the "Bem Sex Role Inventory" (BSRI). The BSRI adjectives used to describe masculinity and femininity include:

Masculinity	Femininity
self-reliant	loyal
independent	cheerful
analytical	compassionate
defends one's beliefs	sympathetic
assertive	affectionate
willing to take risks	sensitive to the needs of others
makes decisions easily	understanding
self-sufficient	eager to soothe hurt feelings
willing to take a stand	soft-spoken
aggressive	warm
individualistic	tender
competitive	does not use harsh language
ambitious	loves children
	gentle

These adjectives are associated with masculinity and femininity, not males and females, but it seems fair to say that, since modern companies are the creatures of males, they will tend to favor or "select for" masculine qualities. It also seems fair to say that at a time of growing consumer activism in areas such as the environment, health, business ethics, pay and working conditions of employees of suppliers in developing countries, diversity, inclusiveness and CSR, and the growing reputational risks of being insensitive to such external pressures, the guiding intelligences of companies need to become more feminine.

Masculine and feminine styles of management complement each other, in much the same way as maternal and paternal styles of parenting complement each other. Since feminine qualities are currently underrepresented, companies that strike a better balance between the sexes on their boards will gain a competitive advantage.

The advantage will not be confined to the tempering of male qualities that lead to error and create reputational risk. We believe that companies with a better balance between the sexes on their boards or executive committees will also be more dynamic. The infusion of inherently masculine organisms with female qualities will create hybrids, which are likely to display the hybrid vigor (heterosis) familiar in animal husbandry – the increase in characteristics such as size, growth rate, fertility and yield of hybrid organisms over those of their parents.

References

1. John Lewis Partnership website: www.johnlewispartnership.co.uk.
2. *The Constitution of the John Lewis Partnership; Introduction, Principles and Rules*, April 2004, (2nd edn).
3. *Integrative Management; Creating Unity from Diversity*, Pauline Graham, Basil Blackwell, 1991.
4. *Mary Parker Follett, Prophet of Management: A Celebration of Writings from the 1920s*, edited by Pauline Graham, Beard Books, 2003.
5. In the company of women: complementary ways of organizing work, Carlotta Tyler, *OD Practitioner*, **34**(3), 2002.
6. *Business and The Feminine Principle*, Carol R. Frenier, Butterworth Heinemann, 1997.
7. *The Red Queen. Sex and the Evolution of Human Nature*, Matt Ridley, Viking, 1993.
8. *The Adapted Mind*, Irwin Silverman and Marion Eals, Oxford University Press, 1992.
9. Measure costs right: make the right decisions, *Harvard Business Review*, September–October 1988.
10. *Reengineering the Corporation*, Mike Hammer and James Champy, HarperCollins, 1993.
11. Leadership & Gender: A Masculine Past; A Feminine Future? 2002, Beverly Alimo-Metcalfe, thematic paper for CERFE project. (CERFE is an independent research organization based in Rome).
12. *General Theory of Employment, Interest and Money*, Macmillan Cambridge University Press, 1939.
13. If you're not serving Bill and Barbara, then you're not serving leadership, Mintzberg, H., in J.G. Hunt, U. Sekaran and C.A. Schriesheim (eds), *Leadership Beyond Establishment Views*, Southern Illinois University Press, 1982.
14. Transformational, transactional and laissez-faire leadership styles: A meta-analysis comparing women and men, A. H. Eagly, M. C. Johannesen-Schmidt and M. L. van Engen, *Psychological Bulletin* 2003, **129**(4).
15. The transformational and transactional leadership of men and women, Bass, B.M., Avolio, B.J. and Atwater, L., *Applied Psychology: An International Review*, 1996.
16. *The Way Women and Men Lead*, R. Kabacoff and H. Peters, Management Research Group, 1998.
17. Think manager – think male, V. E. Schein, *The Atlanta Economic Review*, March–April, 1976.
18. *The Partnering Imperative: Making Business Partnerships Work*, Anne Deering and Anne Murphy, John Wiley, 2003.
19. *A Practical Guide to Alliances*, Booz Allen & Hamilton, 1995.

CHAPTER 7

The experience of women directors

We summarized the views of corporate kings and "marzipan" women about gender imbalances on US and UK boards in Chapters 3 and 4, and reported in Chapter 5 on the progress of a mentoring program designed to bring these two groups together to help to redress the imbalance.

In the next two chapters we summarize the views of two other groups; women directors who have made it through the marzipan to the top and executive search professionals (headhunters) who, as keepers of the gates leading from the marzipan layer to boards and executive committees, exert a strong influence on the gender balance in boardrooms.

As before we set the scene for our interviews by summarizing the latest US and UK figures for women directors and we explain that, since US boards tend to have fewer executive and more non-executive (outside, independent) directors than UK boards, we have taken US boards as proxies for executive committees, on the basis that executive committees were the main source of US outside directors.

We begin with the ex-marzipan women who have passed through these gates in the US and the UK, and the answers they gave us to the questions we put to them.

Reactions to the figures

We asked US directors how they reacted to the 2003 Catalyst *Census of Women Board Directors*, showing that 13.6 percent of Fortune 500 directors were women, 54 companies had no women on their boards and 208 only had one woman.

We asked UK directors for their reactions to Cranfield's *Female FTSE Report 2004*, which showed that women accounted for 10 percent of FTSE 100 board positions and 4 percent executive and 13 percent of non-executive directors.

Most women directors were disappointed to find they were so rare, but were not really surprised. One was slightly surprised by how many companies had no women directors:

> There's no excuse in this day and age for any company not to have at least one woman on its board. The pipeline issue is a red herring. It might be a problem

finding four women for each board, but there are plenty of women; just look for entrepreneurs, for women with experience of running large divisions of large corporates. Companies can't pat themselves on the back for having one woman either. You're looking for the best qualified people – you can't say that women aren't qualified just because you don't appoint them.

"Oh no!", groaned another woman director, on being shown the figures:

This is taking such a long time! I was 32 when I first became a member of an excom (executive committee) below the main board. This issue has been part of my life for the past 26 years. I was on a plc main board at 40. The key experience was seven years on the excom; it mirrored the board, everything was run through it. You could say it was a sort of training ground. I was the only woman on that excom and it's disappointing and frustrating to see that there are still so many boards where women are in the situation I was then; the only woman.

NEDs have changed a lot over the past 25 years. They used to be the wives of the great and the good. On my first board, I took over from the wife of a politician. There has been a professionalization of NEDs since then. The worrying thing is the number of executive directors – the pipeline for EDs [executive directors] hasn't really improved at all.

We asked her whether she thought being appointed an NED at another company improved your chances of being appointed an ED at your own company:

It should help if women get NED positions. An NED role involves much more thinking about stakeholders than a senior executive role; you need to know how the City thinks, for example.

Being an NED also gives you experience of what it's like to contribute to a big board. You don't tend to have much time for what you're going to say and you only get one or two opportunities to speak on a particular topic. Executives are not used to that – you have your say at exec meetings. NEDs have to read what comes through, identify the gaps in the strategy and the challenges, and then make their points succinctly. Executive directors are more partial (they usually present on their parts of the business). An NED has to see the whole picture.

Being an NED is great experience, because it puts you in touch with other views and people from different backgrounds. It's a broadening experience. So, to answer your question, all this experience should help you become a better ED. But if the company sees ED positions as rewards, then the fact that you have been an NED somewhere else won't carry much weight. The core requirement for an ED is performance delivery.

Reasons for the figures

One director suggested:

> Progress is slower now, because of corporate governance requirements. Most companies are looking for people with line, or financial experience. Women tend to be in the "pink ghetto" – pink-collar jobs, such as marketing, HR and communications, that aren't valued at board level" (but see below).

> The problem could get worse. I had to come off a board where I was an NED when a major issue arose at [her employing company]. It is becoming harder to do your day job and serve on another board. US boards demand about five days a year from an NED; UK boards demand eight or nine days and sometimes more, plus site visits, if you really want to understand the company. It's getting harder to do it as a sideline. The advantage for women is that men can't have as many directorships – that should open up opportunities (see box).

Multiple directorships

As we understand it, there are no New York Stock Exchange (NYSE), National Association of Securities Dealers Automated Quotations (NASDAQ), Sarbanes-Oxley Act or London Stock Exchange limits on the number of boards a person can sit on, but there are guidelines. The Institute of Shareholder Services in the US, for example, suggests no more than six. But boards are not bound by guidelines except insofar as they want to be able to tick the relevant boxes in corporate governance scorecards. "The trouble with these rating systems", said a US director, "is that they don't distinguish between people like myself, for whom board service [as an independent director] is a full-time job and people who are also executives."

For audit committees, there are some disclosure requirements. The NYSE, for example, requires a NYSE-listed company to disclose the fact that a member (or members) of its audit committee sits (or sit) on more than three audit committees. The NASDAQ listing agreement requires no such disclosure.

The general point here is that, although there are no legal or contractual requirements for fewer directorships per head, the more rigorous corporate governance climate is having this effect, if only because the added burden of responsibility and accountability it imposes on directors makes it much harder, riskier and thus less desirable to sit on several boards at once.

Another said:

It may be harder to find women if they are not known to you, but there are plenty of serious women out there; you just have to look in the right places. Men look at their own networks – women have to help each other too.

The main challenge is finding women coming up through company roles. They just aren't there in great enough numbers at senior management levels. And many women are not happy to make the trade-offs. International travel, for instance, was a factor in my deciding not to join other companies. We all set our own parameters, but the cutoffs are different for women. If I had a wife it would be easier!

Another director said:

It's very hard to get there. Women have to have a lot of talent, the right blend of experience (which is hard to get), a lot of persistence and the ability to tolerate loneliness.

Experience is important for men too, of course. I've been in on succession discussions at board meetings where men's experience is being debated. The men who get through have made the right moves to be credible. If you don't have a big operational or business focus, you won't be in the running to be CEO. It seems more difficult for women to get these experiences. Companies need to manage women's careers more tightly.

We asked her how someone from the pink ghetto (HR, in her case) had made it onto so many boards:

I was in the right industrial sector, at the right time. Some sectors are more in need of certain functional specialisms than others. Consumer goods is an example of a fast moving sector, which needs marketing experience on the board. Retail is more likely to need HR expertise; it's highly reliant on its people. The technology to deliver the service is minimal, so people really are the biggest asset. I was in the retail sector when my business was in a recovery situation and had to restructure, so my input was needed at the most strategic level.

You can work up through the finance function to get to the board, because finance is always on the board, but that is really the only function where that holds true.

How comfortable are chairmen and CEOs with appointing women?

One female director said:

> Chairmen are comfortable, because they're around women a lot more, but it isn't really about comfort. It's about skills and experience of bottom line roles, such as manufacturing.

> At one time, my company and others like it weren't keen on you taking on other commitments such as NED positions. I had to negotiate to keep my NED position when I moved. That has changed. Many companies see non-executive appointments as executive development opportunities. But there's a problem here – if you were a chairman, would you want someone on your board who was on a career development assignment? But some chairmen do. [See Chapter 5.]

Another thought that most CEOs would be comfortable appointing women, "but they have to have the candidates in front of them and board appointments are normally handled by the independent directors or nominating committees who may or may not appoint headhunters. So it depends who the independent directors come up with. It's not an issue at our company – there are three women on the board, two NEDs and me."

Another said:

> CEOs' initial experience of female directors was mixed. It was the era of academics and women who had retired from government posts. They didn't have the day-to-day experience of the boardroom; knowing other companies, and so on. They weren't as valuable. This may have shaped the views of CEOs of women in general. In my own case, my consultancy background may have been an even harder hurdle for a CEO to get over.

> But the willingness is out there now. The vast majority [she suggested 80 percent] of companies would be delighted to have another highly qualified woman on the board. The problem is headhunters are such a poor interface.

> On the whole, I don't think chairmen demand women on the board. They look for senior executives on boards of other companies. I've spent 10 years in the public sector and there's real political pressure there [for promoting women to senior positions]. Ministers ask questions if there are no women on short lists in the public sector. A quarter of senior civil servants are women now. There's no such pressure [in the private sector] on chairmen or from shareholders. Having women on board nominating committees helps.

Personal experience of appointments

I was put on the [A] board by a headhunter. I didn't apply. I got noticed through my role in [B]. In the case of the [C] board, I was asked to join by the chairman – we had served on another board together and he liked the way I thought and operated. We thought alike, so he asked me to join.

Companies are working hard now to ensure there aren't too many people who serve on each other's boards, because of corporate governance rules. With the first board I was on, I replaced another [B] colleague. When he stepped down they asked me. I was the [B] representative on the board.

Another female director had spent five years at McKinsey:

which gave me a level of confidence and a network. I have used the network of alumni. They are a group of well-connected people who can give introductions. There's a sort of validation about people who have worked at McKinsey – they must be OK. In the same way, I'm happy to meet with McKinsey people.

Cranfield's research of the FTSE 100 found that titles and honors, such as OBEs, give the same kind of validation to candidates in the UK.

"I was the finance director at [a subsidiary]" said another, "and [the CEO of the parent company] brought me up to be FD at corporate level. He took a risk on me. Making the leap from a subsidiary board to the group board was a pivotal move. It gave me good FTSE experience.

"After that I wanted to move into an operational role, and I had also been thinking about private equity. I've never been aware of gender barriers."

Another was appointed as an NED through a headhunter. "The chairman called me through the headhunter. They were very interested in my experience with financial services branding; they were looking for branding experience."

We found the above interesting in light of another woman director's comment that pink-collar functions aren't valued at board level. In this case, marketing experience was a plus point for the company appointing the NED, because, presumably, of its then current strategic priorities. This suggests that the gender balancing of boards may be given extra impetus if and when competitive circumstances give a darker hue to functions that may historically have been "pink".

The director of three US companies attributed her appointments to the fact that, as a senior McKinsey partner:

I was very well connected with a strong market sector specialism. I was a senior partner so my clients were CEOs. I'd been an advisor for a long time, but the

headhunters didn't see my background as suitable for a board. I kept hearing that CEOs wanted someone with bottom line experience, not consultancy.

I got two appointments through direct contacts; someone on the nominating committee recommended me, and I then met the chairman. With the third, one of the board members recommended me to the chairman.

Another director told us she had been appointed by two chairmen who specifically wanted women on their boards:

The first was in 1993, when the chairman used a headhunter – this was unusual at that time. He had three NED appointments to make and wanted one of them to be a woman. He was quite enlightened in that sense, which I think may have been because he was also very active in the arts, and would have come across more women in that capacity. One of the boards I'm on now also used a headhunter.

The chairmen were in the lead, but I also met the CEOs. In one company, I met two other directors, and in the family business where I'm an NED, I met all the board.

Several women said they'd had valuable advice before their appointments to boards by friends, colleagues and acquaintances, including serving NEDs and executive directors. But one woman felt that she would have benefited from more formal "on-boarding":

Looking back I didn't have enough help. There's an opportunity for the IOD [the UK's Institute of Directors], universities and executive coaches to provide more effective training for NEDs and executives so that they come into these roles more prepared for the sort of questions they'll get asked at board meetings. Your role isn't always entirely clear – as an NED you don't run the company.

A US director said:

I had no help at all. I just told headhunters that I was retiring and would be available. I didn't talk to any women directors.

CEOs don't pick board members in the US. The nominating committee has the responsibility to find candidates and recommend them to the chair. But it would be silly to pick someone the CEO might be uncomfortable with. Chairs and CEOs see the list, meet the candidates and offer input, but nominating committees drive the whole process. That's why I tell people to send their CVs to nominating committees as well as to headhunters.

I didn't enlist anyone's help specifically. One of the first boards I was on had another woman director and she was friendly and helpful. We used to have dinner occasionally; I felt she was an ally.

We asked how being on a board matched their expectations.

"I love it!" said one director. "I had a wide variety of experiences, so I thought I could contribute and I can. When you reach a certain level in an organization, where do you get your enrichment from? There are no courses you can go on. It's fascinating to see how people grapple with problems. I have found it an enriching experience. You learn that your way of thinking isn't the only way."

Another agreed that "being involved with an organization at a senior level is exciting", but said "board meetings aren't that exciting!"

One director felt she had made a mistake resigning as an NED, when her day job got particularly difficult. "Perhaps I would have been better advised to have built up a portfolio of directorships, given the difficulties", she mused. "But it's what women do; focus on the job rather than themselves."

"The most interesting and dynamic board I have ever served on was also the most diverse. To enjoy board membership you have to be a fully engaged and able to do advisory work, too. Engagement also depends hugely on the skill of the chairman."

The importance of diversity

"It's really important to have a broad spectrum of opinion", said one. "The board is not there to rubber stamp everything. You need differences of all kinds – gender, race, ethnicity, background and personality."

Another director said:

You can't think differently if you're out of the same mold. You need that spark that comes from difference. Diversity is an intrinsic characteristic of the US. We're a melting pot. It's the hallmark of the US. We struggle with it at the highest level, but that awareness of diversity does provide a context for women to succeed and contribute.

If you're trying to achieve a more diverse workforce, the board supplies instant role models. If there's no diversity on the board, it's like saying "we don't care enough to work hard at it".

It is critical from a consumer standpoint. How many Fortune 500 chairs go shopping? It's more compelling if you have the voice of the woman selling marketing ideas about women inside the company. That's not to say that, in theory, professional marketers cannot represent women, but it's much more powerful in practice when the organization hears the voice of the woman or the voice of the African-American.

"Diversity is important as long as every board member is qualified" said a US director. "I'd go with qualification, if there's a trade-off. Its value is not so much in women understanding women (customers, staff, and so on) as in the range of backgrounds – that's where it's useful. If every director has come up through the MBA route, you don't get enough difference. It's about background and experiences."

The NED of several UK companies said:

Diversity is really important, not just gender and ethnicity. It gives you much more resource to draw on when dealing with uncertainty and the increasingly wide range of issues facing large companies. It means you can draw on critical bits of experience from around the board table. The most diversity I've ever encountered was on [a public sector commission]. We had eight men and seven women; three of the 15 were from ethnic minorities; and their backgrounds included the private sector, education, health, arts and the voluntary sector. This was a huge resource when debating difficult policy issues. There was so much variety of experience and different ways of thinking. The more diversity you have, the greater the chances that, when you have difficult issues to deal with, you will make the right judgments. It's not so important when dealing with the routine stuff.

But to make a board work, you have to have certain things in common – you need to have commonality of values.

"Different people approach things in different ways", said one director. "I think women are more instinctive and more conciliatory in business style. It creates a dynamic. I wouldn't put this on the top of my list. I'd put a mix of business experience and skills first. But in our sector (retailing) gender diversity is important for customer understanding. If there are two people of equal capability, then you should appoint a woman."

"I approach my role, not as a woman, but as a marketing professional", said another. "We do see things differently from men in a lot of areas. We tend to be better at communicating and a lot of what boards do is communication and explaining actions."

An American director recalled:

I was the only woman on the boards of [two big US companies]. I was one of the first women to come through at [B] so I was used to being the "first", or the "only". Some boards have been more welcoming than others. I'm not seen as "one of the guys", but I am seen as an equal contributor.

I'm a member of a group of about 40 women directors who meet from time to time for off-the-record conversations. The quality we have in common (and what I think we bring to boards) is that we are all very straight talking, although we know that it's one thing to say what you think, and another to be heard. Women will say "there's an elephant in the room". Men will dance round it. Women get on with it. On the whole we say what we think in a way that gets heard.

"There could be some sense in which women bring a different dynamic to the boardroom, especially when the board is appointing its first woman", said a US director. "None of the boards I'm on are particularly clubby. I've been gender blind since I was 12. Successful women are much like successful men – smart, decisive, and so on."

"I can't cite personal observations of a style difference", a non-executive UK director said smiling, "because I've never sat on an all-male board! But I do think women are more interested in getting the job done and in moving the business forward. They're not in it for the performance, as such. Most women are pretty direct and use humor appropriately."

Lessons from America

A US interviewee said:

It's not enough to know how to do the job. Others need to know you can do it. Women can help themselves by blowing their own horns more. They have to aim for more financial, accounting, manufacturing and line jobs.

Women must focus on their careers. It's not enough to be smart and female either. To give counsel to a chairman you need experience. In the US, line and operating experience are essential. Independent directors need to test the doability of the business strategy. There are fewer board meetings in the US [than the UK] so their focus is on strategy and statutory financial stuff.

Another American woman suggested the US was:

more of a consumerist society than the UK, and there's more data available about the purchasing power of women. Things in the UK will change as UK consumerism embraces women more.

Also, women's liberation started in the US. I'm not talking about the bra-burning women's lib, but the aspects of women's lib that were about education and opportunity for women. So I'm convinced the confidence of UK women will grow.

Another difference is that in the US people who contribute to non-profits or who head up professional associations are noticed more.

One interviewee advised UK marzipan women to "think small first. The first board I was on wasn't a Fortune 500 company. Small companies with lots of challenges are lots of fun!'
Another suggested that women:

shouldn't have a goal of being on a board. Screen opportunities for your level of integrity and interest and do as much "due diligence" as you can. It's shouldn't be the be-all and end-all. It should be a positive experience. It's certainly not a money issue. You can't want it for superficial reasons.

Women need to network and meet people, so they know who you are. Serve on charity boards, where you get alongside "the great and the good". And find a mentor – that's also a good way to get introductions. Four or five years ago I would have said career progress had nothing to do with who you know. I now think it has a lot to do with establishing connections. Women don't make time for the social stuff. Most women focus their effort on doing the job to the best of their ability. Men focus more on career progression and networking.

A US director said:

Longer term, you have to consider what aspects of expertise will make you an attractive candidate. Women who reach a mid-senior level and then leave corporate life, won't get onto a board. In my case, 30 years of industry experience helped. Think about where your expertise will add value. You can't say "I'm reasonably accomplished, so the phone should ring"! It's like getting a job. Work out what you're bringing to the party and let people know. Head-hunters won't lay pearls at your feet.

You should also network very heavily – women can be naive about what that takes. Every nominating committee has a folder, with notes and comments on each candidate – get into that folder.

Persistence is really important. Getting an NED position can be a tedious process, because the time pressure is never the same as it is for EDs – it can take six months. You have to be patient. You need to work out where your experience is most relevant and be discriminating about what [approaches] you follow up. Learn to present all your experience, draw on it well when you talk and present it firmly. Maintaining your network is very important too. You never know when it will be necessary and when you'll need to draw on it.

We asked why American women did so well in the UK.

"Women have been in and stayed in the workplace longer in the US", said an American interviewee. "I would say the US is 10–15 years ahead of the UK. [The US is ahead, certainly, but the figures don't suggest the gap is that wide.]

"Also when we come here [to the UK] we come into high-profile roles. We're different, so we stand out. That can be bad when we're less qualified, but it's great if we're highly qualified.

Another suggested that women's institutions are more firmly established in the US – "the New York Forum for Women in Financial Services has many more members than the UK Forum, for example" – and that partly because of this, there were fewer Queen Bees in the US than in the UK.

Suggestions for companies

"Companies should look for a wider variety of skills on their boards", said a UK director. "Non-execs have to deal with comp and ben [compensation and benefits] and succession planning, especially now the average CEO is only in the job for about three years, so why not have HR people on boards? But directors need more than one skill. They must also be able to read balance sheets. Having women for women's sake isn't the right approach."

"Companies could cast a wider net amongst women", echoed another. "There is a larger pool of potential talent there, so they should take a chance, it sometimes works and it sometimes doesn't."

Another director suggested:

They should look outside traditional networks and tell their search firms that their lists should be at least 30 percent women, say. If traditional search firms can't do that, go to non-traditional firms.

Within companies, you need to ensure that people filling jobs always have women on their slates. Companies should allow women to fail. Men fail too, but companies should take more risks with women. The most important factor is the tone from the top. If the chairman says nothing about the lack of women, the tone isn't right. He should make his expectations clear and say something when a presentation to the board is made by a group that doesn't include a woman or a black person. The message will soon get through.

Promote managers who value diversity and build mixed teams. Make it clear that the company is suboptimizing talent if it doesn't promote women. Mao said "women hold up half the world", after all.

The figures produced by Cranfield and Catalyst are critical. There should be genuine embarrassment when companies that have no women on their boards are named and shamed. Childcare is a complete red herring at this level.

"The key questions for organizations are: Where do we look for women?' and 'How do we develop women?

"The representation of women is very low near the top", another director pointed out, "so companies need to tackle the issue of women in the pipeline. If there are two people of equal ability in the shortlist for a board position, the woman should be given the position. Positive action is more acceptable in the US than in the UK, but we need to take these sort of steps if anything is to change."
A US director said:

Companies need to think through what other aspects will be valuable. Don't just go for women with bottom line experience – look at different kinds of people. An outside director doesn't need to have run a $X billion company. Look for contribution; be more thoughtful. In the US, boards hire and fire the CEO, and do the comp and ben for other execs. We're an important sounding board for strategy and all sorts of compliance work such as audit and compensation. Companies should look for people with other skills, such as comp and ben expertise, audit skills, and so on, not just bottom line.

A director on one board I serve on and some of her associates have formed a headhunting firm to find women who aren't on everyone's lists. Companies need to push the headhunters more.

Very intensive work is needed on talent management processes. You have to do that for men too. Women have the extra dimension of family contribution (all the research still shows the burden of this falls to women), so they usually have to downplay their careers at some point. Are companies clever enough to listen when a woman says she needs to do this and when she says she's ready to start again? Companies are not good at having conversations with people "in the round" [work–life balance]. It puts pressure on talent management systems, because there is no language for it. Increasingly, men want to have these conversations in the round, too.

Women helping women

"Women at a certain level tend to know each other, but in the UK, the pool is smaller than in the US", said a UK director. "Women should suggest other women for board positions and encourage headhunters to look at other areas such as professional organizations. Women are great joiners."

An American woman also emphasized the role of women's groups, associations and networks:

> Senior women on boards haven't done it on their own. A lot of men and women helped me to succeed. [B] had a good women's community. I try to give something back to professional women's associations by putting women forward for positions, speaking at events and spending some one-to-one time with women.

> We're role models of course, but I worry about people seeing me as having the answer. I view my life in five compartments: work, children, marriage, friends, self. Friends and self don't get as much of my time or attention; that's my trade-off and, for the most part, it works for me. I always tell other women that. We can and should give other women advice. I talk to our women's network about this sort of thing.

"Being on nominating committees, mentoring, sharing experience, suggesting women for jobs, maintaining a network yourself so that you meet new women, offering women advice about their careers when they ask and trying to make them aware how important each choice is", were some things a UK NED said women directors should do to help other women.

Another director said that when "new women join the boards I serve on, I'm usually the one who has the coffee or lunch with them to make sure they settle in. I rack my own memory to find interesting women for available positions. I could do more to pass these on to headhunters."

One reason why she doesn't pass on names to headhunters is that she is not a great fan of executive search firms when it comes to finding and placing non-executive (outside/independent) directors:

> In my appointments the headhunters were fairly useless. I think there are several reasons for them being like this.

> First of all, placing outside directors isn't a high paying part of their service – they do it because they have to. It is as much work as placing a CEO, but it's not remunerated in the same way.

They're also handicapped by the board's specifications. The board may not be in agreement on what's needed, for a start. Some may want international experience, others may want financial experience.

Third, headhunters aren't very creative. They use standard lists with the same people, so the same heavy hitters get recycled. They are not good at catching the "up and comers".

Fourth, headhunters don't tend to challenge board specifications or offer counter suggestions. They won't say some specs are simply not doable. They should challenge. They should say: "we can't find all of this. What do you want to give up from this spec?" They're not good at getting the board to consider someone different. When the board say they want a retailer, their headhunters should say: "have you thought about a management consultant or an investment banker with retail sector experience?"

I realize that their job is difficult and most nominating committees do now put out specifications that include gender and minorities, but they do need to widen their horizons.

She pointed out that as a consequence of the financial reporting requirements in the Sarbanes-Oxley Act, the boards of companies listed in the US were on the lookout for financial expertise and said "the most desired pool is female CFOs".

In the next chapter we summarize the views of executive search professionals, or "headhunters", as they're known, to whom many companies on the lookout for new boardroom talent turn for assistance.

CHAPTER 8

Headhunters

From Palaeolithic times until the early 20th century, from Ireland and the Balkan Peninsula in Europe, to India, Indonesia, Africa, Australasia and South America, peoples ancient and relatively modern removed and preserved human heads.

In most cases the practice of headhunting emerged from the belief that the head contains more or less material soul matter on which all life depends, and that removing the head and capturing the soul matter within it adds to the general stock of soul matter, and thus contributes to the fertility of the community's human population, livestock and crops.

Organizations do much the same in our own time. They don't remove the head from the body, and most of them subcontract their headhunting to external specialists, but the objective is similar – to promote their own fertility and fruitfulness by enriching their community with the skills, talents and experience of outsiders.

The external specialists companies employ to track down talented outsiders play a vitally important role in our story, because they not only find new board candidates; they also screen them and draw up short lists from which their clients make their final selections. In spirit, therefore, executive search firms stand at the boardroom door, checking credentials, welcoming some applicants, turning others away.

Headhunters were involved at some stage, in some way, with the elevation to the board of most of the women leaders whose views are summarized above.

We therefore felt that it was essential, for any book about the paucity of women directors and how to correct it, to seek the views of headhunters on why the gender imbalance on most boards persists and what women who aspire to the board can do to improve their chances of getting short-listed.

We asked them first whether there was any substance to the accusation that most headhunters believe the professional skills required of directors are mostly to be found in Anglo-Saxon men.

"That's just an assertion", said a headhunter. "There obviously are more men than women in business, but many women do possess the necessary skills and many others are quite capable of acquiring them. I don't think that women have to behave like men [to be appointed to boards] either.

What they have to do, is move from being *experts*, to being *authorities* in their fields." Experts, according to the headhunter, support their conclusions with data and analysis, because they are seen by others as being on top of the wave. Authorities are regarded as being ahead of the wave, so people are willing to accept their conclusions without supporting data or analysis.

"I don't see that women are any different from men in terms of skill", said another headhunter, "but it is true that women often come up through functional routes and, as boards get smaller, they shed HR and marketing people. That affects NEDs too; there are fewer women non-execs, because there are fewer women execs." A US headhunter felt that the executive director figures for the UK were worryingly low, because "this means there isn't a big pool for NED candidates."

Another felt there was some substance to the suspicion that headhunters in general felt that the skills required of directors were mostly to be found in men:

Probably quite true. They assume that women "lack impact" and "are too emotional" and they look for those two traits in women. Men start out with these assumptions – they're prejudices, not conclusions based on a woman's behavior in an interview.

I'd ask the question: "what percentage of those women appointed to boards were recommended by women headhunters?" In previous years male headhunters didn't know senior women and would have to come to their female colleagues to ask who those women were.

Another asserted that:

In a short list of four comparably qualified candidates, you could get one woman. If the client was interested in getting a woman, there might have to be trade-offs, because there's a smaller pool of women available. But there are certainly women around who have the skills to do the job, and there is a much higher demand now for emotional intelligence and influencing. In my experience as a headhunter, it's much harder to find these qualities in men. But successful women who are candidates for these positions usually have a very forthright way of communicating and that can be seen perceived by men as too much of a threat.

A US headhunter said:

A dozen years ago, you had to convince people to consider a woman, now it's a given that women should be on boards. Companies are comfortable with women on their boards and they want more of them. The environment is changing. There are more qualified women, which changes the comfort level of men about women. It's important to have the right people on boards, of course (there is no place for tokenism), but the only thing holding companies back from appointing three or four woman to their boards is a lack of qualified women."

Third sector talent

Next we asked our headhunters whether they thought there were any pools of female talent, in the so-called "third sector" (charities, not-for-profits and so on) for example, which headhunters were neglecting.

One felt that it was "very hard to push forward people with not-for-profit backgrounds, because they don't have the commercial experience." Another agreed, but thought this was changing:

I think that voluntary or not-for-profit board work has been seen to be more of a "club" environment – women having coffee, chatting round the issues – rather than being commercially orientated. But many charity organizations have "professionalized" their boards in the last few years and it's much more appropriate now to look at those boards to identify talent. But I don't disagree that, if you go back a few years, the quality of those boards was at best average. There were a few that were exceptional, more professional, but generally they were much less commercial than they are today.

At a conference at London's Cass Business School on third sector NEDs in March 2005, the CEO of an international charity, who had run a FTSE 100 company and was an NED on the boards of two others, said a lot of what he does was very similar to a private sector CEO's role. "There's a gap, but you can bridge it. You have to accept the rules of the game; that the role of companies is to generate wealth, for example. Some people in charities don't accept this. But top charity CEOs are a damn good bunch!'
Another said:

There's a bigger area they [headhunters] ignore and that's academia. For example, a member of the monetary policy committee [the Bank of England body that sets interest rates] was a professor in development economics at Cambridge. The client was a commercial organization operating in the third world, so the experience was relevant. So, no, there is crossover from non-commercial sectors. In fact, managing a board of trustees is more difficult than managing a board of directors – there are more of them and they're accountable to nobody.

A speaker at the third sector conference said academics brought a number of valuable qualities to a board. They were smart, intellectually curious, had independent perspectives, understood young people, tended to challenge conventional wisdom and, because most of them thought constantly about the future, were good early-warning systems.

Another headhunter suggested that it was horses for courses:

> I would say that, in terms of recruitment, it's the responsibility of the head-hunter to break down the competences and skills required. For example, a mutual [a financial services company owned by its customers] might want someone with experience of a consensus environment. For a plc, you have to ask yourself how critical it is that the candidate has experience of the plc world. Rather than taking things at face value, headhunters should ask what it is that the client really requires.

> You can push back. You have to be educated about board structure and know what clients really need. The plc environment is obviously different (six-monthly reporting to the stock exchange and confidentiality issues), but a lack of plc experience is not an insurmountable obstacle.

Another US headhunter said:

> We used to look for women who were running divisions, or were the CEOs of smaller companies. That's changed now. Active CEOs aren't serving on as many boards, because it takes too much time and there's an increased risk, which the rewards don't justify. CEOs are also being prevented by their own boards from serving on others. So we have to look for different kinds of people now. Because of Sarbanes-Oxley [section 404 of the legislation obliges boards to sign off financial statements] there has been a demand for finance, but there is a limited pool of finance people and boards are now looking at other areas, such as HR and the law. A million women have legal backgrounds, so that is great news!

> This loosening up of the definition of "ideal board candidate" completely changes the talent pool – "unknowns" are going onto boards now. Companies say: "We need marketing expertise, so go out and hire a marketing person."

> The process of recruiting directors has changed. It used to be the CEO who recruited, but boards are taking responsibility now through the nominating committees which may not be chaired by the CEO so there's less recruitment going on "in own image".

> We used to do three types of search for a CEO, a woman and a member of an ethnic minority. We're still asked for women, but more often these days it is:

"We want a CFO, and we would prefer her to be a woman." I always put a woman on a slate. There are starting to be enough women to be considered.

A man and two women do our searches. If a woman is doing the search, then there will be a more conscious look for women and it's likely that a woman search consultant will simply know more women.

Strategic career planning

We asked headhunters whether they felt women who wanted to be appointed to a board needed to be more strategic about career counseling, planning and coaching.

One headhunter said:

I'm not sure about that. Most careers just happen – successful people have drive and ambition. You can have three siblings in the family; a postman, a teacher and the chairman of BP. You need to be determined. I actually believe it is driven entirely by want. What do women want? One of the things I think that women are more honest about than men is that there are some trade-offs. You can't have it both ways. You can't be a hands-on mother and a supportive partner, and be as successful at work. You have to make choices and women are more honest about those choices – if that's not being "strategic", what is?

Another thought men were just as, if not more, reluctant than women to get career advice, and to plan. A third suggested that, these days, women were probably more strategic about their careers than men:

Historically, women were probably less strategic, but in my experience of successful career women, they know exactly what they want. They struggle to get the appropriate support, or leverage themselves, in the way a young male professional is able to. It's more difficult for a woman to appear as organized or as strategic. But it's quite old-fashioned to regard women as less strategic. I think some are probably more strategic than men. Women know exactly where they want to get to, but they're less ruthless and take more time to get there. Their elbows are less sharp and they don't project their thoughts, desires and aspirations as early on in their careers or at critical career stages. Organizations and society need to support women so they can do that.

Another US headhunter said:

Women need to be prominent. You need to be well known and respected in your company, your community and your industry. If you live in Cincinnati you should be known in Cincinnati; you have to have a presence. Women tend to keep their heads down. They should hold not-for-profit roles, be involved in their industry associations, and so on. Going to a directors' college doesn't give you that.

We asked her if women should be sending their CVs to nominating committees as another interviewee had suggested: "The protocol's quite odd", she said. "It's still better to have someone else vouch for you and write on your behalf, rather than send your own CV."

We asked whether headhunters felt that women's priorities changed in their mid-to-late thirties.

One said:

They often want something more flexible, where they're allowed to be more of an individual operator, doing e-mails at home after leaving work at 6.00pm to put the children to bed. Nicola Horlick [a prominent UK fund manager] said superwoman doesn't exist and if she did, she would have bags under her eyes, greasy hair and broken nails. The women who make it to the top are usually strong, competent, don't need close management, read all the newspapers, apply themselves, are hard-working and focused and set out the basis on which they're willing to work.

"Culture is important" said another. People don't feel they can be honest and say they need to leave work because their child is sick. That's one reason why civil servants say that the private sector is macho and self-centered."

Another headhunter went on:

This is the childbearing age group, and there is a dilemma for successful women. Without getting too mother-earthy about it, no matter how committed you are to your career, you want to give your children the chance to perform as well, or better than you. Children aged five to eight are terribly demanding. You want to be great at everything, but you have to choose where you cut the slack. In the UK it's very hard to decide to work 9 to 5. It's the clients, more than the employers. I have a client who told me that a criterion for selecting a head-hunter was that "you will be available on a 24/7 basis".

There's also the international piece. There's far more demand now to take tele- and video-conferences and so on at extreme ends of the day. So, if you've got Middle East and US clients, it can become an intolerable challenge for some people. Your children get up and go to bed, and you never see them. Most consumer clients are 24/7 businesses. They couldn't give a damn about your work–life balance. If you want to work with them, you have to accept their 24/7 lives. If you're managing global companies, that's how it is.

I'm not hearing people saying they don't want women – I am experiencing a range of other dimensions that are making it more difficult for women.

But another suggested:

It doesn't have to be that way. Women tend to agonize about whether they're going to pay too high a price for their success. "Am I going to lose my children; my husband?" Because they have more on their agendas on the whole than men, they look for compromises. Mobility creates issues that women tend to be more honest about than men.

As a headhunter, you look at track records, international background, the variety of experience, the size of company, the scale of issues addressed, sector experiences, and so on. A lot of women will steer clear of international work, because they can't travel for three months a year.

Another suggested that men questioned their ambition and drive at that age as much as women:

Many men I meet today in their thirties are actively seeking new and different directions that may be new and different careers. Women obviously face a similar dilemma, particularly if they're married and want children. They are still, and are still expected to be, the primary carers for children, so they have to juggle time and careers more, and that often gives the impression that they're less hungry and ambitious. But these days, I meet more highly moti-vated women in their early forties than men.

But I do think it's true that women get frustrated with the politics, and leave to do something else. It is not lack of ambition, but frustration. I know of many women who've retrained and done something different, because they were fed up with the politics.

Fitting the image

We asked headhunters if they agreed that, to attract their attention, women needed to make themselves "look like" candidates.
One said:

That's not a gender issue. If the first impression a man gives is deeply unattractive or inappropriate (nylon socks, sandals, lederhosen, for example) it will work against him. What we wear to work is camouflage; clothes shouldn't get in the way of what you think. Don't make the way you look an issue. The CEO of [an international bank] came in on a dress-down Friday wearing a silk batik shirt and tailored slacks. He looked the bee's knees – for the beach. His secretary said: "What on earth do you think you look like?" and reminded him that he was having lunch with the governor of the Bank of England. He'd forgotten and had to go out and buy a suit. It's no good looking "a" part, you have to look "the" part.

Hairstyles can be problematic – men with shaved heads, for example. There is a line between what is deemed acceptable and unacceptable. Hair looking scruffy and unkempt is a disadvantage for both men and women.

Another agreed that appearance was not a gender issue:

One of the current real-life issues I am concerned about is weight. I have had a number of situations recently, with very senior appointments, where the client felt that it would be inappropriate to short-list overweight people. There is no doubt that, in some sectors, such as pharmaceuticals, being overweight is seen as inappropriate. That applies to males and females. The inference is that over-weight individuals lack self-control.

I CAN'T QUITE PUT MY FINGER ON IT —
BUT WE SHOULD DEFINITELY TAKE THE ONE IN THE MIDDLE

Image is important for men and women; you must project yourself as having stature, presence and instant impact. But you don't have to conform to the stereotype of the tough, ballsy, New York-type women executives. There are plenty of well-groomed, well-dressed and very friendly and feminine female executives. Take X [CEO of a UK media group] – ferociously bright, highly numerate and very creative. There's no debate about her ability, but she has French manicures and a Gucci handbag, wears peep-toe shoes and her office is full of flowers.

Looks are important in a telegenic age – you don't see many 18-stone male CEOs. Some women don't take appearance seriously enough. They turn up with plastic carrier bags, and they're not dressed properly for that unexpected meeting. If you want to be upgraded on a plane, don't wear trainers. It's how we assess each other. Lots of women look messy (hair not properly cut) and don't present themselves well. Invest in clothes. If you want to be on the board, you need to think about where you shop. Quality clothes are important.

"Do women sometimes rule themselves out?", we asked.

"Totally true, and often deliberately", said a headhunter. "There's a woman at [a law firm]. She's ace: bright, focused, charming. She rates 10–11 out of 12 and has been managing partner for 10 years. They asked her to become senior partner last year. It was a fantastic opportunity. But she said no, because she would have to travel the world, glad-handing. Men think that's glamorous. She signed up to do another stint as managing partner instead."

Another thought women put themselves at a disadvantage, by being adamantly less mobile. "Within the current social climate, men are more likely to be willing to work away from home for most or all of the week. Women who have children are not prepared to do that. They are prepared to be away part of the week, but not five days a week, every week."

Two headhunters thought that some women ruled themselves out in interviews by equivocating too much:

Sometimes, in thinking out loud, women open up to the extent that they verbalize the compromises, conflicts, and concerns and thus appear less than single-minded. There's a slight element of being unnecessarily tentative. You should do your thinking off-line. You have to get the person who's interviewing you to offer you the job. You can't turn down a job that hasn't been offered.

I think women are inclined to be more self-doubting; more realistic about their relative strengths and weaknesses and less confident. In the initial interview stage, and the initial approach stage, women will tell you five reasons why they

SHE'S MORE CAPABLE — BUT HE *LOOKS* THE PART

could do the job, and five reasons why they couldn't. Men will just tell you the five reasons they could do it. Women are much more honest about their overall abilities. Men will come in and say: "I've read the specification and I meet all the criteria." Women will come in and say: "I've read the specification; I meet six criteria, but would need to reach bench-strength on these six others."

Dos and don'ts from headhunters for aspiring directors

Be very clear about why you're appropriate, and leave your interviewers in no doubt about how much you want to do the job. But emphasize what you can contribute, not what you think you'll get out of it. Don't say "the reason I want the job is because of what I can learn from it!" You've got to feel you're there as a major player, not a spectator or an occasional bit-part actor. If you make it easy for people to be positive about you, they'll be more inclined to support you.

In any role there's the good and the bad; the exciting and the boring. You have to appear to be up for all of it – it's a table d'hôte menu, not à la carte. It's a package. You can't do a top job unless you move outside your comfort zone. A new role, such as moving from London to Singapore (or vice versa) for a year, may be part and parcel of it. It gives credibility at a level you've never previously operated at and exposes you to the board.

Present yourself as gender-neutral – let others ponder the gender-positive aspect. Remember that when you join a board, you do so not as the delegate of a faction or special interest group, but as a representative of all the organization's stakeholders. But that said, recognize that the marketplace is demanding the emotional intelligence skill sets more usually associated with women than men. Recognize that your gender's skill sets are in demand and don't underestimate their value and importance.

Be well groomed from top to toe. Your appearance should be appropriate and professional; not too severe, that's a common mistake, but well tailored.

A lot of women suffer from the interloper syndrome, and it comes across. Sometimes they're a little bit too jokey; some witter on too much; others do the "nodding donkey" bit – women are notorious for nodding their heads in meetings – and are too willing to please. Be confident and succinct. Speak clearly and authoritatively, and don't be afraid to "sell" yourself, by talking about your achievements and the value you will bring. One of the challenges for women who want to get on boards is to be seen by (usually male) interviewers as approachable, competent and professional.

There is always a limited number of outstanding candidates for every board position. Able women should never underestimate their ability and scarcity in the marketplace or assume that there are gender barriers where none exist.

You have to accept that large companies are political organizations and be willing to engage in the politics. It's not hard – 90 percent of politics is good manners. The political effectiveness of "please" and "thank you" should never be underestimated.

Find a senior male mentor – you need male input, because your interviewers will usually be men. Few men have had much exposure to professional women and most have certain preconceptions about them. Although they would never admit it, some are intimidated by them. Others dislike emotion in women. Be candid about your communication style and how you operate at an executive management level, but be very careful about how you talk about your family and your extracurricular activities; they may be seen as distractions. It is OK for a man to talk about shooting, golf and putting the children to bed – that's not seen in the same way. It is more difficult for a woman to talk about herself without triggering prejudices about emotional capacity, time and the ability to juggle domestic commitments and deal with conflict.

Any other comments?

Finally, we asked our headhunters for any other comments.

> We do get requests from chairmen. They sometimes say they would prefer to have a woman, and genuinely mean it. But companies are more risk aware now and many more jobs stipulate "must have proven experience in X".

> There's also the globalization issue – it imposes certain restrictions on what's acceptable or unacceptable in relation to gender for companies with representation in the Middle East, for instance. It's a new dimension that wasn't there five or ten years ago.

> I've not witnessed companies actively not wanting to appoint a woman, but there are international and economic factors that are still acting against the appointment of women.

> There's a sort of smirk that appears on male faces when you mention women and leadership – "Oh, this thorny old issue again" – but there's a growing awareness that women can bring distinctive qualities to a board. Women are good at multitasking. Men are more linear in their approach to work; they focus on one thing at a time. You need both approaches – you have to deal with things in line-abreast as well as in line-astern, because you may not always have the time to deal with things systematically. Men have to learn that command and control isn't the only management style that's effective; women have to learn to focus and prioritize, and that consensus management isn't enough on its own.

This echoes our discussion of complementarity in Chapter 6.

One final observation from a headhunter:

> I still think that, behind every successful woman there is a man who plays a supportive role to his partner and fundamentally holds the family together.

At the third sector conference, a senior City figure urged headhunters to become "passionate exponents of diversity", so that clients didn't "rotate the same old names". He warned them that if they didn't "wake up and start being real advisers", instead of "circulating photocopied CVs", they would "lose their business to online recruiters".

CHAPTER 9

Priming the pipeline

Bush fire

The head of HR at a FTSE 100 company had supported the formation by some of the group's senior female executives of a "women's network". He could scarcely have done otherwise. The CEO was in favor for one thing and for another, the HR director knew these women. He liked and respected them and it was clear from his conversations with them when they proposed the network that they would have got together anyway if the company had withheld its approval or refused to provide administrative support and a modest budget for expenses.

But the HR director wasn't prepared for the reaction.

The half-a-dozen or so emails from men, after the formation of the women's network was announced in the house journal, wanting to know when the men's network would be launched, were predictable enough. They were answered by an article in the following issue of the journal by one of the founders of the women's network. She explained why the network was necessary by giving figures for the representation of women in senior management positions and said that men were welcome to attend the network meetings. The token male opposition died down. It had been rhetorical, rather than heart-felt. Most male managers knew the women had a point.

It was the reaction of other women in the company that was alarming.

A large number of female middle managers asked to join the network. The founders were caught off-guard; they hadn't planned to move on to that stage right away. They supported the applicants, however, and urged them to form their own regional networks. Many did. When these regional women's networks were announced, dozens of female junior managers asked to join them. They in turn were urged to form their own, local networks. Many did.

The HR director took one of the founders of the original network aside and expressed his concerns. "You're lighting fires all over the organization – they might start burning out of control." She thought for a moment, smiled and shook her head. "No. They'll shed more light."

Action has consequences, but so does inaction. If that HR director who was alarmed by the fires started by the women's network (see box) had opposed the network, it would have "emerged" anyway, and would probably have bred its regional and local counterparts. But these "unofficial" networks would have been different. Born of frustration, they would have been less formal, more isolated from the organization, more likely to be opposed to the male majority and perhaps more subversive.

Ralph Stacey, a pioneer of the application of the science of complexity to business and management, says that inside every apparently stable company there is a "shadow" company trying to destroy it. This is both inevitable and as it should be, according to Stacey, because organizations will only be innovative when they're both stable and unstable at the same time.[1]

The legitimate and shadow systems need each other. The legitimate system is needed to provide stability. The shadow system is needed to bring about change. The legitimate system changes by adopting attributes of the shadow system, or having them thrust upon it.

Whether or not their members realize it, women's networks (whether official or unofficial) are shadow system institutions that are trying to replace incumbent, male-dominated hierarchies with more gender-balanced management systems.

At root, they're not the creatures of the enlightened CEOs and HR directors who sponsor and support them. They "emerge" spontaneously from the tension between the female-dominated marketplace and in many cases workforce, and male-led companies that are becoming ever more dependent on the skills and talents of women.

The HR director's alarm at the spontaneous combustion that occurred at his company after the senior women's network was announced is understandable. But, although the fires seemed to be out of *his* control, they were not out of control. The human need to belong and retain the support of friends and colleagues is a powerful form of control, but it is exercised not by an individual, but by the group as a whole. As Stacey put it: "There is control, but no one is in control."

Smart company leaders understand the power of these deeply buried tensions and forces driving the evolution of business. And, although they know that they can't control them or predict their consequences, they also know that it's fruitless and even dangerous to resist them. Companies must maintain their stability, but remain open to challenge from their shadow systems. It is a tricky balancing act. How can companies respond to the gender challenge in a safe, measured way that preserves their stability, while promoting their adaptability?

We offer two kinds of answer to this question in this chapter and the next. In this chapter we focus on what women can do in the short and medium terms to further their careers while companies remain male-dominated, and how companies can work with them. In Chapter 10 we provide some practical advice on how to promote long-term cultural adaptation to the tension between the female-dominated marketplace and the male-dominated company.

Some of these prescriptions aren't always obvious to the leaders of large companies, who, for good business reasons, want to get more women into top management, but are wary of making inappropriate or politically incorrect moves.

Before getting into the prescriptive detail, however, three general points about interventions need to be made.

Men

A certain amount of opposition from men to interventions that favor women is to be expected, because at first sight they seem discriminatory and it stands to reason there can be no pro-female discrimination, without anti-male discrimination. That is why many people, and not only men, object so strongly to women-only short lists. UK readers will remember the outrage that greeted New Labour's demand for women-only short lists of prospective parliamentary candidates before the 1997 general election. The victory of the male heir apparent to a safe Labour seat in Wales in the 2005 general election, when he stood as an independent after a woman-only short list had robbed him of his seat, may have reflected the inequity that voters saw in women-only short lists.

Senior male managers are not normally concerned. They have reached the top already, so they have nothing to lose personally from policies that favor women. And from their elevated vantage points, they see the need for such policies more clearly than less senior males. Male middle managers, however, can see such interventions as obstacles to their advancement.

So, quite apart from the legal considerations, it is essential to position any pro-female intervention as "affirmative action", designed to level the playing field by correcting a market inefficiency, rather than "positive discrimination". Targets are OK, but quotas that reserve, say 30 percent, of senior positions for women are not.

Our colleague Lesley Brook recalls many discussions where positive action (or indeed any talk of gender diversity) was met with strong resistance and concerns about "lowering the standards" or "damaging our meritocracy". But as Lesley says: "the truth is that, for many organizations, a focus on diversity and inclusion is a first step toward a true meritocracy, free of the unintended bias that has historically worked in favor of one group to the exclusion of others."

There is, however, a danger that prospective male employees may be put off by aggressive, in-your-face interventions. They might see them as signs of an institutionalized female bias and ask themselves whether they have what it takes to succeed in the organization.

Although these understandable male objections and misgivings are no reason to refrain from pro-female interventions, they do emphasize the importance of openness and good communications. If men are welcome at women's network meetings, for instance, there is a good chance that they will realize why the women's network is necessary and become more aware of the richness of the female managerial talent pool.

In time, they are likely to notice other benefits. They will see that the interventions they felt threatened by are boosting the confidence and thus the effectiveness of their female colleagues, and contributing to business performance improvements from which everyone gains kudos and material benefits through performance-related reward systems. They may also begin to see such policies as part of a rational long-term corporate strategy and realize, as one of our "marzipan" women put it, that it is "cool and sharp and business focused" to enter into the spirit as well as the letter of the strategy by promoting, developing and otherwise sponsoring women.

The emergence of women's networks as new political powers in companies can also produce changes in or clarifications of company policies, such as the introduction of flexible working or the publication of hitherto unofficial promotion criteria that are of benefit to all.

Diversity and inclusion

Some women object to the bundling of the gender issue with other inclusion issues, such as ethnicity, sexual orientation, disability, age, and so on, into the portmanteau term "diversity". They object, not because they see these other issues as less important, but because they see them as fundamentally different. They worry that handing the gender issue over to what might be called the "diversity industry" leads to a one-size-fits-all approach that takes insufficient account of the problems peculiar to the gender issue.

Women feel the predicament of women personally, not as a micro-component of an overarching problem of equality and human rights that can be addressed by statements of intent to comply with grand policy declarations issued by remote institutions.[2] It is not the macro-inequity that bothers women so much as the micro-inequities they encounter each day in the workplace (see Chapter 10 for more on micro-inequities).

We have some sympathy with this view. The differences between the issue of gender and other inclusion issues do require a separate stream of activity for each. But they are members of the same class of issue (those concerned with exclusion), they share the same goal of inclusion and they demand the same kind of intervention. It makes sense, therefore, to plan, orchestrate and manage all the separate streams of activity within the same strategic framework.

But although there are good practical as well as philosophical reasons for consolidating the management of exclusion issues, they should be analyzed separately, because the reasons for exclusion differ. An understanding of the reasons for exclusion because of gender confers some understanding of the reasons for exclusion because of ethnicity or sexual orientation, but not the whole picture. Once the scale and nature of all exclusion problems are fully understood, however, they can be brought together and dealt with alongside one another.

Gender may not be the most important exclusion issue, but it's clearly the largest, because it involves much the largest excluded group. Age may soon mount a challenge for that dubious honor, but for the moment the scale of the gender issue and the sheer conspicuousness of women's absence from top management put gender in the driving seat of the diversity movement.

It is, therefore, natural for companies concerned about exclusion to focus on gender. It is the big issue and can blaze a trail that other excluded groups can follow. The formation of a women's network can stimulate the formation of other new networks, for example, because the predicaments of women will often exemplify the predicaments of other excluded groups.

Going with the grain

The final point we want to make before embarking on specific prescriptions is that corporate cultures vary enormously and an approach to intervention that is appropriate for one company may do more harm than good in another.

In companies with "laid-back" cultures, an informal approach that persuades and cajoles, rather than instructs, is usually best. Relaxed and flexible cultures won't take kindly to minutely specified initiatives and hosts of new institutions labeled with TLAs (three-letter acronyms). It is not the way they're used to working and changing. In other companies, particularly large global companies with far-flung workforces, bureaucracy and clearly specified procedures, performance measures and incentive systems are often the essence of the culture and a powerful instrument of change.

One company we've worked with has achieved considerable success in filling its female executive pipeline and improving the gender balance at the top of its management hierarchy with a program of intervention that seems to outsiders to be absurdly complicated and bureaucratic. At another company with a more action-oriented culture, similar success is being achieved by a much simpler program based on three or four key initiatives.

The basic principle is horses for courses. All change programs, not just those related to gender, have to go with the grain of the culture, because you can only change a culture from within.

Bearing these points in mind, we now turn to specific prescriptions for filling the pipeline and increasing the representation of women on boards in the short and medium terms, while the longer term initiatives discussed in Chapter 10 take effect.

Analysis

As we noted in Chapter 1, the Cranfield *Female FTSE 100 Report 2004* measured the fullness or otherwise of the UK pipeline for women directors by asking FTSE 100 companies the percentage of women they employed in junior, middle and senior management positions. Only 12 companies supplied information and we suggested that some of them might have done so because they felt they were ahead of the game in this area. It is likely that some (quite possibly most) of the 88 companies that declined to respond to the pipeline questions did so because they simply did not know the answers and were disinclined for one reason or another to seek them out.

Since the tension and lost opportunities that require a company to develop what we call a "gender pipeline strategy" are to do with numbers, the first step is to look at the figures. They need to know the scale of the problem at their own companies in particular and at large companies in general. They need to have the information the Cranfield researchers asked for (see Chapter 1) at their fingertips and know how their numbers compare with the averages for all companies and for those of their closest rivals in the war for talent.

They should look for anomalies – areas or levels of the business where the proportions of women managers are particularly low or decline particularly steeply.

The results of this comparative quantitative analysis of gender will often be surprising, may sometimes be alarming, but will always be illuminating. We were surprised, for example, when one or two of the chairmen who agreed to act as mentors for senior women in other companies in our Cross-Company Mentoring Programme (see Chapter 5) said that there were no suitable women candidates for mentoring in their own management pipelines.

Quantitative analysis gives shape to the problem – qualitative analysis is needed to give it substance. This will take various forms, but the objective is always to get women who are or have been employed in relatively senior positions in the company to talk candidly about their experiences. Some men are astounded when they discover how different the experiences of their female peers have been to their own and what a struggle it has been for women to clamber up to their level. An added complication is that when senior women are asked about the barriers they have encountered climbing the hierarchy, some say they have not been discriminated against because of their gender.

The numbers can come in handy here. It's hard for anyone, man or woman, to continue to deny discrimination when confronted by statistics showing, for example, that women account for 35 percent of junior managers, 28 percent of middle managers, but only 13 percent of senior managers. There is a dawning realization that the sharply contrasting pictures of female and male progression painted by the numbers cannot be fully explained by the usual references to child rearing and historical patterns of participation in college education.

Interviews with junior and middle managers may help to explain why certain women whose abilities were expected to take them further are reluctant to put their feet on the next rung of the career ladder. Is it because they have looked up and don't like what they see or what it would take to get there? If so, why do they stay? Because they're comfortable where they are? If they lack self-confidence, is it because of the male culture? What can be done to encourage them to reach higher? Could coaching or mentoring boost their self-confidence, renew their hunger for promotion or rekindle their desire to realize their potential?

Turnover rates among female employees may well have fallen in recent years as improvements in maternity provision have boosted the numbers who return from maternity leave. But as Sylvia Hewlett and Carolyn Luce reported (see Chapter 2), 37 percent of highly qualified American women (and 43 percent of those who have children) quit work voluntarily, against 24 percent of men, and barely a quarter of high-flying women leavers return to full-time jobs.[3] Interviews with women who are about to leave or have already left may help to explain why an organization is finding it harder than its rivals to keep able women and induce those who leave to return.

Focus groups and informal meetings over dinner can also shed light on the barriers women see to their advancement and other reasons why they might be inclined to leave.

And don't forget the men. Interviews with men at a similar career stage to female interviewees can act as a control group for the research and help distinguish general from gender-specific career development problems. They can also produce original insights of their own about gender barriers. Men will often see or understand things men do consciously or unconsciously to obstruct women of which the obstructed women themselves are unaware.

In addition to revealing gender-related career development problems, these interviews may also reveal more general talent management problems of the kind ScottishPower has been trying hard to solve (see box).

Talent management at ScottishPower

ScottishPower plc is an international energy business listed on the London and New York Stock Exchanges. Through its operating companies, it provides electricity and/or gas services to about six million homes and businesses in the western US and throughout the UK. It generates electricity, operates and maintains power delivery networks and provides a full range of energy supply services, including metering, billing and call center support. In the US, its activities extend to coal mining and gas storage/hub services, and, in the UK, to the supply of gas to its customers.

The company employs over 14,000 people in the UK and the US. Its board and executive team include individuals from a variety of backgrounds with wide experience in the energy industry and international business community. It has three US-based women on its board and there are many more women in top management posts and in the "talent pipeline" in both the UK and US.

ScottishPower is wholly committed to talent management. The executive team meets regularly to review the talent pipeline, and CEO Ian Russell meets senior executives identified as "high potential".

Of the 250 most senior managers in the senior management group, 60 are seen as "high potential". ScottishPower develops them for larger, more complex roles, as part of succession planning. The development program includes:

- attendance at internal development programs
- attendance at a range of executive education programs at leading world business schools
- cross-company career moves including international assignments
- internal mentoring
- external coaching.

ScottishPower was one the first participants in the FTSE 100 Cross-Company Mentoring Programme. At the time of writing, Chairman Charles Miller Smith was a mentor and two senior ScottishPower women managers were mentees.

Evangelism

Once the scale and nature of the problem are well understood, the next step is to broaden awareness of the issues within the organization, and recruit support and generate pressure for change.

The results of the research will often speak powerfully for themselves. In many cases there will be a general awareness that something's wrong – that there are many men, but very few women at the top of the organization, for example – but little understanding of the extent of the problem or the origins of the imbalance. Publishing numbers showing at what levels in the management hierarchy the number of women declines most sharply will create a demand for explanations and focus attention on the key areas.

The results of the qualitative research published in the form of anecdotes or anonymous quotes in the house magazine, or videos of actual interviews, or dramatized versions of them, using actors, can be very powerful at this stage.

In addition to building awareness, the results of the analysis will also provide an empirical starting point for developing a plan of action, and help to identify who needs to be engaged if the plan is to be implemented successfully.

One of the most important, but also the hardest, tasks at this stage is to choose the right sponsor for the campaign. The obvious choice is the most senior female executive in the organization, but she might not be the best choice. Some women at the very top of organizations, who have the "ear" of their CEOs and chairpersons, and who effectively represent their gender on their boards, do not acknowledge that there's a soluble problem.

Not long ago we were invited to lunch by the newly appointed chairman of a large engineering company to talk about gender imbalances on boards. When we arrived we found that our host had also invited his most senior female executive. It quickly became clear that this talented and successful woman didn't share our belief that something could and should be done to redress the gender imbalance at the top of the company. She acknowledged there was a problem, but insisted there was nothing that could be done about it in the short or medium term and that the imbalance would "work itself out" in the long term.

We knew from other conversations we'd had with the chairman that he didn't agree with his female colleague on this matter, but we could also see how difficult it would be for him, given her attitude, to assemble a coalition within the company powerful enough to get much done.

We don't know why she took that view. It may have been because the company was in a very "male" industry (see Chapter 3) and she thought the current gender imbalance was thus natural, and in no need of correction. We know, however, that some other senior women like being the sole representatives of their gender at the top of their organizations. It gives them a cachet among their male colleagues, which would be diluted by the arrival of more women. They may, therefore, see it as in their interests to do nothing and "pull the ladder up behind them", so to speak. This is known as the Queen Bee syndrome. Other successful women, who wouldn't go as far as making it harder for other women to join them, still feel that, since they got to the top, despite the obstacles, they are under no obligation to make the climb any easier for other women.

Although rare, in our experience, these attitudes can make it hard to gather the momentum needed to address gender imbalances on boards. Senior women speak with great authority on gender issues. If they tell their male colleagues that nothing needs to be done, who can gainsay them?

It goes without saying that, if there is such a person, she would not be a suitable sponsor for a gender-balancing campaign. Another woman – perhaps a non-executive director, or better still a senior male executive – should be asked to fill the role.

Executive coaching

There comes a stage in the careers of many able and ambitious women when they begin to feel a little like a fish out of water. Perhaps it's because the fundamental "maleness" of organizational hierarchies (see Chapter 2) becomes more abrasive and harder for women to tolerate, the closer they get to the top. Or perhaps it's because there are simply many fewer women at the top. Those that make it into the "marzipan" layer often begin to feel very exposed and isolated from the gender solidarity that may have sustained them in their climb through their organization's middle ranks. A number of women leaders we have spoken to have mentioned this feeling of being alone – of being unable to look sideways and see other women working at the same level.

Whatever the reasons, some women lose self-confidence as they approach the board. Relationships that were easy and warm before become more difficult and complex. Minor actions and casual remarks acquire new significance in the rarefied atmosphere. Personal strategies and tactics that worked well enough previously seem less effective. The unspoken language of status and politics that most men seem to understand intuitively is harder for women to grasp. They begin to feel they are walking through minefields where one false step might be disastrous. They begin to fear they're "losing it" and become anxious and stressed. For some, a deep-seated fear of being "found out", almost as if they were impostors, becomes self-fulfilling. Recently promoted men often feel this too of course; that they're not up to the big job, with its daunting challenges. But, perhaps because they have more male role models to emulate, men tend to get over their self-doubts more easily than women.

'It's only me," said the senior partner of a large consultancy, running a major business area. She is able, respected by her colleagues and clients alike and regarded as an invaluable asset by her fellow senior partners. But deep down she still sees herself as "little me" and, by inference, is still not convinced her job can be really that important if she is the one who is doing it.

IT'S ONLY LITTLE ME!

© Barbara Shore

Self-deprecation and an apparent lack of self-esteem aren't uncommon among women who have been promoted to senior positions.

A woman recently promoted to the board was finding her new role stressful. She was relatively young, extremely able and was getting plenty of support from her chief executive and peers. But she felt overworked and began to wonder if she was really up to it. The chief executive suggested that she be assigned a "coach", to help her overcome what they were convinced was just a transitional problem.

Although paid for by the employer, the executive coach works, in strictest confidence, for and in the interests of the executive to whom he or she is assigned. Clearly, there are potential conflicts of interest here, and they do arise. They are surprisingly rare, however, and can always be resolved without compromising the coach's primary duty to the person being coached.

Coaches focus on the person rather than the position and nothing about the person being coached is irrelevant or off-limits. Sometimes an apparently trivial remark can reveal thought processes that are preventing the client from developing good business practices. The experienced business coach is always alert for such signs.

At one early coaching session, for example, the conversation turned to the client's daily routine.

"I leave home at seven, walk to the station and normally get to work soon after eight. I like to be in when the others arrive."

"Why stand on the train? It must be packed at that time of the morning. You could have a car pick you up, couldn't you?"

Her coach was pointing out that, by using the cars their positions entitled them to, her fellow male directors claimed quiet stress-free time to think about the issues and problems of the day – time which she was denying herself. They clearly valued their work and preparation time more than she valued hers. This was par for her course. She always seemed to be putting herself last.

The issue here wasn't her lack of assertiveness, but her lack of focused control over her working life and the low value she attached to her job and herself. Once the coach had identified and pointed out these traits, the client could begin to address them.

Another coaching client was the senior IT manager of a public sector organization, who had been headhunted from the private sector. She was offered a coach because her director thought she would need some help in adjusting to working in the public sector. In the event, she did have adjustment problems, although her coach soon discovered that these were as much to do with her diffidence (and an insufficient understanding of how business was conducted at senior levels) as they were with the move from the private to the public sector.

Although highly effective in meetings with her team, in the big set-piece meetings in her new job, she was slow to speak, somewhat passive and thus relatively invisible. Her coach realized that she did not understand that, at the level she had now reached, meetings were vitally important theatre. She was used to doing business and taking real decisions at meetings. She didn't realize that at these exalted levels, quite a lot of the horse-trading was done in corridor chats and coffee-room conversations before the formal meetings.

Her coach explained how such high-level meetings actually worked and urged her to use her voice – always speak at meetings, participate, register her presence – but also to ensure that meetings were not her only platform for exerting influence and asserting herself. She has changed her behavior as a result, found her voice and proved her value. Nowadays, she is not content simply to fill gaps in conversation – she is seen as wise and authoritative, and has been invited to sit on other boards.

It's undoubtedly true that some newly promoted men are also hesitant and fail to grasp right away how the rules – of meetings in particular and the game in general – change at senior levels. But, perhaps because of their innate aptitude for hierarchy climbing (see Chapter 2) and the existence of more senior male role models, they soon learn how to participate effectively. In our experience, women are more reluctant to "occupy the space" associated with the new job, especially if they feel they have not fully mastered it. Men are perhaps more prepared to take chances in areas they have not fully mastered.

A third example of the use of coaching concerned a newly promoted woman at a leading UK bank who, initially, did not like the idea of being assigned a coach. She felt that this might imply some sort of inferiority or remedial need. As a courtesy to her boss – since he had asked her to – she went to see a coach and after an awkward, inconclusive discussion, the prospective coach asked the woman if she would be interested in two observations about her body language during the meeting. The woman nodded a little hesitantly and sat down again.

'You were sitting on the edge of your seat", said the coach. "Your back was not supported. You weren't occupying your space – you looked temporary, as if you didn't really believe you had a right to be sitting there. And, when you talked, your whole body tended to slump slightly to the left – you were effectively telling your listeners you were off-balance." The observations led to a more open conversation and a series of coaching sessions that have helped the client not simply to occupy, but to use her personal space. The sessions were successful, because the coach was able to move the relationship on into areas of potential business benefit. The best coaches have plenty of direct, personal experience of what it feels like to sit in the hot seat at the top of an organization.

Some women come to senior jobs feeling that they don't belong there – that they are, in some sense, interlopers, or pretenders. With that underlying sense, they often find it difficult to be explicit about their ambitions. In extreme cases they may hardly dare to admit to having any. As one coach put it, they need to "buccaneer a bit" and take a few more risks. The role of the coach is often to convince the clients that they have a right to be there, and must "occupy their space" effectively. Such coaching often has the effect of showing the female client that she is there, as much because of who she is as a human being, as of what she does in her operating role.

Taking control in this way can be disconcerting at first, because it means that, instead of reacting passively to events, the female executive has to take the initiative and make things happen. This may require her to set down the basis on which she's willing to work, which she may well have seen successful male colleagues do. Some female executives newly appointed to boards can get sucked into the maelstrom of committedness. They must not fall in love with the organization, because the organization can't love them back.

As these cases show, coaching can help recently promoted women deconstruct and understand their experiences, thoughts and feelings. They may prefer informal structures and relationships, but when moving up to a senior role, they are entering a level where structures and relationships may be a good deal more formal. They must learn to live with that. And although they may loathe office politics, they must recognize that they now work at a level where politics are endemic and unavoidable. Despite their gender's general dislike of "politicking", many women turn out to be very good at it, not by becoming more like men, but by using their feminine qualities effectively.

Coaching can be a great help here. By "strengthening the musculature" of a female executive – building up inner resilience to support her competence – a coach can give the sponsoring company access to more of her potential, more quickly.

Coaching is not for everyone. Some women always feel included and have the self-confidence, when elevated, to occupy their new spaces unaided. Other women will find that, when adjusting to the challenges of high office, the personal support and professional counsel of an experienced, business-oriented coach is invaluable.

Mentoring programs and role models

Coaching (personal, confidential, one-to-one support) isn't for all levels either. It is relatively expensive and should be reserved for those who hold (or are likely, within a relatively short time, to hold) high office. It's particularly useful in helping executives to acclimatize to the rarefied atmosphere at the top of organizations. It focuses on traits and behavior and helps a client to apply her skills and competence effectively.

Mentoring is a less expensive and less intensive way to provide one-to-one support for people heading for the top. It's particularly useful for those who have yet to reach a level where a coach would be either appropriate or economically justifiable.

The European Coaching and Mentoring Council tried for many years to define the two activities and distinguish them from each other. It abandoned the attempt. There are so many variations of each that encroach on the other's territory that the line between coaching and mentoring is, and will always remain, blurred. It may help to think of them as points on a continuum of one-to-one support activities for executives, with mentoring at the lighter end of the spectrum and coaching at the heavier end.

Thus, coaching relationships will involve regular monthly or more frequent meetings and in-depth examinations and analyses of how the individuals fit their talents and personalities to the jobs in hand, and the relationships surrounding them. In mentoring relationships, individuals might meet their mentors only once a quarter, and the focus is on examining career progress and, for the mentors, ensuring that the mentees think through major career decisions when the need arises.

For practical reasons involving confidentiality and trust, coaching has to be performed by someone outside the organization. Although mentoring can also be provided by someone outside the organization (see Chapter 5), it's more often provided by someone senior within it, although there is always a need to ensure that the "someone" has no personal interest in the career of the mentored individual.

Putting it another way, within most large organizations, one could say that coaching involves a relationship between an executive and an outsider that is focused on personal as well as professional and leadership development, while mentoring involves a relationship between an executive and a senior insider focused on career development. A coach helps a coachee realize his or her potential, as a human being as well as a professional, but a mentor helps a mentee to advance his or career in the organization to which both belong. The FTSE 100 Cross-Company Mentoring Programme is unusual, in that the mentors and mentees work at *different* organizations, but in most other respects it conforms to the classical mentoring model (see Chapter 5).

One possible reason why the Programme has worked so well is that, although mentor and mentee do not share an organization, they share a milieu – the "space" on and around the board. As one mentor was at pains to emphasize, when he talked about "the gap", the differences between that space on and around the board between companies are less significant, in some respects, than those between that space and areas lower down the hierarchy within the same company. By and large, women appear to find it harder than men to negotiate the gap between a position where the board is out of reach, to a position where it is within touching distance.

Mentoring, whether intercompany or intra-company, can help both women and men acclimatize to this near-board milieu much faster than would otherwise be possible and thus to prepare themselves for their eventual elevation.

Career development programs for women

Action is also needed to encourage more women to put themselves forward as candidates for high office, particularly at the levels where the analysis shows sharp declines in the number of women being promoted or applying for promotion. This is the pipeline problem. However eager the organization's leaders may be to promote more women to top jobs, there is little they can do if there are no women eager and qualified for promotion lower down the hierarchy. Career development programs specifically targeted at women can help fill that pipeline if they follow some simple design guidelines.

They should involve plenty of group work and cover general issues, such as career planning, self-confidence, flexible working hours and environments and differences between male and female communication and leadership styles. In addition to general topics the program should also cover matters that have been revealed by the initial analysis or otherwise become apparent that are peculiar to the industry or the organization.

All-female group work is important for two related reasons. First, because it ensures that the real issues are brought out into the open more easily, and thus made more discussable. Opening up issues that women are aware of as personal problems, but have never talked about or had reason to believe may be shared by others, can be very cathartic. "Oh my goodness", one woman might think, when hearing a woman she hardly knows from some other part of the organization describing perfectly her own feelings of frustration in a group setting, "it's not just me!"

For many women, the experience of being part of an all-female "cohort", as the modern, still military parlance has it, in a work environment is quite new. Many find the opportunity it offers them to review their career goals and development with female colleagues motivating and empowering.

The second related reason why group work is important in women-only career development training is that it can create the kernel of gender solidarity from which a women's network might then emerge.

But acting as a Trojan Horse or prototype for a women's network is not the main objective here. The programs we are discussing are designed to give women the confidence to keep going, and help them learn some of the skills they need when applying for senior jobs, such as marketing themselves with well-crafted CVs, canvassing the personal support of senior executives for their candidacies and generally raising their personal profiles.

Feedback from one all-female work group included:

"Women in organizations need an extra hand like this to climb over or avoid crashing into barriers."

"It addressed many barriers to progression and advancement. It was fantastic to be together with an all-female group."

"It made me more aware of the importance of impact and exposure. I came away with some great ideas."

The shape and balance of women-only career development training programs will inevitably be seen as a reflection of what the leadership perceive as the key problem areas, so great care is needed when designing them.

Childcare and flexible working

A year or so ago we were invited to 11 Downing Street, in London (the home of the UK's Chancellor of the Exchequer), to discuss what could be done to get more women onto the boards of large companies. We were surprised when the discussion quickly turned into a debate about childcare.

We were surprised, not because we do not believe that childcare provision is both important and essential for women's advancement in organizations, or that there is no more to be done in this area, but because so much has already been done, by both companies and governments in recent years, that it is no longer reasonable to blame the absence of women in boardrooms on the lack of childcare provision and inflexible working arrangements.

Climbing the ladder up to the boardroom is not, of course, the ambition of every woman and we're not suggesting it should be. For those who do choose to climb, however, different barriers will appear at different stages.

Figure 9.1, developed by a WDoB member Hilary Samson-Barry, head of child health, maternity and women's health at the UK Department of Health, illustrates the point. Companies need to help women to negotiate these steps.

On the gender front in the war for talent, good childcare provisions and flexible working are "qualification criteria" – if you don't provide them, you have no hope of becoming an attractive employer for able and ambitious women. The objective for companies trying to attract more women should be to satisfy "differentiation criteria"; qualities that can earn the company a reputation for regarding their lack of senior women as a serious problem and for developing bold, innovative approaches to solving it.

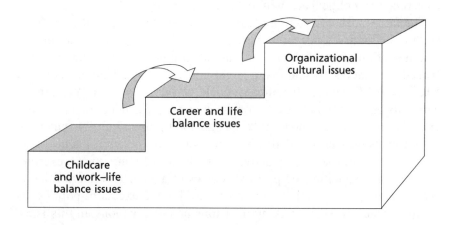

Figure 9.1 Moving on up: issues that affect the career progression of women

Aurora Gender Capital Management, for example, provides an invaluable web-based service (Where Women Want to Work) for women who want to compare potential employers according to how well they "qualify" in terms of their women-friendly policies and the extent to which their gender-balancing strategies and initiatives "differentiate" them from their peers.[4]

Ambitious women who have reached or are about to reach the marzipan layer from which board candidates are selected will, in most cases, have long since sorted out their childcare arrangements, although elder care issues could be looming. The women-only career development training discussed above should ensure that women are aware of statutory and corporate childcare benefits and provisions and know how to use them, but most of the time should be devoted to career-related issues, such as the tendency of women to lack confidence at senior levels and differences in male and female management, communication and leadership styles.

The work–life balance is no longer a female-only issue nor, at a time when the population is aging and elder care is a growing issue, is it just related to child-rearing. In their 2005 paper *Kaleidoscope careers,* Mainiero and Sullivan urge companies to "redesign the way work is done" to support work–life integration for men and women.[5]

Women's networks

Most women say they loathe organizational politics and there is no reason to doubt them. We don't much like it ourselves, but we recognize that we have to engage in it; indeed, we recognize that writing this book could be construed as a political act, with political objectives.

The fact is that, whether business women like it or not, politics, defined as "the art and science of government ... the form, organization and administration of a state" (OED), is an integral part of organizational life. Indeed, it is inconceivable that a large, integrated organization, such as a FTSE 100 or Fortune 500 company, could be free of politics. When many gather together to pursue a purpose, such as creating value for sharehold-ers, what we mean by the term "organizational politics" always emerges, or "raises its ugly head" (depending on your point of view). It's the name we give to clearly necessary activities, such as assigning power, exerting influence and soliciting support for courses of action. It is not politics as such that people (including men) object to. It's the excess of politics, its inappropriate use when making decisions and dispositions and its isms, such as nepotism or cronyism, which many men and even more women find intolerable and unfair.

There is nothing right or wrong about organizational politics – it just is.

But it gets out of hand. It can insinuate itself into areas it doesn't belong and make a mockery of commitments to principles such as fairness, inclusion or promotion based purely on merit. Paracelsus, the 16th-century physician who attributed medicinal properties to opium and mercury, said: "The poison is in the dose." It is true of organizational politics. Some is healthy. Too much can be addictive and dangerous.

The fact that politics is necessary and inevitable in large companies, and the wealth of anecdotal evidence that women don't like politics as much as men (there's no evidence that they are any less adept at it), and are less willing to "play" it, creates a bias in favor of men, particularly within organizations where the politics has become pathological.

Establishing a women's network can help to remove or at least offset that bias. As a more or less formal way to bring women in the company together, a women's network seems at first sight to be no more significant than a bunch of guys in the habit of meeting for a drink after work. But, as we noted at the start of Chapter 2, women as women in the organization, have more to talk about than men as men in the organization. As a shadow system institution (see above), a women's network can acquire considerable political power that can be used in pursuit of agendas that bring about significant change. A study by Demos, the UK think tank, found that women's networks can promote diversity by challenging invisible structural obstacles.[6]

In one case, a high priority for a new women's network was to establish the criteria that senior managers used to judge individual potential. Its queries revealed a lack of transparency, which led to clarifications that were of benefit to all employees.

As well as giving women a voice, supporting their development and being an autonomous power base from which to seek information, exert influence and challenge policies and decisions, women's networks also give their members a new place to shine. The founders, leaders and active members of women's networks tend to become better known in the formal as well as the shadow organization. The Demos study found that over a third of members felt that they had gained more confidence from their involvement in women's networks.

Our own experience is that women's networks help members to hone their own networking skills, make connections in the formal organization, and expose junior and middle managers to senior role models.

There are some downsides, however. There is a risk, for example, that the isolation of the women's network from the formal organization will make it a safe, comfortable haven for some women, and thus weaken their engagement with the formal organization. There is also a danger that some women will become accustomed to exercising power and exerting influence collectively, through the network, and cease to challenge decisions and debate issues as individuals. We believe, however, that the collective ability to challenge provided by women's networks more than compensates for these risks.

There's another risk; that the extra confidence that a women's network gives to its founders and leading lights will make these able and politically adept women more aware of their worth, more ambitious and more inclined to move on to more high-powered jobs elsewhere if they find their abilities are not recognized in their own company. The women's network at one company we know of was founded by a group of eight women in 1997. They still meet once a year for lunch. At the 2004 lunch, only two of them still worked for the company where they had jointly created one of the first formal women's networks at a major UK company.

The increased self-confidence and political adeptness that women's networks can give to their members are among their most valuable outputs, but they will be lost to others if the company fails to anticipate and accommodate them. Women's networks should be seen as training grounds from which new leaders are likely to emerge from time to time. They should be watched, as well as listened to, and given political, administrative and financial support, so that while not part of the formal organization (that would be fatal), they are not too isolated from it either.

They can become valuable resources for the company too. As well as keeping leaders honest about the hard business issues relating to gender, they can contribute to a variety of business activities from new product design and marketing, to strategy formulation and stakeholder management (CSR programs, and so on).

Ford has used its women's network to provide insights into some aspects of car design; Barclays, the UK retail bank, gets advice from its women's network when developing products aimed at women.

PwCwomen, the women's network at PricewaterhouseCoopers, was formed three years ago and its achievements have already been recognized in the UK by the campaigning group, Opportunity Now. It focused initially on providing personal development for women in the firm, but is now trying to embed the network into the business by involving its members in other areas, such as attracting women clients and recruiting more women to the firm. Sarah Churchman, PwC's head of student recruitment and diversity, says that PwCwomen "is contributing significantly to realizing the firm's declared vision of becoming a 'leader in its chosen markets and a great place to work'".

Recruitment

To end at the beginning, strategies for recruiting talented women are also necessary to prime the talent pipeline with a good blend of the genders in the first place.

Attracting young women with advertising designed to appeal to them and assigning female company representatives to milk-round duty in schools and on university campuses are now par for the course. These are not enough on their own, however, because attracting female applicants is one thing, and choosing the best women and persuading them to join you, instead of one of your competitors, is quite another.

A deeper adaptation of the front end of the pipeline to the female half of the marketplace can only be achieved when the company's selection criteria and competence frameworks are fully aligned with the company's declared recruitment strategy and prevailing market conditions. The fact that there is a clear recruitment strategy doesn't guarantee this, because, as we saw in Chapter 6 in another context, people responsible for recruitment may be the unwitting thralls of some defunct builder of competence frameworks.

Thorough reviews of the organization's recruitment processes and selection criteria are essential to identify hidden gender biases, and both men and women must be trained to avoid them. Critical process reviews of this kind are routine at some companies. At Shell, women's network members advocated such reviews and reforms and successfully pressed for their introduction.

Nudging the culture

All these initiatives (coaching, mentoring, development, women's networks and recruitment criteria reviews) can help to bring more women up through the pipeline and into senior positions. But, as more or less permanent features of the corporate environment, they do more than that. They make the leadership's interest in and commitment to addressing gender issues visible; they establish precedents and principles that guide and encourage other excluded groups; and the evidence suggests that they have a positive overall effect on HR practices and the working climate.

In short, they act as catalysts for the long-term cultural changes we discuss in the next chapter.

References

1. *Complexity and Creativity in Organizations*, Ralph D. Stacey, Berrett-Koehler, 1996.
2. Fairness for all: A New Commission for Equality and Human Rights, DTI Cm 6185, May 2004.
3. Off-Ramps and On-Ramps. Keeping Talented Women on the Road to Success, Sylvia Ann Hewlett and Carolyn Buck Luce, *Harvard Business Review*, March 2005.
4. www.www2wk.com.
5. *Kaleidoscope careers: An alternate explanation for the "opt-out" revolution*, Lisa A. Mainiero and Sherry E. Sullivan, Academy of Management Executive, 2005.
6. *Girlfriends in High Places*, H. McCarthy, Demos, 2004.

CHAPTER 10

Changing the game

The main challenge in a major change program, such as the integration of a significant acquisition, the creation of a new business, or some kind of fundamental cultural transformation, is to prepare the people involved for their new roles.

Theatrical techniques can be helpful here. In one variation on the theme, a group of people are asked to "act out" their future roles themselves, in a specially commissioned play under the guidance of an experienced director.

"We had gathered together various parts of the business, to create a brand new business", a participant recalled. "We were starting with a clean sheet of paper, but the people brought a lot of baggage with them. The director ran some rehearsal games first to remove our inhibitions and then we acted out the post-merger situation. People became very open, major issues came to the fore and the solutions became obvious. We designed the new business during that session."

In other cases professional actors take the roles of the main protagonists and employees are invited to criticize the performance afterwards.

In one such case, a company's top 200 managers were invited by their CEO to watch a play about the company set in the future. Professional actors were hired to play the dramatis personae. The CEO was played by a woman. It was once traditional in the English pantomime for the leading man to be played by a woman, but this was not England and the actor playing the CEO was not masquerading as a man. After the final bows had been taken, members of the audience were asked to comment on the performance.

"I couldn't take the scenario seriously", said one.

"Why not?", asked the CEO.

"Because we'll never have a female CEO in my lifetime."

Such incredulity is common and stems from the rarity of women CEOs. In her book, *The Naked Truth*, Margaret Heffernan tells of an encounter she had in Boston in 2000 when she was CEO of the US business services group, CMGI.[1]

I was riding on the elevator at work when the doors opened and a young woman got on. After a few seconds of the usual silence, she looked at me and said, "Excuse me. Are you Margaret?"

"Yes," I answered, not knowing what to expect next.

"I just wanted to meet you and shake your hand," she said. "I've never met a female CEO before."

The incredulous member of the audience of that play with a female CEO gave the CEO of the day an unlooked for opportunity to express what he regarded as an important aspect of his vision for the company. He told the skeptic and the rest of the audience that he wanted them all to be able to foresee a time in the not too distant future when a woman held his job.

Vision

A few companies, very few, have or have had female CEOs, so it is not hard for their employees to imagine having another one. Unless, of course, she has failed and opinion has since converged on the view that her failure is attributable to her gender. (Can anyone imagine a male CEO's failure being attributed to his gender?)

For most companies, however, becoming relaxed about the prospect of having a female CEO is a sign of the kind of long-term cultural change we discuss in this chapter. It is evidence that the company's employees as a discrete social group have overcome, or are in the process of overcoming, their unconscious conception of their organization as inherently male.

But it would be wrong to couch the vision in these specific terms. What is needed is not a belief in the plausibility of having a female CEO at some time in the not too distant future, but a belief in the need for a culture without prejudice that does not exclude anyone from high office on grounds of gender (for the purposes of this book), race, religion, and so on.

The ideal of an *inclusive culture*, where everyone has an equal opportunity to realize his or her potential and where difference is valued rather than merely tolerated has, when expressed with conviction, a powerful appeal to people of both sexes. The belief that things work better when everyone is respected and treated fairly, when promotion and rewards are based solely on merit and when the market for talent and ability is free and unbiased is widespread. Most people, particularly those brought up within a liberal democratic tradition, would subscribe to it without hesitation.

The belief that, in an organization in which women account for one-third of the workforce, there should be, other things being equal, a one-in-three chance that the next CEO will be a woman follows from this general belief in the desirability of a fair, even-handed allocation of power and reward. It's the "normal" state of affairs. A wish to promote more women to senior positions can and should be characterized as a wish to bring normality to an organization, or class of organization, that has been burdened for various reasons with an abnormal gender balance at the top.

The indisputable fact that there are fewer women in senior executive roles in business than their representation in the population and their power as consumers warrant is a consequence, not of women's relative competence or conscious male prejudices, but of an inefficiency in the market for human capital. Women have a lot to contribute to the governance and guidance of companies and if the market for executive talent were efficient, they would occupy a much larger proportion of senior and board positions than they do currently.

But it is one thing to recognize the existence of these inefficiencies and quite another to correct them. Their roots run so deep, and are so tightly woven into the fabric of organizations, that we cannot expect the market's own self-correcting quality to remove them any time soon. There is much to be gained from such a removal, however, and a company that gives the self-correcting mechanisms of its own internal talent market a deliberate nudge toward a better (more value-creating) gender balance is likely to achieve a significant competitive advantage (Figure 10.1).

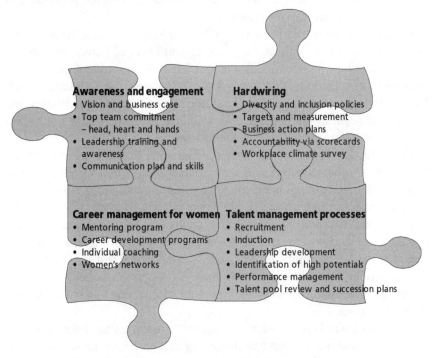

Figure 10.1 Sustaining competitive advantage
Source: Brook Graham LLP, April 2005, www.brookgraham.com

High-level commitment

It goes without saying (although practically everyone who writes or speaks about change says it) that successful change requires active commitment at the top. To stand any chance of success, efforts to achieve a better gender balance on boards must be sponsored and actively supported by leaders who acknowledge, and are determined to capture, the value that more women directors will bring to boards.

Gender-balancing initiatives will never create much value for shareholders if their objective is to enable the company to tick the boxes of political correctness. They must be seen as important strategic investments designed to achieve long-term improvements in governance and management.

It is much easier for a CEO to recognize the company's gender imbalance as a problem that needs to be solved, however, than for him/her to understand the nature and origins of the problem and work out how to solve it.

In companies where solid progress is being made toward solving the gender imbalance problem, you will usually find CEOs and other senior leaders who see value in gender difference and are, therefore, investing personal time and effort in investigating the details of the problem and searching for a portfolio of solutions.

Company leaders can brief themselves in various ways. To acquire a general picture of the subject, they can read articles and books, such as this one, and study the latest national statistics. To build a picture of the issue for their own organizations, they can ask for the internal data, including feedback from focus groups, employee attitude surveys and exit interviews, and so on, and seek the knowledge and guidance of those within the organization who know and care about such issues.

One effective method is to assign a "personal learning partner" to the CEO (and to other directors and senior executives, if that seems appropriate). The detailed arrangements may vary, but the basic idea is that there's one particular woman who the CEO meets informally three or four times a year, say, and to whom he can turn for counsel and explanations if gender problems or puzzles arise. An advantage of this arrangement is that, although the relationship has to be strictly confidential if it is to feel "safe" for the leader, it can do much, through a process of osmosis, to foster mutual understanding between the company's leadership and senior women in the workforce.

One final point here. Leaders should never assume that, once achieved, the inclusive culture they have been seeking will be self-perpetuating. It may become so eventually, but it will be under constant threat in the meantime from the temptation during a business downturn to revert to the "old ways" and see gender-balancing initiatives as luxuries which the company can no longer afford. The leader must keep gender initiatives going through fair weather and foul and through successive generations of leadership, as Unilever has done (see box), and must continually reaffirm their importance.

Diversity at Unilever

The diversity program at the consumer products group Unilever was launched under the joint chairmanship of Niall Fitzgerald and Antony Burgmans, and continues to receive strong support from Patrick Cescau, the current CEO. The program is based on the belief that Unilever's culture has to become more feminine.

The early focus was on women and local employees who the company regard as "key resources". Unilever started monitoring attrition and promotion rates in these groups in 1992.

As Rhodora Palomar-Fresnedi, the group's global diversity director, neatly puts it, the focus on numbers "gets it started, but doesn't get it going". The driver of change at Unilever has been the evolution of a philosophy of inclusion and embracing difference, exemplified by the practice of "looking through a diversity lens in everything we say and do".

The main focus has been on the top 200 executives. Current initiatives for promoting inclusion and focusing the Unilever diversity lens on gender and nationality in particular, include the following.

1. Reciprocal mentoring
This was initially targeted at gender. The top seven executives all agreed to mentor a senior woman, and be mentored by her. The mentors offer career advice and their mentees help them to understand what it's like to be a woman in Unilever.

The program began in 2002 and was evaluated in January 2004. The results were very encouraging. Mentors appeared to have learned a great deal about the predicament of Unilever's women, particularly about the attitudes and expectations of generation X women, and their mentees were much more aware of the nature of the work of senior executives.

2. Getting into the skin
A leadership program for high potentials based on Unilever's strategy of connecting better with the consumer. The idea is to "get into the skin" of someone entirely different – actually to experience diversity, rather than merely learn about it. In a widely acclaimed speech at the European Women in Leadership Conference in Geneva in June, 2003, Fitzgerald described his own experience of getting into the skin of a "down and out".

3. Top-level commitment and leadership communication
Senior leaders make themselves visible and audible on the subject of women in leadership. Fitzgerald's Geneva speech, another by Fergus Balfour, Unilever's senior VP leadership development, in September 2003 at the European Council for Work, Life and Diversity in Brussels and a third by Palomar-Fresnedi at Oxford University's Business Economics Programme in July 2004 have been circulated within Unilever and published on the website, leaving employees in no doubt about how seriously their leaders take the issue.

4. Traffic lights
Having recruited the leadership to the cause, the company is targeting the group's 223,000 employees around the world. "Global diversity councils" are being established and a "traffic light" system has been introduced for the seven directors. Each director has a diversity plan he or she reviews in a private session with the diversity director at which the two judge whether progress is green, amber or red.

Hard-wiring the system

It is not enough for an organization's leaders to be convinced of the need to get more women onto the board. The conviction must reach deep down into the culture, because it's only from the cultural depths that women who are more than mere tokens will rise to the top echelons of management. Senior women hired from outside can help, by acting as role models and catalysts, but the main, long-term objective must be to attract ambitious young women to relatively junior jobs, by persuading them that their talents will take them higher in your company than they would in other companies.

Once the commitment of the leadership has been won for the cultural change needed to achieve a better gender balance, senior managers must be persuaded to sign up to it and act accordingly. This is vital, because if the commitment to change is not shared at all levels of management, too few women will enter the pipeline from which future leaders emerge.

The measures needed to hard-wire a company's commitment to appointing more women to senior positions are no different in principle from those needed to achieve any major business change – develop a strategy, derive business plans and targets from it, construct appropriate measurement systems and make appropriate adjustments to reward and recognition systems. In short, build a control, measurement and reward environment that encourages employees to act in ways that will lead to the achievement of the strategic objective.

Diversity at TNT

TNT is a global provider of mail, express and logistics services. The group employs over 163,000 people in 64 countries and serves over 200 countries. The topic of diversity and inclusion was first discussed in early 2004 and the company has taken carefully planned steps to introduce it to its workforce.

Support from the top
Adam Travis, TNT's diversity manager, is responsible for implementing diversity within TNT. He says: "Our approach with this initiative is pragmatic. Whilst we need to ensure that TNT senior management fully understand it so that they can support it and "walk the talk", we also want to engage with employees and get regular feedback."

Links and networks
Diversity represents change and TNT has put in place a practical framework to build longer term change. Continues Travis: "Rather than appointing diversity champions from the center, we asked for volunteers from the different business units and countries to be the links between employees and head office. We provided toolkits, guidelines and suggestions, but they are responsible for implementing diversity in their own areas. No two initiatives are the same, because we have so many different nationalities, cultures and ideas. We also created a network for the professional development of women, which provides opportunities for mentoring, sharing best practice and career progression."

Investors in People (IiP)
TNT Express, one of three divisions in the TNT Group, is the first ever company to achieve worldwide IiP recognition and Travis wants to ensure that the diversity initiatives are aligned with IiP. He says: "By embracing our different cultures and ideas, we are encouraging everyone to perform well. Diversity and inclusion and IiP work naturally together."

It is true that targets for people variables are more difficult to develop and police than those for financial variables, but they are used routinely in such areas as recruitment and headcount reductions. Denise Kingsmill's report on women's employment and pay included a section on the management of human capital[2] and the "intangible assets monitor", developed by Karl-Erik Sveiby, the Swedish knowledge management guru, is a well-proven tool for measuring and managing intellectual capital.[3]

It's a cliché in business that you get what you measure, so if you want to know whether a diversity program is a real strategic commitment, or just a cosmetic, nice-to-have point-scoring initiative, you need look no further than the measurement and incentive systems associated with it.

Wal-Mart responded to widespread criticisms of its labor practices in June 2004 by linking executive bonuses to the company's diversity goals and setting up an in-house compliance group to oversee pay and hours. CEO Lee Scott announced at the annual meeting that executive bonuses would be cut by up to 7.5 percent in 2004, and up to 15 percent in 2005, if the number of women and members of ethnic minorities hired as managers was not proportionate to the number of female and ethnic minority applicants.[4]

That Royal Dutch/Shell Group was taking diversity and inclusion seriously became evident in 1997, when the company published global workforce goals and processes for measuring progress toward them. A central component of Shell's sophisticated and widely admired diversity program is its global diversity and inclusiveness (D&I) standard developed by the Global Diversity Council at the request of the oil group's governing body, the Committee of Managing Directors. It was introduced worldwide in 2002.[5]

The D&I standard provides high-level guidance for diversity management and applies the lens of diversity to areas such as leadership, governance, the development of strategy and objectives, support systems and the deployment of resources. To promote and establish the new standard, the group included diversity measures in its performance "scorecard", introduced a diversity reporting system for leaders of the country businesses and required all senior managers to attend "diversity awareness" sessions.

The most appropriate hard-wiring techniques will vary, of course, and will typically emulate approaches that have been effective in the company in the past. But, generally speaking, large, complex, widely dispersed, global groups must go about things in more systematic ways than smaller companies with more closely knit workforces and more intimate cultures.

The initiatives, interventions and prescriptions described in this chapter and in Chapter 9 presuppose the existence of some kind of agency (a change team, or a political coalition within the organization) that may have been formally constituted or may have emerged spontaneously from the tensions discussed in Chapter 9. Whether its origins are official or unofficial and whether it operates formally or informally, this group will usually be the driving force behind an organization's efforts to bring more women through the talent pipeline and ultimately onto the board.

If the group is informal and unofficial, it may be useful to endow it with formal status, as the organization's official diversity council. In such cases, the CEO or another senior executive should be appointed chair of the council, or whatever name seems most appropriate, to convey how seriously the leadership takes the issue. As the saying goes, "what interests my boss fascinates me."

Micro-inequities

One of us was sent a copy of an old cartoon, showing six people sitting at a long table. A man, presumably the chairman, is sitting at one end of the table, two men are sitting on his left, another two men are sitting on his right and, next to them, furthest from the chairman, there is a woman. The caption reads: "That's an excellent suggestion Miss Triggs. Perhaps one of the men here would like to make it."

Ring any bells?

We would be astonished if it rings no bells with some female readers. That men do not hear women in meetings as well as they hear other men, and do not attach as much value to observations and suggestions made by women as they do to the same observations and suggestions made by men, is so common a complaint that it has almost become a cliché.

A friend of ours has encountered the phenomenon so often that she has devised a routine response. "Do you know," she says innocently to the male colleague who has unwittingly stolen her thunder, "I totally agree. My idea sounds so much better coming from you."

This strangely selective male deafness in meetings in which most attendees are men is an example of what are now commonly called "micro-inequities".

As the name implies, a micro-inequity is a minor unfairness or discourtesy that is no big deal on its own, and certainly nothing worth making a fuss about, but which, when combined with other micro-inequities, can add up to a deeply frustrating environment for an ambitious woman (see box).

Micro-inequities often cited by women

- People, including customers, suppliers and colleagues, address one of your junior male colleagues in the mistaken belief that he's senior to you

- Challenging tasks are given to male colleagues, while your work is "over-checked"

- You're left off distribution lists or information given to male colleagues is withheld from you

- Emails that start: "Gentlemen and ... Claire"

- You're interrupted at meetings, or your contributions are ignored

- A man brings up your earlier, ignored idea at a meeting as his own

- Rolling eyes, sighing, lack of eye contact when you speak

- Team-building functions are inappropriate (quad-bike racing, for example), or at awkward times (golf on Saturday, for example)

- Male executives talk to you about themselves at social functions and express no interest in you

- You frequently find yourself the only woman at a dinner, conference or team meeting, and miss out on "chats in the corridor"

- Whenever the subject of diversity is mentioned, everybody looks at the women in the group

Men can be victims of such discourtesy too, particularly when they are new to their jobs and have yet to "occupy their space" (see Chapter 8). In our experience, however, women are victims of such micro-inequities more often, and some are quite gender-specific. For example, one of us discovered some months after she had been appointed to a new job that the rest of the team were in the habit of having a drink together in a pub every Friday evening after work. It was not her "scene", but it may have been important, and it was certainly a relevant feature of the team culture. She was not told about it. The men said afterwards that they assumed she would be doing the weekly shop on a Friday evening.

A female South African executive, who'd been an ardent rugby union fan all her life, discovered – purely by chance – that her company had a corporate hospitality box at Newlands, where the big international rugby matches are played. Her elation at the discovery turned to dismay and frustration when she was told that her male colleagues were automatically put on the circulation list for big match tickets.

There is nothing deliberate or consciously discriminatory about a micro-inequity. When a man becomes aware of having made such a faux pas, he will often be dismayed and offer profound apologies.

That's what makes micro-inequities so hard to eradicate. Their origins are below the threshold of conscious awareness. They are woven into the fabric of the organization; embedded in the deep culture of the inherent maleness of hierarchical organizations (see Chapter 2). But, at a subliminal level, they characterize an organization and how women come to see their role and value in it. A senior male executive who has studied micro-inequities, says they are "multiple small injustices, which wear you down over time".

PINTS ALL ROUND ?

© Barbara Shore

With cultures, the devil is in the detail; in the micro-messages employees and other constituencies are constantly transmitting and receiving. It is no comfort to individuals that the organization's official culture is open and meritocratic, if the micro-messages they are receiving day in, day out make them feel excluded and undervalued. On its own, each micro-message is insignificant. Taken together, they are probably the most corrosive form of discrimination in modern organizations. They need to be exposed and flushed out of the culture.

Being aware of these micro-inequities and their micro-messages is half the battle. When women become sensitized to micro-inequities and can name the minor irritations they felt previously but could not articulate, they can ask the perpetrators to stop doing it. To take an example from a different context, "sexual harassment" seemed undiscussable until we gave it a name.

Recruiting sympathetic male allies can help too. One of us had a colleague who was sensitive to micro-inequities in meetings and spoke up when he saw her being over-talked.

Meeting behavior is particularly important, because, as we pointed out in Chapter 9, the meeting is the stage. It is where people see you in action. Your performance at meetings affects how other people regard you and talk about you. Someone once said that "in meetings, people are either talking, or waiting to talk". Our view, based on our work with women in groups and one-to-one coaching sessions, is that most women regard meetings, not as theatre, but as collaborative quests for insights and solutions.

Human resources

The organization's HR function will be in the front line of any attempt to change its culture, but it would be unwise for a leader to assume that HR will automatically support and grasp the need for initiatives designed to remove gender barriers to advancement.

The HR function attracts more women and often values them more highly than other business functions. But that does not necessarily mean that HR staff are aware of the gender barriers in other areas of the business. Nor does it mean that, when they are aware of gender barriers, they wish, regard it as part of their jobs or feel equipped or empowered to remove them.

They are a key group, however, in any culture change program and efforts should be made from the outset to engage their support, brief them on the numbers and objectives and provide them with any training they may need to understand the problems and find solutions. If HR is not fully engaged and informed, the chances of a successful outcome are slim.

HR systems and processes should be reviewed and modified, if necessary, to ensure that the fundamentals of attraction, recruitment, development, promotion and retention are at the least unbiased. This is easier said than done, of course, because bias takes many forms. Some of them are so subtle as to be almost invisible. Others that were visible once may have dropped below the threshold of conscious awareness and are working their mischief unseen and unchallenged. As we noted in Chapter 6, the competence frameworks used for promotion and recruitment can remain effective carriers of prejudices and bias that were officially purged many years previously.

Some forms of gender bias in recruitment processes are illegal now. In the UK, for instance, it is against the law to ask a woman during a recruitment interview about her childbearing plans. At some companies, the spirit as well as the letter of this law is complied with, and discrimination on such grounds has disappeared. At other companies, the discrimination lives on in disguise.

Reviews of systems and processes must, therefore, be very thorough. In the US, people talk of viewing systems through different "lenses". Reviewing HR systems and processes through a gender lens could reveal instances of bias that would not have been detected by a neutral review, and may also reveal opportunities to tune HR processes in ways that make the organization more attractive to women.

We would argue that if company leaders regard the lack of women at or near the top of their organizations as a problem that needs to be solved, it is not enough merely to ensure that HR processes comply with the law and have been purged of any obvious bias. They should actually be geared for women. For example, purging HR processes of the macho, military-type language that is still so common in business will remove a deterrent for women.

The HR function can make or break an "assault" on gender barriers. It must be engaged, informed and fully motivated, with appropriate qualitative and quantitative targets. It must also understand the all-important difference between positive/affirmative action, which is a powerful weapon in the war against bias, and positive discrimination, which is unfair and can cause a great deal of trouble.

Change on three levels

To achieve the deep, long-term cultural changes needed to bring more women up to board level, change is required in three areas; individual, team and systems (Figure 10.2).

We naturally look at the world and other people through the lenses of our own experiences, backgrounds, cultures, values and beliefs. In short, we create stereotypes. A culture can only become genuinely inclusive when its members look deep inside themselves, at their assumptions and beliefs, and identify, understand and, if necessary, modify or abandon the attitudes and stereotypes guiding their behavior. This can be difficult, and those assigned

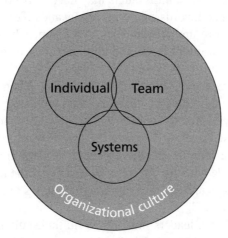

Figure 10.2 Change on three levels
Source: www.brookgraham.com – Jan 2005

SORRY, WHAT DID YOU SAY ?
-I WAS JUST WORKING ON MY NEXT WITTY COMMENT

to help others to understand and adjust their habits of mind should tread softly. The objective should not be to shame men into changing their behavior by confronting them with a catalog of their sins, but to help them to see how attitudes and assumptions they consciously abhor may still affect their behavior at a subconscious level.

Within groups or teams, individuals may need to become more aware of how their behavior and words are perceived by and affect others. They must learn to receive more and transmit less; to listen, when previously they might have merely waited to talk, and to understand, when previously they might have preached. If they see others behaving in ways that exclude, stereotype or oppress, they should challenge them. When forming teams or work groups, they should value difference and inclusion as much as camaraderie, and actively try to form productive cross-gender relationships. Team leaders must learn to recognize the power of difference and how to use it. As a senior female executive put it: "It's not enough to surround yourself with people who are different. You only get the real benefits if you value the differences and create a climate that allows everyone to bring all of themselves to work."

At the system level, leaders must try to rid their cultures of gender bias and barriers by developing the tools, processes, systems and institutions required to make their corporate cultures inclusive. They must set targets and provide the resources to achieve them, measure progress toward those targets and make people accountable for them. Above all, they must promote and exemplify the desired behaviors and see to it that everyone, at every level, understands the business benefits of inclusion.

References

1. *The Naked Truth: A Working Woman's Manifesto on Business and What Really Matters*, Margaret Heffernan, Jossey-Bass, 2004.
2. The Kingsmill Review of Women's Employment and Pay, Department of Trade and Industry, 2001.
3. *The New Organizational Wealth. Managing and measuring knowledge-based assets*, Karl-Erik Sveiby, Berrett-Koehler, 1997.
4. *Wal-Mart Links Executive Bonuses to Diversity Goals*, The Associated Press, June 4, 2004.
5. www.shell.com – About Us – Commitments, Policies and Standards.

CHAPTER 11

Any other business

It will surely not have escaped the notice of the reader that we believe that the boards of our large companies would be more effective and create more value for shareholders if they included more women.

"But what", we hear readers ask, "do you mean by 'more?'" A few more? Quite a few more? Many more? If 10 percent of FTSE 100, 14 percent of Fortune 500, 16 percent of S&P 500 and 17 percent of Fortune 100 constituent directors are insufficient, what would be sufficient, appropriate or satisfactory? What would "good" look like in terms of the gender balance on the boards of our largest companies? It's a fair question and one we have wrestled with endlessly while writing this book.

Our first inclination was to avoid the question altogether, and content ourselves with a simple "more", on the grounds that mentioning any number would be invidious and arouse howls of protest from some people for being too high and from other people for being too low.

We toyed with the idea of putting "significantly", or "substantially" in front of the "more" and explaining our imprecision by suggesting that the appropriate gender balance on the board will vary from company to company, from industry to industry and from time to time. It will vary according to such circumstances, but we know that doesn't excuse us from coming up with an overall, average, "other things being equal" figure.

"More" did not seem enough. It was ducking the question. We felt we had to come up with a number. But what number?

One of our marzipan women told us that although she was "not sure what the figure should be", she was "not in the 50 percent camp". She thought that if women held 20 percent of "serious and not token" board positions "that would be good" (see Chapter 4).

On reflection, we wondered why she was not in the 50 percent camp. And although we recognize that a rise from current levels to 20 percent women directors would be a significant increase, particularly if these appointments also increased the proportion of women executive directors, 20 percent did not seem to us to be enough. It seemed a reasonable medium-term target, within five years, say, but not a satisfactory end point.

We approached the question by reviewing the positions we had taken earlier in the book. We have said that it is not seriously disputed (even by

Larry Summers, president of Harvard, who got into hot water for citing research showing that men were disproportionately represented at the top and bottom of science test scores) that talents and abilities are distributed equally between the sexes (see Chapter 2). We have aligned ourselves behind those, like Carlotta Tyler, who believe the male and female leadership approaches are complementary, in the sense that they produce better decision making in combination than either produces on its own (see Chapter 6). We have noted that some qualities most often found in women are more sought after today, as companies move away from command and control leadership to more consensual styles.

In the end, we realized that there were two questions. First and most important is the question of what percentage of women board members companies should be aiming for in the medium term. On this we're in agreement with the WDoB recommendation that, on average, FTSE 100 constituents should be aiming to increase the percentages of women EDs from 4 percent to 10 percent, and women NEDs from 13 percent to 25 percent by 2010. These increases have the merit of being achievable and, because two women on a board make more than twice the difference of one, achieving them should have a disproportionate effect on the quality of management and governance, and sensitivity to the gender of the marketplace.

The second question is: what's the long-term equilibrium gender balance on company boards? There is nothing prescriptive about our answer, we're just speculating, but, given the even distribution between the sexes of talents and abilities, and the basic complementarity of male and female leadership styles, we see no reason to suppose that the long-term equilibrium gender balance on the average company board will be very different from 50:50. It could favor men very slightly, because of women's childbearing role, but research already quoted (see Chapter 2) found that 93 percent of women who take career "off-ramps" want to return and those who return to business do so, on average, after barely a year.

We should emphasize again that these are average numbers. We're not saying that women should account for 10 percent of EDs and 25 percent of NEDs at every FTSE 100 company by 2010 and neither are we predicting that women will account for 50 percent of every company's board in the long term.

The average long-term equilibrium gender balance might be less than 50 percent women in certain industries, such as mining and engineering, and more than 50 percent women in other industries, such as cosmetics and grocery retailing. And whatever balance is appropriate for the industry might vary at particular companies from time to time.

So, if in theory the long-term equilibrium gender balance on the boards of our largest companies is 50:50, what are the prospects of getting there in the foreseeable future? Or, to put it another way, what business risks will a company incur, if it decides to take no action to increase the number of women on its board?

We believe that the risks are considerable for the reasons discussed in earlier chapters, but they are impossible to quantify and, although there are good reasons to believe movement toward the equilibrium position will pass a "tipping point" at some stage and begin to accelerate rapidly, it's impossible to predict when that point will be reached.

Each company must make its own judgements about the scale of the risk, and what to do to combat it. But when making such judgements, companies should look beyond the pressures for change in their own organizations and listen for signals presaging change emanating from the global environment.

We identified some signals earlier:

- the 17 percent and 24 percent proportions women accounted for of new appointments to FTSE 100 and S&P 500 boards respectively in 2004
- the increasing proportions of first and higher degrees awarded to women
- the change in the gender of the customer
- the albeit inconclusive evidence that companies that have women on their boards create more value for their shareholders than those run by all-male boards
- the growing suspicion, in societies made sensitive to corporate wrong-doing by a crop of corporate scandals, that women directors can help to improve standards of corporate governance.

In a speech at Independence Hall, Philadelphia, on July 4 (US Independence day), 1994, the Czech statesman and dramatist, Václav Havel, said:

I think there are good reasons for suggesting that the modern age has ended. Today, many things indicate that we are going through a transitional period, when it seems that something is on the way out and something else is painfully being born. It is as if something were crumbling, decaying, and exhausting itself, while something else, still indistinct, were arising from the rubble.

It seems to us that the same can be said of the business world today. Many things indicate that we are going through a transitional period, when some of the old ways of business are on the way out and new, more feminine ways are coming in.

Scandinavia

In 2002, Norway's Minister for Trade and Industry proposed legislation for a mandatory gender balancing of the boards of Norwegian companies.

The Norwegian Parliament passed the law in 2003, but left the date it came into effect up to the government. The controversial legislation gives "publicly restricted companies", which include stock exchange listed companies, just three years from the law's effective date to bring the proportion of women on their boards to 40 percent.

Government ministers, employers and other interested parties discussed the implementation of the legislation at a conference in Oslo on May 27, 2005. Marit Hoel, director of the Centre for Corporate Diversity, presented a paper based on her report *Women Board Directors and Executive Directors in Norway 2005*, which showed that Norwegian companies had some way to go to reach the 40 percent target, but progress was accelerating sharply. In 2004, women accounted for 16.9 percent of board directors. By May 2005, the figure had risen to 22.5 percent in stock exchange listed companies.

A comparative pan-Scandinavian study by Hoel and her colleagues showed how legislation and the threat of legislation can drive the evolution of board composition.[1]

In 2003 the Swedish government announced that it would legislate to oblige listed companies to ensure that women accounted for at least 25 percent of board members by the end of 2004. In 2003, Swedish companies appointed 102 women to their boards. In view of this response, the government decided to postpone the legislation, but watch developments closely. In 2004, Swedish companies recruited 53 women directors. By the time of writing, July 2005, the number recruited since the end of 2004 was 34, bringing the proportion of women directors of listed companies to 17.9 percent.

The Danish government decided not to legislate in this area, but has urged companies to appoint more women directors. The number of women on boards in stock exchange listed companies in Denmark as of May, 2005 was 35, less than 9 percent of the total.

Hoel said: "This is the nearest we can get to a controlled experiment. The Nordic cultures are similar, and many of the same women serve on boards in each of the countries so the talent pipelines are the same. What makes the difference is the threat of legislation."

The Norwegian government got the message, and announced that the law would be implemented with one change: instead of the dissolution proposed in the original law, other sanctions, still to be decided at the time of writing, would be imposed on companies that failed to reach the required 40 percent target. The effective date was to be announced when the new sanctions were agreed.

Sweden's Minister for Trade and Industry attended the Oslo conference last May and also got the message. Sweden plans to enact legislation similar to Norway's in 2006.

Ruter Dam (Queen of Diamonds), a pioneering Swedish management development program for women business leaders founded and run by Gunilla Arhén, has been operating since 1987.[2] The one-year program consists of seminars, company visits, both external and internal mentoring by CEOs and an alumni alliance for networking after completion of the program. Roughly two-thirds of the 700 or so Ruter Dam alumni have been promoted at least once and of the 125 most powerful women in Swedish business listed in the Swedish business journal *Veckans Affärer* in March, 2005, 40 were Ruter Dam graduates.

An analysis of women directors in Europe published in the Cranfield School of Management's *Female FTSE Report 2004* showed Norway was fourth, behind Latvia, Romania and Slovenia, in a ranking of countries by the percentages of women directors at their top 50 companies. At some 16 percent, Norway's percentage has a way to go before it complies with the new law, but it was roughly the same as the SSBI figure for S&P 500 constituents and higher than the FTSE 100 figure.[3]

Eastern Europe

What's happening in Eastern Europe? Is a different, more feminine business culture rising from the rubble of Communism? Maybe. In addition to Latvia, Romania and Slovenia, Estonia, Bulgaria, Slovakia and Hungary also ranked above or well above the EU average. But Slovenia stands out, with a GDP per head of US$18,540 in 2002 making it one of the richest of the Eastern European economies, and women accounting for 22 percent of the boards of its 50 largest companies.

Citing other research, the Cranfield authors say that women account for 29 percent of Slovenia's legislators, senior officials and managers; 55 percent of professionals and technical workers; 12 percent of parliamentary seats; and 15 percent of minister level jobs. "Gender equality is notably high in Slovenia", say the report's authors, "following official communist policies to eliminate discrimination. Women are accepted as leaders … [and have] invested more than men in education over the last two decades."

The small size of Eastern European economies makes them implausible "prime movers" of a worldwide shift toward more gender-balanced boards. But they are rapidly becoming more integrated with the European and world economies and their increasingly important role as low-cost manufacturing locations is exposing large US and Western European companies to their more feminine management cultures.

Western Europe

In 2004 the European Professional Women's Network (EPWN) launched the EPWN European BoardWomen Monitor (www.europeanpwn.net) in conjunction with executive search firm Egon Zehnder to track trends in the gender composition of the boards of the top 200 companies in Western Europe.[4] The figures show that Western European companies have fewer women on their boards than Eastern European and North American companies – women account for 8 percent of total board positions; 62 percent of the 200 companies have at least one woman on the board; only 28 percent have more than one.

The monitor divides Western Europe into three groups:

1. *Trailblazers* – 14–22 percent women directors. Norway, Sweden and Finland are the only trailblazers

2. *Middle-of-the-roaders* – 6–10 percent women directors. Germany, the UK, the Netherlands, Switzerland, Austria and France

3. *Slow going* – 2–4 percent women directors. Denmark, Spain, Belgium and Italy.

The board monitor found that the Western European "marzipan" layer (or top management as the monitor calls it) consists of 5 percent women. Action is being taken in the Netherlands, one of a number of Western European countries where the gender composition of board pipelines is seen as a problem. A group of influential men and women in Amsterdam, led by Mirella Visser of the Amsterdam branch of Paris-based EPWN, launched Vrouwen in Beeld (Women in the Picture) in September 2004. Impatient with excuses for the 7 percent of Dutch board positions held by women, such as "we can't find qualified women", the group published a list of senior women to showcase the talent available to companies wishing to appoint women to their boards.[5] The group's high-powered advisory board includes the European commissioner Neelie Kroes and Antony Burgmans, chairman of Unilever.

Elsewhere in Western Europe, cultural, historical and social factors appear to be implicated in country differences. Of the 41 women directors of the French companies tracked in the monitor, almost half are family or union representatives. In the 15 Italian companies in the survey, 2.2 percent of board seats are occupied by women compared to the Western European average of 8 percent. The survey concludes that Italy's traditional male-dominated society, insufficient childcare infrastructure and lack of female-friendly companies are the main reasons for Italy's bottom place in the ranking.

EPWN and Egon Zehnder distinguish the Corporate Challenge (preparing women for leadership roles), from the Political Challenge (crafting policies and nurturing cultures that support women's careers).

Asia Pacific

On March 31, 2005, the ailing Japanese supermarket group Daiei announced that it had appointed Fumiko Hayashi, former president of BMW Tokyo, as *shacho* – a Japanese title that can mean company president, CEO or director. She became Japan's first female CEO of a Nikkei 225 company when a new Daiei leadership team took over at the end of May. Commenting on the appointment, a representative of the Industrial Revitalization Corporation of Japan (a government-backed corporate rehabilitation body to which Daiei had turned for help) said Ms Hayashi had been chosen because the troubled chain's revival required the "housewife's touch" and her appointment would help to present a favorable image of Daiei to the general public.[6]

As the appointment was being hailed as a major breakthrough for women into the previously all-male preserve of senior Japanese executives, there was another shock. It was announced on April 8 that Ms Tomoyo Nonaka, a former TV journalist, would on June 29 become chairman and CEO of Sanyo Electric, which was expected to post a record loss of $1 billion for the year to the end of March 2005.[7]

Both companies were in dire straits when they appointed women leaders, but Hayashi had an impressive leadership track record behind her (at BMW Tokyo and Volkswagen Group Japan), and since quitting television in 1996, Nonaka had served on several government advisory committees and corporate boards, including Sanyo's. They may fail, of course, and if they do, their failures may be attributed to their sex. But if they succeed, other leading Japanese companies may start looking for female directors and leaders.

Some see the appointments as a new variant of corporate Japan's relatively recent habit of appointing foreign leaders, in the persons of Carlos Ghosn at Nissan and Howard Stringer at Sony. "Japanese companies often need some outside pressure or shock to change, even if they know the direction they should be heading", Yuki Sugi, an analyst at Lehman Brothers, told *Business Week*. "Employing a female leader could be … like having a foreigner."

There are other signs of a major change in corporate Japan's attitude to women. Matsushita Electric announced an increase in the number of women managers of 170 percent in 2004, and in February 2005, Nissan announced that by 2007, it wants to triple the number of female managers to 120 – 5 percent of the total, compared with the Japanese average of 2.8 percent and a mere 1 percent in the auto sector. Announcing the target, CEO Ghosn said: "We want to be a company that talented capable women want to join, to contribute to, and, ultimately, to lead."[8]

A special issue of *Asia Pacific Business Review* in May 2005 included eight articles on women in management in the region. Their gist was that there's a growing acceptance of female managers, but many of their male colleagues still see them as less capable than men and business careers are generally less open to Asian women.

These appointments of Hayashi and Nonaka to ailing Japanese companies, and the reactions to them, bring to mind research by Professor Alex Haslam and Dr Michelle Ryan of Exeter University, in the UK. They found that, as well as facing the so-called glass ceiling, women face what they called a "glass cliff". Their analysis of the performance of FTSE 100 companies before and after the appointments of men or women to senior executive positions found that companies were more likely to appoint women when they were performing relatively badly.[9]

The appointment of Kate Swann as CEO of troubled UK retailer W.H. Smith in November 2003 was a case in point. Ryan and Haslam suggested that their findings were a problem for women, because their chances of succeeding as CEOs were less than those of men, who were more often appointed CEOs when the hiring companies were doing relatively well. If W.H. Smith continues to struggle or gets "taken out" by a private equity firm at a low price, for instance, investors could put the blame on Swann and her gender.

But there's another possibility. The Chinese word for "crisis" consists of two characters; one standing for "danger" and the other standing for "opportunity". If, as Ryan and Haslam suggest, there is a new tendency for companies in the UK (and Japan too it seems) to appoint female CEOs *in extremis*, it seems entirely possible that in the not too distant future female CEOs will earn a reputation for being turn-round specialists and so become the favored gender for institutional investors when replacing the CEOs of underperforming companies.

It is too early to tell for Hayashi and Nonaka at Daiei and Sanyo, but the auguries look good for Swann at W.H. Smith. The company recovered strongly in 2004. Results for the six months to February 28, 2005, showed profits before tax, goodwill, amortization and exceptional items up 32 percent on the same period the previous year, to £70 million. Swann reported that £13 million of cost savings had already been achieved and the company was on schedule to deliver the three-year cost savings of £30 million that she had predicted.[10]

Canada

In addition to growing pressure from their female employees and their need to respond to wider global developments of the kind described above, large companies are also being pressed on gender issues by politicians, pressure groups and other external institutions in several developed countries.

The Canadian campaign to get more women into boardrooms began in the 1970s and was initially led by individuals. Toronto philanthropist Bluma Appel, for example, used her formidable reputation and influence in the 1970s to push Canada's major banks to include at least one woman on their boards.

The modern campaign began in 1998, with the first Catalyst census of women directors in Canada. Four years later the business journalist and feminist Doreen Mckenzie-Sanders finessed the suggestion that there were not enough suitably qualified female board candidates by publishing a comprehensive directory of women board candidates called *Women in the Lead*. A new edition appeared in 2004 and an electronic newsletter was launched in early 2005.[11]

Another key milestone was the publication in 2002, by the Conference Board of Canada, of a study entitled "Not just the right thing, but the bright thing," showing that boards with women significantly outperformed all-male boards on key corporate governance measures.[12]

Canada's most comprehensive women on boards initiative was started in 1999 by Canadian Women in Communications (CWC), a national organization of 1400 members promoting the advancement of women in the communications sector. It began tracking the number of women on boards of the top 50 companies in the communications industry in 1999, and launched its first initiative the following year.[13]

CWC's campaign is multifaceted. The CWC President, Stephanie MacKendrick explained:

> With no ability to enforce compliance we knew our strategy had to focus on persuasion and establishing ourselves as a credible source for tactical advice and practical support. We worked with a top notch advisory council to make sure our goals were ... achievable, then went directly to the industry, and asked key companies what they were doing to find women board candidates and how could we help them.

The CWC campaigners are systematic and relentless. They research the dates of company annual meetings to find out when board nominations take place, contact CEOs to ask whether they have board vacancies and if so, what they are doing to find suitable women candidates and send the CEOs articles and studies showing the bottom line benefits of women board members. MacKendrick said:

> In some cases, we send copies of the *Women in the Lead* directory, or refer them to the Conference Board research and the Catalyst census, which lists ... women already on the corporate boards of Canada's top companies. We ... don't take no for an answer, but in a way that addresses the best interests of the companies, the industry and the highly qualified women who have so much to offer.

The pressure has worked. The number of Canada's 500 largest companies with all-male boards fell 13 percent between 1998 and 2003, but the number of companies with all-male boards within the group targeted by CWC fell by 60 percent between 1999 and 2005. Women currently hold 18 percent of board positions in Canada's communications industry, compared to the 11 percent of board positions they accounted for in the top 500 companies in 2003.

CWC provides corporate governance and financial literacy training sessions and career advice for members, and maintains links with organizations that recruit not-for-profit board members. Its next step is a mentoring program to match powerful mentors with highly qualified women candidates. The mission for the mentors is to get their mentees placed on boards within a year and to spend another six months helping mentees adapt to their new roles.

Catalyst, CWC and Canada's Institute of Corporate Directors (ICD) staged a one-day "summit" in 2004 to discuss key issues and bring business leaders and women candidates together. Beverley Topping, ICD president and CEO, is encouraging women to enroll in ICD's Corporate Governance College; a joint venture with the University of Toronto's Rotman School of Business, which provides governance training and "an opportunity for women to network with high-profile board directors who recognize that, in the current governance climate, even the experts need formal training."

The USA

The Conference Board Inc. in New York, to which the Conference Board Europe and the Conference Board of Canada are affiliated, is an august, extremely influential not-for-profit, which helps to set the agenda for the contemporary business debate. It has been putting the case for more diversity on boards for many years now, frequently quotes Catalyst's research, and organizes Women in Leadership conferences in Europe and the US.

Its Global Corporate Governance Research Center, members of whose advisory board include two major US pension funds, the California Public Employees' Retirement System (CalPERS) and Teachers Insurance and Annuity Association College Retirement Equities Fund (TIAA-CREF), published a report on board diversity back in 1999. It included an argument for diverse boards that we had not encountered before. At a Conference Board Business Roundtable in 1997, an experienced litigator suggested that "if a company were to find itself … [in court] with a class-action suit, the presence of minorities on the board who appeared to be actively involved in the company's business would "play" better before the jury".[14]

It seems a trivial, even disingenuous point, but it is part of a serious general argument about the increasing importance of reputation in a world where traditional company differentiators, such as price and quality, have lost their potency, the enormous financial risks associated with damage to reputations, and the qualities that customers, suppliers, prospective employees and the public at large infer about companies from their boards.

This seemed to be one of the reasons for the appointment of Fumiko Hayashi as CEO-designate of Daiei (see above).

Apart from the support of influential institutions, such as the Conference Board, the American campaign to get more women onto the boards of leading companies is being pursued by individual advocates. Prominent among them is Susan Schiffer Stautberg, president of PartnerCom Corporation, a search firm that assembles and manages corporate advisory boards.[15]

Advisory boards are becoming increasingly popular in the US. They comprise experts in various fields who advise their formal boards on risk analysis, strategy development, security, innovation, new technologies, marketing or any other area in which the company needs guidance and counsel.

Companies like them, because members are paid per meeting, rather than the increasingly expensive annual fees outside directors require to compensate them for their legal risks; advisory board members like them, because they offer board-type experience without the fiduciary responsibilities and the expensive directors and officers liability insurance premiums.

Stautberg told us:

> These are not governance; they're purely advisory and growing in popularity the whole time. They are very hot for family-owned companies. They can be convened around a specific issue or for a period of time. One example of how they can help was when a cosmetics group decided to go into women's health

and wellness. They came to me to help create an advisory board, including women doctors and healthcare writers. Advisory boards bring others to the attention of the CEO.

She sees them as a great opportunity for women eager to raise their profiles and test the water at board level.

But that is not all Stautberg is doing to promote women directors. Several women directors we spoke to urged us to talk to her. One of them said that she was "doing more for potential women directors in the US than any other person I know". She founded Belizian Grove, a well-known retreat for women leaders, the Women Corporate Directors (WCD) dinner series for directors and women at comparable levels in government and academia and the On Board Bootcamp.

Stautberg says the inspiration for the WCD dinners was that women "needed to know what questions to ask and how to ask them at board meetings". The group includes about 450 serving women directors. They help each other and dine together in Washington, Chicago, Boston and New York. The WCD held its first annual conference in March, 2005. The heading on the conference invitation read: "Like an airline pilot, a corporate director has hours of boredom, punctuated by moments of terror."

On Board Bootcamp is a two-day board preparation for men and women who are not yet on boards, run in New York and Washington. "It's also about getting the word out", said Stautberg. "People know about the boot camp."

Several of the marzipan women we talked to (Chapter 4) emphasized the need for training for aspiring directors.

Toward equilibrium

If all the straws in the wind discussed above add up to what John Naisbitt would call a "megatrend", three questions arise:

- What will business be like after the megatrend has fully matured and women occupy half the seats in the average corporate boardroom?

- How long will it take to reach a long-term equilibrium position?

- What intermediate transitional steps along the road should companies measure their progress by?

The answer to the first question is anyone's guess and will certainly vary enormously according to geography, circumstances and industries. Only very broad, impressionistic, partial answers are possible at this stage.

We can be fairly confident, however, that the differences between business as it is, and business as it will be when equilibrium is reached, will be just as evident in the relationships between large businesses as in the management styles within them. The female preference for collaboration and cooperation over out-and-out competition, for example, will probably lead to a sharp acceleration of the current growth in joint ventures, strategic alliances and other forms of partnership.

Relationships between big business and society at large, which have always been tense and have become more so in recent years, are likely to improve as the female preference for consensus and stability begin to settle long-running disputes about tax and CSR, and help both parties to reach an agreement on the meaning of the term "good corporate citizen".

In terms of geography and timing, there are signs that Northern Europe will take an early lead in the long march toward equilibrium, although we doubt whether the results of the legislative approach to gender-balancing boards with which some Scandinavian countries are flirting will prove sufficient on their own. Interested parties in Scandinavia recognize the need for the cultural change that emerges from the search for competitive advantage.

When speculating about interim and transitional steps toward equilibrium, it is worth pondering for a moment the implications for our argument of the idea that one of the most important responsibilities of a leader is to prepare for his or her succession, on the basis that a success that falls apart on the departure of its chief architect is no success at all.

Consider Avon Products, the US "direct sales" cosmetics group, where Andrea Jung has been CEO since 1999 and chairman since 2001. According to the company's website, this self-styled "company for women" is the world's largest direct seller. After over a decade of residence, it has almost become a permanent member of Fortune's "most admired companies" and is one of Fortune's "50 best companies for minorities". It has been judged to be among the "100 best corporate citizens" for six consecutive years by *Business Ethics*. It has been ranked the top company for executive women by the National Association for Female Executives. According to *Business Week,* Avon is among the "top 100 global brands" and has been voted "most trusted brand" on three continents.[16]

With over 86 percent of its management positions and 50 percent of board seats occupied by women, it could also be called "the company of women".

With all these awards and approbations, a cynic might suspect shareholders have been neglected. Not a bit of it. During Jung's leadership, the S&P 500 index has fallen by 18 percent while Avon's stock price has risen 135 percent.

We spoke to Jim Preston, Andrea Jung's predecessor as CEO and chairman from 1988 to 1998. These were also years of great achievement, with revenues rising from $3 billion to $5 billion, a doubling of the number of sales representatives to 2.6 million, and 10 years of uninterrupted growth in revenues and earnings. There were other, less tangible achievements. Avon became the first major cosmetics manufacturer to ban animal testing and it was during Preston's leadership that the ground was cleared for the emergence of Avon as "the company of women".

Preston recalled:

Avon sells over 99.9 percent of products by women to women, but for many years, women were underrepresented at board level". "The company was unique – I felt you could make a strong case [for more women] throughout the organization and at board level. I also thought that unless you tap into the talents women have, you are neglecting 50 percent of the talent in today's world.

The women's movement in the US began in the mid-1960s, so women have been in the pipeline and been earning their spurs professionally for many years now. There's an incredible pool of talent now that didn't exist previously, so there's no excuse for the paltry numbers in the Catalyst research. Why haven't corporations done more? The only answer is that they don't think it's important enough. They may think it's unimportant because they're not women's companies like Avon, but that ignores the talent argument.

Women and men think differently, solve problems differently. Their brains are wired differently. They have a different perspective and thinking. Why would you not want to tap into that? Why would you not want people on your board who think differently?

In the 1980s and 1990s, [executive] search firms would give you academics and people from not-for-profit organizations, if you told them you wanted to appoint a woman to your board, and the women they gave you were already on many other boards.

When I became an executive at Avon, I was surprised by how few women there were at senior levels. I used to tap into one woman for advice and counsel and I asked her why she wasn't an officer. She said she thought she'd got as high as she could go; everyone above her was a man. She told me stories about how she was treated, as the only woman in meetings – that made a big impression on me.

In the 1970s, Avon was sliding and was in serious trouble by the 1980s. It struck me that we were a woman's company, and had to have people who could understand our consumer base.

I hired Andrea Jung about 11 years ago. I had a picture on my office wall of "Four footprints of leadership evolution", ranging from a gorilla print through to a man's print and finally a dot (representing a stiletto heel). She asked me at the interview whether it was for real and I listed all the women that Avon had by then, in senior positions. She says that was one of the main factors behind her joining.

That's another reason for having women on a board; if you want to attract the brightest and the best, you have to show you have got women at the top otherwise top female talent won't come to you.

If you have women in senior leadership positions, you need to have them on your board. I told Catalyst in 1995/6 that in my lifetime I believed there would be a woman chair of Avon, and that in my tenure as chairman we would have 50 percent women on the board.

I told the search firms I wanted to see female candidates on their slates and asked consultants who were working with Avon if they knew of any good women in other companies. That's how Brenda Barnes (recently appointed CEO of Sara Lee) came to Avon from Pepsi.

It wasn't difficult to persuade the guys. One of the most powerful events once we had a few women on the board was when we were viewing forthcoming commercials. The men didn't think they were very good – they didn't think the brand was clear enough. The women said: "Are you kidding? They're great – they really speak to us!"

A change has to come from the top. Most CEOs and business executives will only do things that are in their interests. When you can point out it's in your self-interest to have the very best talent, they'll pay attention. The very best talent isn't just found in the male population.

Whenever people ask me what made the difference at Avon – what turned the company round – I always say it was the people, but specifically women.

Conclusion

We have argued in this book that men and women lead differently, that, for historical reasons, business organizations bear the imprints of masculine values, norms and patterns of behavior and that, as a result of this, the cultures of companies frequently don't "fit" women, particularly at senior levels where women remain thin on the ground.

Two consequences arise from this. The few women who do manage to reach the top of large companies often feel abraded by the cultures they find there, and women just below the board, who look up at the tip of the management pyramid, often decide not to participate, because the price they will have to pay seems too great.

Despite the exhortations of governments and external and internal lobbying groups, innovations such as the Cross-Company Mentoring Programme in the UK and the goodwill and commitment of many top male executives in the UK and US, the resultant "lop-sidedness" at senior levels in organizations is, as a consequence, proving hard to correct.

But it must be corrected, because powerful, impersonal forces, in the form of intensifying competition for managerial talent and the inexorable march of demographic change, will require it. The Western world is running out of white males under 45, who have been the source of the vast majority of our business leaders up until now. In the UK they will account for barely a third of the workforce, for example, in seven years.[17] Our leading companies can't continue to rely on them for over 80 percent of their boardroom needs, especially not at a time when the pressure of corporate governance reforms obliges them to reduce their non-executive commitments.

They are going to have to bring up the reserves and the only reserves that are available in the UK and US in sufficient numbers are women. As we've seen, many women are ready, willing and able to help out, but they are going to want some changes. Not enough of them are prepared to work in and lead organizations that retain cultures that are fundamentally "male". They're too abrasive for one thing, and for another they prevent the emergence of the synergies associated with the complementarity of male and female styles of management and leadership. A new compact between the sexes must be reached about how our large companies are organized, managed and led, that makes them better adapted to and more welcoming for women.

Leadership models, which worked well enough before these demographic changes began to gather momentum and before the emergence of women as the buyers of the majority of goods and services, are fast approaching their sell-by date. New leadership models and corporate structures need to be developed that are more in tune with the gender of the marketplace and the needs and preferences of the female executives who companies need to attract and keep if they are to remain competitive.

It will no longer be enough to get women "in" for consultation. They will have to be deeply and daily involved in high-level decision making and the formulation of strategy. Their voices must be heard alongside those of men in the highest echelons of corporate management and given equal weight and legitimacy. We believe that the skills, qualities and aptitudes, and the styles and approaches to leadership, of men and women are complementary. We need all of them to tackle the complex, difficult and urgent problems that face us in the early 21st century.

References

1. www.mangementwomen.no.
2. www.ruterdam.se.
3. *The Female FTSE Report 2004*, Cranfield University School of Management.
4. EPWN European BoardWomen Monitor, 2004.
5. www.vrouweninbeeld.nl.
6. Japan's top firms to get first female president, Leo Lewis, *The Times*, March 3, 2005.
7. Can Tomoyo Nonaka get Sanyo back on the beam?, Ian Rowley and Hiroko Tashiro, BusinessWeek online, May 9, 2005.
8. *Business Week*, May 2, 2005.
9. The glass cliff: Evidence that women are over-represented in precarious leadership positions. M. K. Ryan and S. A. Haslam, *British Journal of Management*, 2004.
10. www.whsmithplc.com/grp.
11. www.womeninthelead.ca.
12. www.conferenceboard.ca.
13. www.cwc-afc.com.
14. *Board Diversity in U.S. Corporations*, The Conference Board, 1999.
15. www.partner-com.com.
16. www.avon.com.
17. UK Census, 2002.

A NOTE ON METHOD

A substantial part of this book (that is, most of Chapters 3, 4 and 7 and much of Chapter 5) consists of the results of "qualitative research".[1] We have sought to understand the experiences of men and women already on boards and women seeking board positions, by talking to them, rather than trying to measure that experience and capturing it in numbers. We're acutely aware of the dangers inherent in this approach, especially with regard to the stance that the researcher adopts to questioning, interpreting and the whole process of enquiry. We employed procedures designed to minimize, or at the least hold up to public view, any factors that might skew the results in the direction our preconceptions dictated.

The term "grounded theory" comes nearest to defining our approach.[2] It is a method of handling, organizing and analyzing unstructured, qualitative material that acknowledges the contributions of researchers as participants in the process and their essential involvement in it. It means a particular body of knowledge is "grounded" in, or emerges from, the experience of those involved in it, both researchers and participants.

To understand people's experience, we engage with them in an exploration of what the experience is like for them – how they themselves see the world. But researchers have to be careful not to get sucked too far into the participant's world; they must maintain a distance or separateness if the exploration is to be meaningful. We are seeking to make explicit what is otherwise taken for granted and, in doing this, to generate new ideas. Features of qualitative data are:

- Consistency of outcome may be a feature, but the context may also form a crucial part of the story. In this study, for example, the fact that many of the subjects were women was important, and their work settings may also have influenced the stories they told.

- Making sense to the reader is important. Ideas should hang together in ways that evoke responses, such as agreement or disagreement.

- Ideas on cause and effect may emerge, but loose ends can be left.

- Measurement is not necessary to the telling of the story.

- The aim is interpretation; the possibility of going beyond the data.

Three problems with this method

1. The story can't escape its context. For example, many of the subjects were senior women, not junior women or men, so we cannot say that our conclusions apply to junior women and men.

2. Accounts and interpretations can never be conclusive. Time passes. We can only capture a moment in time, a snapshot.

3. The researchers' previous knowledge of the subject and the impact of the subject of study on the researchers both produce a potential for data distortion.

Some solutions

We took various steps to ensure the trustworthiness of the research:

- We adopted a clear approach. Everything we did was well documented.

- We went to great lengths to devise a robust structure for the face-to-face enquiry (see below) that disciplined, but didn't straitjacket the exploration.

- We selected interviewees to achieve a spread of experience, in terms of geography and industry sectors, to ensure that our findings would have the potential to be widely applicable.

- We designed the project carefully and identified responsibilities.

- Our interpretation process consisted of:
  - producing an account from each individual meeting
  - identifying the broad themes, individually for all accounts
  - examining the account again from "events" that cluster under the themes, in order to help refine them, identify different levels of theme and also to help illustrate them
  - applying a similar content analysis approach to the aggregate of themes from all interviewees, to identify what is common and what is distinctive about each experience

- We applied quantitative measures where these were appropriate. For the most part, this applied to demographic data.

- By the writing stage, we found it was possible to link the findings of our research to other relevant work in the field.

The questions we asked

We asked all our interviewees a set of basic questions:

1. Name

2. Age

3. Role/position

4. Brief role/position description/board positions held

5. Industry/enterprise/field of work

6. Length of time in present role

In addition we asked each member of each group of interviewees the same set of questions, although we did not insist that all be answered.

Questions put to FTSE 100 chairmen and chief executives (Chapter 3):

1. What is your reaction to the Cranfield figures?

2. Why do you think there are so few women directors on FTSE 100 boards?

3. How comfortable are you about appointing a woman to your board?

4. Have you ever appointed a woman to your board?

5. What was your experience of this?

6. How did you manage the process?

7. What part did you play personally in the process?

8. How important is it to have a diverse board?

9. What dimensions/aspects of diversity do you think are important?

10. What differences do women make to boards?

11. What do women need to do differently to achieve executive and non-executive board positions?

12. What do FTSE 100 companies need to do differently to increase the number of women on their boards?

Questions put to S&P/Fortune 500 chairmen and chief executives (Chapter 3):

1. What is your reaction to the Catalyst figures?

2. How comfortable are you about appointing a woman to your board?

3. Have you ever appointed a woman to your board?

4. What was your experience of making that appointment?

5. How did you manage the process?

6. Did you personally play a part in the process?

7. How did you manage your colleagues on the board through the process? Was appointing a woman director an issue?

8. How important is it, in your view, to have a diverse board?

9. Which aspects of diversity do you think are important?

10. What differences, if any, do women make to boards?

11. What do women need to do differently in order to achieve inside or outside director positions?

12. What action would you recommend should be taken by US companies to increase the number of women on their boards?

Questions put to UK "marzipan" women (Chapter 4):

1. What is your reaction to the Cranfield figures?

2. Why do you think there are so few women directors on FTSE 100 boards?

3. How comfortable are you about being appointed to a FTSE 100 board? Is it one of your ambitions?

4. Have you ever put yourself forward for a non-executive board position? If so, what was your experience of this? How did you go about it? For example, did you approach a headhunter?

5. Have you ever been in the running for an executive appointment?

6. If so, why were you not appointed? What reasons were you given for not being appointed? How satisfied were you with those reasons?

7. What part did the CEO or chairman of the company play in the process?

8. What help did you enlist? Did you have any coaching? Did you talk to any women directors on your board?

9. Is having a diverse board important? If so, why, and what aspects of diversity do you think are particularly important?

10. What differences do you think women make to boards?

11. What do women need to do differently to achieve executive and non-executive board positions?

12. What actions would you recommend should be taken to increase the number of women on FTSE 100 Boards?

13. What will you do if you are not appointed to the board within the next few years?

Questions put to US "marzipan" women (Chapter 4):

1. What is your reaction to the Catalyst figures?

2. Why do you think there are so few women on Fortune 500 boards?

3. How comfortable are you about being appointed to a Fortune 500 board? Is it one of your ambitions?

4. Have you ever put yourself forward for an independent/outside director position? If so, what was your experience of this? How did you go about it? For example, did you approach a headhunter?

5. Have you ever been in the running for an inside or outside director appointment?

6. If so, why were you not appointed? What reasons were you given for not being appointed? How satisfied were you with those reasons?

7. What part did the CEO or chairman of the company play in the process?

8. What help did you enlist? Did you have any coaching? Did you talk to any women directors on your board?

9. Is having a diverse board important? If so, why and what aspects of diversity do you think are particularly important?

10. What differences do women make to boards?

11. What do women need to do differently to achieve inside and outside director positions?

12. What actions would you recommend should be taken to increase the number of women on Fortune 500 Boards?

13. What will you do if you are not appointed to the board within the next few years?

Questions put to mentors in the Cross-Company Mentoring Programme (Chapter 5):

1. Why did you agree to participate in the FTSE 100 Cross-Company Mentoring Programme?

2. How is it going?

3. What have you learned so far?

4. Have there been any surprises?

5. Is there anything else you would like to add?

Questions put to mentees in the Cross-Company Mentoring Programme (Chapter 5):

1. How many meetings have you had so far with your mentor?

2. How is it going?

3. What benefits have you derived so far from mentoring?

4. Is there any other feedback you would like to provide?

Questions put to UK women board directors (Chapter 7):

1. What is your reaction to the Cranfield figures?

2. Why do you think there are so few women directors on the FTSE 100 boards?

3. How comfortable do you think most chairmen are with appointing women to their boards?

4. How did your own appointment come about? For example, did you put yourself forward to a headhunter? Were you approached?

5. What part did the CEO or chairman of the company play in the process?

6. What help did you enlist? Did you have any coaching? Did you talk to any women directors on other boards?

7. How important is having a diverse board?

8. What dimensions/aspects of diversity do you think are important?

9. What differences do women make to boards?

10. What do women need to do differently to achieve executive and non-executive board positions?

11. What should FTSE 100 companies do to increase the number of women on their boards?

12. How does being on a board match up to your expectations/career aspirations?

13. Is there anything more that existing women directors can do to help other aspiring women?

Questions put to US women board directors (Chapter 7):

1. What is your reaction to the Catalyst figures?

2. Why do you think there are so few women directors on Fortune 500 boards?

3. How comfortable do you think most CEOs are with appointing women to their boards?

4. How did your first appointment come about? For example, did you put yourself forward to a headhunter? Were you approached?

5. What part did the CEO or chairman of the company play in the process?

6. What help did you enlist? Did you have any coaching? Did you talk to any women directors on other boards?

7. How important is having a diverse board?

8. What dimensions/aspects of diversity do you think are important?

9. What differences do women make to boards?

10. What do women need to do differently to achieve insider and outside director positions?

11. What actions would you recommend should be taken by companies to increase the number of women on their boards?

12. Is there anything more that existing women directors can do to help other aspiring women?

References

1. Our thanks to Clare Huffington, Director of The Tavistock Consultancy Service, for these notes on grounded theory.
2. *Handbook of Qualitative Research Methods for Psychology and the Social Sciences*, J. Richardson, BPS Books, 1996; *Doing Qualitative Analysis in Psychology*, N. Hayes (ed.), Psychology Press, 1997.

FURTHER READING

Armstrong, Michael (ed.) (1992) *Strategies for Human Resource Management: A Total Business Approach*. London: Kogan Page.

Aurora and Caliper (April 2005) The DNA of Women Leaders: a research study.

Band, William A. (1991) *Creating Value for Customers: Designing and Implementing a Total Corporate Strategy*. Canada: John Wiley & Sons.

Bourez, Véronique (2005) *Women on Boards: Moving Beyond Tokenism*. France, European Professional Women's Network, Women@Work No. 2.

Brancato, Carolyn Kay and Patterson, D. Jeanne (1999) *Board Diversity in U.S. Corporations: Best Practices for Broadening the Profile of Corporate Boards*. New York: The Conference Board.

Bryce, Lee (1989) *The Influential Woman – How to Achieve Success in your Career and still Enjoy your Personal Life*. London: Piatkus.

Burke, Ronald J. and Zena Burgess (2003) "Women on Corporate Boards of Directors". *Women in Management Review*, **18**(7). Bradford, West Yorkshire: Emerald, published in association with the Equal Opportunities Commission.

Charan, Ram; Drotter, Stephen and Noel, James (2001) *The Leadership Pipeline, How to Build the Leadership-Powered Company*. San Francisco: Jossey-Bass.

Dickson, Anne (1982) *A Woman in Your Own Right*. Aylesbury: Quartet Books.

DTI (2004) Fairness For All: A New Commission for Equality and Human Rights. Cm 6185.

Facing the Challenge: The Lisbon Strategy for Growth and Employment. Report from the High Level Group chaired by Wim Kok. Luxembourg: Office for Official Publications of the European Communities, 2004.

Gallagher Hateley, B.J. and Warren H. Schmidt (2001) *A Peacock in the Land of Penguins*. San Francisco: Berrett-Koehler.

Garratt, Sally (1998) *Women Managing for the Millennium*. London: HarperCollinsBusiness.

Garratt, Bob (1997) *The Fish Rots from the Head: The Crisis in Our Boardrooms: Developing the Crucial Skills of the Competent Director*. London: HarperCollinsBusiness.

Godfrey, Joline (1992) *Our Wildest Dreams: Women Entrepreneurs Making Money, Having Fun, Doing Good*. New York: HarperBusiness.

Hansard Society (1990) The Report of The Hansard Society Commission on Women at the Top. London: A.L. Publishing Services.

Helgesen, Sally (1990) *The Female Advantage: Women's Ways of Leadership*. New York: Doubleday.

Herera, Sue (1997) *Women of the Street: Making it on Wall Street – The World's Toughest Business*. New York: John Wiley & Sons.

Higgs Report (2002) http://www.dti.gov.uk/cld/non_exec_review/pdf/higgsreport. pdf.

Hite, Shere (2000) *Sex & Business*. London: Pearson Education.

Hofstede, Geert (1991) *Cultures and Organisations: Software of the Mind*. Maidenhead: McGraw-Hill.

Hosmer Martens, Margaret and Mitter, Swasti (1994) *Women in Trade Unions: Organizing the Unorganized*. Geneva: International Labour Office.

Howe, Elspeth and McRae, Susan (1991) *Women on the Board*. London: Policy Studies Institute.

Huffington, Clare, et al. (2005) *Working below the surface. The emotional life of contemporary organizations*, Tavistock Clinic Services, Karnac.

Institute for Public Policy Research (2004) *Race Equality: The Benefits for Responsible Business*. IPPR.

Kabacoff, Robert I. (1998) "Gender Differences in Organizational Leadership: A Large Sample Study". Portland, ME: Management Research Group.

Kets de Vries, Manfred F. R. (1995) *Life and Death in the Executive Fast Lane*. San Francisco: Jossey-Bass.

Kolb, Deborah M., Williams, Judith and Carol Frohlinger (2004) *Her Place at the Table: A Woman's Guide to Negotiating Five Key Challenges to Leadership Success*. San Francisco: Jossey-Bass.

KPMG (2004) Pressing strategic issues for leading FTSE organisations. "You're invited: Diversity programs make commercial sense too", *Performance Plus*, April Issue 5.

Lehan Harragan, Betty (1977) *Games your Mother Never Taught you: Corporate Gamesmanship for Women*. New York: Warner Books.

Litwin, George, Bray, John and Lusk Brooke, Kathleen (1996) *Mobilizing the Organization: Bringing Strategy to Life*. Hemel Hempstead: Prentice Hall International.

Lloyd, Tom (1990) *The "Nice" Company*. London: Bloomsbury.

Loden, Marilyn (1985) *Feminine Leadership: or How to Succeed in Business Without Being One of the Boys*. New York: Times Books/Random House.

Ludeman, Kate and Erlandson, Eddie (2004) "Coaching the Alpha Male", *Harvard Business Review*, May.

Mann, Sandi (1995) "Politics and Power in Organizations: Why Women Lose Out" *Leadership and Organization Development Journal*, **16**(2).

Markillie, Paul (2005) "Crowned at last". *The Economist*, April 2–8.

Marshall, Judi (1984) *Women Managers: Travellers in a Male World*. Chichester: John Wiley & Sons.

Marshall, Judi (1995) *Women Managers Moving On: Exploring Career and Life Choices*. International Thomson Publishing Europe.

Mattis, Mary C. (2001) "Advancing women in business organizations: Key leadership roles and behaviors of senior leaders and middle managers". *Journal of Management Development*, **20**(4).

McCracken, Douglas M. (2000) "Winning the Talent War for Women: Sometimes It Takes a Revolution" *Harvard Business Review*, November–December.

McDougall, Linda (1998) *Westminster Women*. London: Vintage.

Miles, Rosalind (1986) *Women and Power*. London and Sydney: Futura Publications.

Myers, Isabel Briggs with Peter B. Myers (1995) *Gifts Differing: Understanding Personality Type*. Palo Alto: Davies-Black Publishing.

National Work–Life Forum Report (2000) *Breakpoint/Breakthrough: Work–Life Strategies for the 21st Century*. London: The National Work–Life Forum.

Palframen, Diane (2004) *Work–Life and Diversity: Local Needs and Business Relevance Drive Success*. Brussels: The Conference Board Europe.

Pease, Allan and Pease, Barbara (2001) *Why Men don't Listen and Women can't Read Maps*. London: Orion Books.

Peiperl, Maury A., Arthur, Michael B., Goffe, Rob and Harris, Timothy (eds) (2000) *Career Frontiers: New Conceptions of Working Lives*. Oxford: Oxford University Press.

Peters, Helen and Kabacoff, Rob (2002) "A New Look at the Glass Ceiling: The Perspective From the Top". MRG Research Report: *Leadership & Gender*.

Radcliffe Public Policy Institute and The Boston Club (1999) *Suiting Themselves: Women's Leadership Styles in Today's Workplace*. Cambridge, MA: The Radcliffe Public Policy Institute.

Rees, Deborah (June 2004) "Women in the Boardroom: A Bird's Eye View" (Change Agenda Series) London: Chartered Institute of Personnel and Development.

Ridley, Matt (2003) *Nature via Nurture: Genes, Experience and What Makes us Human*. London: Harper Perennial.

Rosener, Judy B. (1990) "Ways Women Lead" *Harvard Business Review*, November–December.

Ross, Dr Karen (2000) "Women At The Top 2000: Cracking the public sector glass ceiling". London: The Hansard Society.

Rubin, Harriet (1997) *The Princessa: Machiavelli for Women*. London: Bloomsbury.

Scott-Morgan, Peter (1994) *The Unwritten Rules of the Game*. New York: McGraw-Hill.

Silverman, I. and Eals, M. (1992) Sex differences in spatial abilities: evolutionary theory and data, in J. H. Barkow, L. Cosmides, J. Tooby (eds) *The Adapted Mind*, Oxford University Press.

Slipman, Sue (1986) *Helping Ourselves to Power: a Handbook for Women on the Skills of Public Life*. Oxford: Pergamon Press.

Smith Institute (2000) *Women in the New Economy*. London: The Smith Institute.

Swan, Jonathan and Professor Cary L. Cooper (2005) *Time, Health and the Family: What Working Families Want*. Working Families and Professor Cary Cooper.

Taffinder, Paul (1995) *The New Leaders: Achieving Corporate Transformation through Dynamic Leadership*. London: Kogan Page.

Tait, Ruth (1995) *Roads to the Top: Career Decisions and Development of 18 Business Leaders*. Basingstoke: Macmillan Business.

Tannen, Deborah (1995) "The Power of Talk: Who Gets Heard and Why", *Harvard Business Review*, September–October.

Tannen, Deborah (1992) *You Just Don't Understand*. London: Virago.

The Psychologist (August 2004) Intersex Special Issue, **17**(8).

Thomas, David A. and Ely, Robin J. (1996) "Making Difference Matter: A New Paradigm for Managing Diversity" *Harvard Business Review*, September–October.

Thomson, Peninah, Goyder, Mark and Roberts, John (2003) "Corporate Governance, Leadership and Culture Change in Business". London: Royal Society of Arts.

Thomson, Peninah, Coleman, John and Graham, Jacey (2004) "Demographic Change; the FTSE 100 and Women Directors on Boards". *Talking About*, (2).

Tomkins, Richard (2005) "Macho business muscle gives itself a feminine makeover, *Financial Times*, May 17.

Tyler, Carlotta (2002) "In the Company of Women: Complementary Ways of Organizing Work". *OD Practitioner*, **34**(3).

Tyson Report (2003) http://www.london.edu/tysonreport/Tyson_Report_June_2003.pdf.

Van Velsor, Ellen and Martha W. Hughes (1990) *Gender Differences in the Development of Managers: How Women Managers Learn From Experience*. Greensboro, NC: Center for Creative Leadership.

Vinnicombe, Susan and Bank, John (2003) *Women with Attitude*. London: Routledge.

Wallace, Wanda T. (2004) "Reaching the Top: Five factors that impact the retention and effectiveness of the most talented senior women". Leadership Forum Inc.

Walter, Natasha (2005) "Prejudice & Evolution", *Prospect*, June.

West, Lucy and Milan, Mike (2001) *The Reflecting Glass: Professional Coaching for Leadership Development*. Basingstoke: Palgrave – now Palgrave Macmillan.

Wilkinson, Helen, Howard, Melanie with Sarah Gregory, Helen Hayes and Rowena Young (1997) *Tomorrow's Women*. London: Demos.

Wirth, Linda (2001) *Breaking Through the Glass Ceiling: Women in Management*. Geneva: International Labour Office.

Wittenberg-Cox, Avivah and Milan, Margaret (2005) *Women, Careers and Competitive Advantage in the New Millennium*. Women@Work No.1 EPWN.

INDEX

A

activity-based costing 117–18
advice 48–53
affirmative action 156
age–experience correlation 37
aggressive tax planning 17–18
Alimo-Metcalfe, Beverly 120–21, 123–4
all-female cohort 170
Alliance for Board Diversity 13
ambition 23–4, 62, 66, 83–4, 148
amortization 199
analysis 159–61
androgyny 5
Anglo-Saxon culture 45
anomalies 159
anxiety 61
any other business 192–208
    conclusion 206–7
    toward equilibrium 203–6
Appel, Bluma 200
appointment to major company's board 68–70
Arhén, Gunilla 196
arrow and spiral 114–17
artificiality 49
Asia Pacific 198–9
Asia Pacific Business Review 199
attraction 37
attunement 2
Aurora Gender Capital Management 172
Aviva 60
Avon Products 204–6

B

B2B 6
B2C 6–8
baggage 177
Bakker, Peter 119
balance between the sexes 2
balancing act 155
Baldauf, Sari 29
Balfour, Fergus 182
band nine 38
Bank of England 88, 144, 149

Barclays 174
Barnes, Brenda 29, 206
BBC 88, 108, 115
behavior shift 96
being table d'hôte 152
Belizian Grove 203
Bem Sex Role Inventory 125–6
Bennis, Warren 114
best practice 47
BMW Tokyo 198
board experience 70–71
body language 167
Boeing 41
Booz Allen & Hamilton 124
botanical metaphors 115
BP 59–60, 146
bridging the gap 87–110, 169
    FTSE 100 Cross-Company
    Mentoring Programme 92–4
bringing women forward 81–3
British Airways 60
Brook, Lesley 156–7
brownie points 3
BSkyB 60
BSRI *see* Bem Sex Role Inventory
buccaneering 167
Bulgaria 196
bump of locality 22
burden of tax 18
Burgmans, Antony 181, 197
bush fire 154–5
business benefits of inclusion 191
Business Ethics 204
business process re-engineering 117–18
Business and The Feminine Principle 115–16
business-to-business company *see* B2B
business-to-consumer company *see* B2C
buying decisions 1

C

Californian Public Employees' Retirement System 202
calmness 43, 119

CalPERS *see* Californian Public Employees' Retirement System
camouflage 149
Canada 200–201
Canadian Women in Communications 200–201
candor 93
capability 81
career counseling 146
career development programs for women 169–70
Carr, Roger 108
Cass Business School 144
casting a wide net 138
catalog of sins 190
Catalyst 10–11, 14, 27–8, 34, 50, 127, 201–2, 205–6
catharsis 170
causative link 12–13, 57, 120
Census of Women Board Directors 34, 127
Center for Work–Life Policy 28
Centre for Corporate Diversity 195
Centre for Economic and Business Research 7
Centrica 60, 108
Cescau, Patrick 181
CEW *see* University of Michigan Center for the Education of Women
Champy, James 117–18
change 189–91
Change Partnership 87, 92
changing the game 177–91
    change on three levels 189–91
    hard-wiring the system 182–4
    high-level commitment 180–82
    human resources 188–9
    micro-inequities 185–8
    vision 178–9
charisma 123
charities' talent 144–6
childbearing 3, 37, 55–7, 61, 85, 147, 188
childcare 170–2

Sapere Aude

**TODD WEHR
MEMORIAL
LIBRARY**

Viterbo University
900 Viterbo Drive
La Crosse, WI 54601
608-796-3269

DEMCO